Professional
Academic
Writing

in the
Humanities
and
Social Sciences

Susan Peck MacDonald

Southern Illinois University Press
Carbondale and Edwardsville

Printed in the United States of America
Designed by Jolene Faye Hamil
Production supervised by Natalia Nadraga
97 96 95 94   4 3 2 1

Library of Congress Cataloging-in-Publication Data

MacDonald, Susan.
    Professional academic writing in the humanities and social
sciences / Susan Peck MacDonald.
        p.   cm.
    Includes bibliographical references and index.
    1. Authorship. 2. Humanities—Authorship. 3. Social
sciences—Authorship. 4. Scholarly publishing. I. Title.
PN146.M33   1994
808'.066001—dc20   93-11095
ISBN 0-8093-1930-6   CIP

The paper used in this publication meets the minimum requirements of
American National Standard for Information Sciences—Permanence of
Paper for Printed Library Materials, ANSI Z39.48-1984. ∞

CONTENTS

PREFACE

Increased attention to the social contexts of writing provides the intellectual framework that will be obvious in what follows. But long before scholarship in rhetoric turned its attention to contextual variation, my experiences as writer, teacher, and administrator were leading me toward a growing sense of the strangeness writers feel as they move from one discourse community to another.

As a new academic trying to publish literature articles in the 1970s, cut off from any research network, I grew increasingly puzzled by the seemingly capricious and inconsistent critiques that accompanied journal submissions. As a teacher of "basic writing" students, I was frequently jolted by the ways students failed to observe conventions that were, I soon realized, not intuitively obvious except to a trained academic. In the 1980s, I entered enthusiastically into administering a program in writing in the disciplines because I wanted to integrate writing instruction with disciplinary knowledge. I discovered, however, that undergraduate writing tasks outside the freshman composition course could be oddly divorced from professional disciplinary axiomatics—and that course readings often presented students with competing models of discourse to imitate. I encountered new graduate students in literature distressed by the seemingly esoteric language of graduate school after having entered graduate school because of a love of literature. Out of such experiences of pain and confusion has grown my conviction that academics need to do a better job of explaining their text-making axioms, clarifying their expectations of students at all levels, and monitoring their own professional practices.

My intellectual indebtedness will be apparent in the pages that follow, but several additional influences have been crucial. Charles Cooper has been particularly supportive and inspiring from the beginning of this project; I am grateful not just for his encouragement and unfailing good cheer but also for the insights into text making, genres, and teaching that have resulted from our daily work in administering writing programs at the University of California, San Diego. M. A. Syverson also has been particularly helpful, both as the coder who helped me with the empirical study reported in chapter 6 and as a reader of stages of the manuscript. Other faculty and graduate teaching assistants too numerous to name in disciplines in the humanities and social sciences in UCSD's Third College have indirectly contributed insights. I thank them for responding patiently to my queries or for holding their own disciplinary convictions so strongly as to convince me of how deeply disciplinary convictions shape our academic work. I also thank nearby writing adjunct program administrators—Joan Graham, Ellen Strenski, and Muriel Zimmerman—for frequent conversations about administering a program to integrate writing and disciplinary knowledge; their conversations have helped strengthen these same convictions about the difficulties of negotiating disciplinary boundaries.

I thank the reviewers for Southern Illinois University Press for comments on an earlier version of this manuscript and thank the anonymous reviewers of earlier versions of chapter 2 in *Written Communication* and *College English*; Roger Cherry and readers at *Written Communication* were especially helpful with the recent article here revised as chapter 6. I thank Avon Crismore and William Vande Kopple for helpful comments on the relation between metadiscourse and my epistemic categories (chapter 6). Finally, I thank my family for their patience and encouragement.

Grateful acknowledgment for permission to reprint is extended for: "Problem Definition in Academic Writing," *College English* 49, no. 3 (Mar. 1987): 315–31, reprinted in revised form in chapter 2, copyright © 1987 by the National Council of Teachers of English, reprinted with permission; "Data-Driven and Conceptually Driven Academic Discourse," *Written Communication* 6, no. 4 (Oct. 1989): 411–35, reprinted in revised form in chapters 2 and 3 by permission of Sage Publications, Inc., copyright © 1989 by Sage Publications, Inc., all rights reserved; "A Method for Analyzing Sentence-Level Differences in Disciplinary Knowledge Making," *Written Communication* 9, no. 4 (Oct. 1992): 533–69, reprinted in revised form as chapter 6 by permission of Sage Publications, Inc., copyright © 1992 by Sage Publications, Inc., all rights reserved.

Patterns of Variation

CHAPTER ONE

Introduction

From academic fields as diverse as rhetoric and composition, sociology of science, philosophy of science, anthropology, history, and literary theory, a growing consensus has emerged that written knowledge is more than merely a pale reflection of reality or a translation of already formed thought. The consensus takes different forms and is fed by different traditions, Continental and Anglo-American, but one common denominator is to perceive writing as constructing or constituting thought, rather than merely translating or superficially dressing thought. With this consensus, direct examination of written texts becomes more important, and academic writing begins to share in this new attention. Signs of such attention are evident in the curricular innovations of "writing across the curriculum" or "writing in the disciplines," and though these curricular movements arose from competing premises, enough new courses and programs have been developed over the past decade to suggest considerably increased interest in academic writing.[1] At the theoretical level also, discussions of the importance of rhetoric, the untenability of positivism, the incommensurability of scientific paradigms, the interpretive nature of history and anthropology, or the subjective component in literary interpretation have all warranted extending our discussions of the rhetoric of the academy.

In the exceedingly complex specialization of the modern university, however, even an emerging consensus struggles against specialist fragmentation, unconscious remnants of previous practices, competing theories, and gaps between theory and practice. Contradictory premises coexist, and despite ample theoretical warrants for extending such examination to professional academic writing, examinations have proceeded haltingly. This halting progress is partly the result of institutional inertia: departments previously unconcerned with the rhetoric of inquiry have been slow to reshape their practical missions and institutionalized structures even though they have accorded more theoretical importance to rhetoric. Rhetoric and composition studies, consequently, remains a somewhat despised stepchild at many universities, particularly at the research university.[2]

But fuller examination has also been slow in coming because the tools for such analysis are insufficiently developed. Particularly in the humanities and social sciences, full investigation of academic writing remains to be accomplished. As David Russell has written, "Scholars have just begun to study the rhetoric of academic disciplines and other professional communities on a case-by-case basis, to analyze the interactional rules, tacit and explicit, which govern the knowledge-making and communicating activities of various discourse communities and subcommunities. . . . [O]nly such sociorhetorical analysis, discipline by discipline, will provide a foundation on which to construct meaningful generalizations about how writing works—and how students learn to make it work" (14).

The purpose of this book is to examine variations in academic writing in the humanities and social sciences through perspectives from three sources: (1) a converging body of theory suggesting that academic text making will reflect knowledge-making activities specific to disciplinary fields, (2) sample texts and disciplinary issues in three subdisciplinary fields over the last decade or two, and (3) a rhetorical and linguistic perspective on issues that are often posed as epistemological or ideological, rather than textual issues.

I will look at academics' textual practices, going beyond the simplistic descriptions that sometimes populate our textbooks (e.g., scientists use the passive) or the misleading "rules" we think we work by but violate in practice. Our explicit accounts of academic writing have often been molded by philosophies we no longer believe, by shibboleths we have accepted without reflection, or by decontextualized half-truths that do not reflect the complexity of actual practices. I will discuss why we have ample theoretical warrant for assuming there to be important differences in the writing of the differing disciplines, how we might describe those differences, and how different kinds of text making may reflect differing kinds of knowledge making current in the humanities and social sciences.

My exploration is focused on four interactive elements in the academy: (1) written texts, (2) knowledge-making goals and practices, (3) disciplinary communities, and (4) professionalism. In this chapter, I will first explain the role each of these four elements plays and then describe the structure of the book.

The Importance of Written Texts

In the now largely abandoned objectivist model in epistemology, writing could easily be seen as the relatively unproblematic transcription of thought.[3] This assumption has often been involved, for instance, when philosophers argued about epistemology, historians argued about narrative and analysis, or literary scholars argued about interpretations. In such instances, academics have readily assumed that key disciplinary issues could be resolved without explicit reference to the ways in which they were written. In other words, academic writing has received relatively little attention until recently because it has been taken for granted, assumed to be transparent (see Russell). If not seen as transparent, writing has long been seen as an all-purpose skill, an ability to translate thought with correctness and grace, but a skill unaffected by particular disciplinary problems or knowledge-making processes within specific disciplines.

With such a view, methods courses in academic disciplines have been able to focus on inquiry in ways that divorced inquiry from writing. In psychology, methods courses could focus on types of studies, experimental design, and how to collect data. Philosophers of history could concern themselves with epistemological questions about causality quite unrelated to the problematics of constructing history texts. When historians have argued with each other about the relative merits of narrative and analysis, they have often talked about history itself or interpretation, scarcely differentiating those arguments from arguments about textual practices.

Literary studies, the academic homeland of textual studies, has, perhaps, been even less aware of its own textuality. Absorbed by the interpretive problems of literary analysis, literary scholars have often treated their own academic texts as transparent—or as transgressing unspecified conventions. In the last decade, literary theory has produced a flood of journal articles and monographs about the problematics of interpretation but has said comparatively little about the *textual* features through which literary theories and interpretations are constructed. By comparison to the amount of work on theory or interpretation, there has been little explicit discussion of crucial practices of text making in the field, such as how critical texts may be organized, how arguments may be warranted and substantiated, or the underlying rationale for choosing what to cite, where in one's text to do so, and how to choose from the explosion of material in print that which is relevant for citation.[4] Recent discussions show that literary scholars are beginning to pay more attention to the language of their own texts, but even these growing discussions, as I will argue in chapter 7, can suffer from confusion about how larger purposes may be connected to linguistic and rhetorical variations.

Elsewhere in the humanities, there are signs of increased recognition of the importance of academics' own texts; Clifford Geertz's 1988 *Works and Lives*, for instance, discusses how anthropologists "have traced their difficulties in constructing such [ethnographic] descriptions to the problematics of field work rather than to those of discourse" (10). Rosaldo comments, similarly, that "the human sciences have . . . only recently noticed that their work is written" (33). Yet except for work in rhetoric and composition, much examination of academic discourse still focuses on stances, philosophies, interpretations, or concepts rather than texts. But however much texts may contain and be partly generated by philosophies, they are not the equivalent of philosophies. Writers with similar beliefs might create vastly different academic texts, just as writers with dissimilar beliefs might write similar texts. To say of an academic that she is a social historian tells us relatively little about how she constructs her texts. To say someone is a Renaissance New Historicist may, among insiders, tell something of how a particular academic constructs his texts, but such identifications—"He is a Renaissance New Historicist," "She is a feminist critic," "He is a cultural materialist"—give primary importance to ideology or schools of interpretation, rather than to written discourse, while texts remain unexamined.

Such identifications are of no help for a number of purposes: they do not help a discourse analyst interested in greater descriptive power; they do not help novices trying to gain access to the discourse of a community; they do not help professionals trying to initiate novices into academic communities; and they do not help any of us scrutinize or reflect upon our own practices as professional writers. Without more rhetorical and linguistic description, such identifications as "she is a social historian" constitute only vague gestures in the direction of textual practices that are largely unexplored.

Yet the conceptual underpinnings of this older neglect of academic text making are largely eroded. In the emerging consensus, the conviction that written knowledge is constructed and that our thoughts are not merely forced on us by reality leads to recognizing that knowledge claims are constructed, negotiated, and made persuasive through written texts.[5] As embodiments of socially negotiated inquiry, texts bear witness to their social origins, and so the increasing social emphasis should lead to fuller, richer, and more numerous studies of academic text making. The field of rhetoric and composition studies has already begun to pay increasing attention to discipline-specific variations in academic texts (e.g., Bazerman; MacDonald; Berkenkotter, Huckin, and Ackerman; Fahnestock and Secor; Myers; Hansen; Schwegler and Shamoon; Swales; Dillon). But in comparison with the amount of work on academic inquiry—on the philosophy, history, and sociology of science, for instance, or on the problematics of literary interpretation—the amount of attention to actual textual practices in the academy, particularly in the social sciences and humanities, is still relatively meager.

The increasingly "social" focus of much recent work in rhetoric and composition has both increased and diluted the focus on academic texts because while it has led to interest in textual variation, it has also led beyond texts to the circumstances surrounding their construction. We now have important studies of the social dynamics of disciplinary classrooms (e.g., McCarthy, Herrington); the social contexts of invention (LeFevre) and composing (e.g., Myers, Brodkey, Geisler, Porter); the contribution of writing to disciplinary learning (e.g., Ackerman, Faigley and Hansen, Langer and Applebee, Marshall, Newell, MacDonald and Cooper, Walvoord and McCarthy); and individual learners (e.g., Berkenkotter, Huckin, and Ackerman; McCarthy; North). But the increasing emphasis on the social contexts of academic writing should not imply that texts themselves are unimportant. Texts provide one of our richest sources of information about social practices, and at the same time texts are not simply epiphenomena; they help create communities (Bazerman), they act on us, they shape how we relate to each other as professionals and shape what we can and cannot do.

Though it would be useful to develop ways of describing the whole spectrum of academic writing, I limit myself here to writing in the humanities and social sciences because they have been relatively neglected while scientific and technical writing have received more attention. That fact alone is noteworthy. Although analysis of discourse has come largely from fields situated in the humanities or humanistic social sciences, the preponderance of attention to scientific discourse among these disciplines suggests two possibilities: that humanists and social scientists are still alternately fascinated by and envious of the prestige of science and tend to take their own discourse for granted. The first of these two possibilities is worth weighing. Works which have been influential in undermining "foundationalist" notions and showing the social construction of academic knowledge—for example, Kuhn's *Structure of Scientific Revolutions*, Latour and Woolgar's *Laboratory Life*, Gilbert and Mulkay's *Opening Pandora's Box*—have tended to be works written by scholars in the humanities or social sciences about work in the physical sciences. Perhaps those of us in the "soft" sciences and humanities envy our more prestigious colleagues in the "hard" sciences and want to bring them down to our level.

Or perhaps our attention is simply better captured by the relatively exotic writing in the sciences, writing that is markedly not natural to us. In the field of rhetoric and composition studies, scientific and business writing have for some time been recognized as not natural—not the sort of thing we teach in freshman composition, for instance, and therefore marked by being treated in separate courses. The institutionalized assumption, in the past, has been that anyone could learn generic "writing" at the freshman level in a composition course but that the marked (non-natural) conventions of scientific or business writing could only be undertaken after this more natural writing was learned at a relatively elementary level.[6] With increased awareness of the constructedness of scientific accounts or the importance of rhetoric in inquiry, however, we also have ample reason for considering the constructedness of accounts in the humanities and social sciences, and doing so involves exploring how texts are ordered, issues are defined, sentences are constructed, or inferences are made explicit in written language.

Knowledge-Making Goals of the Academy

Broadly speaking, academic prose has evolved as a vehicle for constructing knowledge claims: for wielding ideas, constructing categories and concepts, weighing competing abstractions, assessing the relation between claim and evidence, developing careful distinctions, and taking us out of the ephemerality of individual instances so that we can learn something about our past and our present, while attempting to control or improve our present. This generalization can, of course, be qualified in any number of ways if we consider the variations of purpose, subject matter, and level within the academy. Not all levels of the academy function to create new knowledge: students' writing, administrative writing, or grant writing, for instance, all serve purposes different from making new knowledge. Furthermore, the academy itself contains contradictory purposes evolving from the mixed origins of the modern American university (see Russell, Graff, Novick, Berlin). Such tensions will be part of my examination, but the generalization that academic writing is distinguished from other kinds of writing by its knowledge-making function serves as a useful starting point for examining variations within the academy.

I restrict my examination here in a number of ways: excluding from consideration writing within the academy that, for instance, performs administrative functions, transmits knowledge for novices, or translates knowledge for non-experts. With all but the cutting edge of professional academic writing eliminated, then, academic writing might readily be described as a vehicle for constructing and negotiating knowledge claims. This description may sound consistent with older foundationalist assumptions about knowledge and objectivity, but my focus is on the goals of varying textual practices and the processes of negotiation embedded in them, rather than on whether the results indeed constitute new knowledge or not.

Even with that caveat, however, there are at least two partial alternatives to viewing professional academic writing as a knowledge-making enterprise. Neither of these alternatives need undercut my examination here, but they both require some explanation.

The first alternative comes from studies in the sociology of knowledge or rhetoric of inquiry suggesting that the "knowledge" arrived at in academic texts is often more provisional and more historically situated than it admits to being. Herbert Simons, for instance, has described the new academic field of rhetoric of inquiry as dominated by the trope of irony, the debunking mood; and Pearce and Chen define the rhetoric of inquiry as operating to counteract "an untenable model of scientific discourse envisioned as detached, neutral, unbiased, and objective" (119).[7]

But even if knowledge making does not occur in a pure, objective form, the goal of creating knowledge still makes academic writing different from, for instance, murder mysteries or technical instructions. Whatever self-interest or social contingencies enter into academic texts, there are also attempts at genuine knowledge making and whether we judge them to succeed or fail must depend, in part, on understanding how they are made, what forms they take, and what are the ways in which communal processes of decision making are textually shaped. The debunking mode runs the danger, then, of erasing important differences within academic inquiry through focusing too absolutely on whether pure knowledge can or cannot be achieved.

Another tendency within the debunking mood should also give us pause. If we conceive of academic fields as arrayed, more or less, on a continuum from the "hard" sciences to the "soft" humanities, debunking studies tend to be directed at fields that are "harder" than the field from which they are written. That is, sociologists of science may debunk the work of "hard" scientists; literary theorists may debunk the work of "hard" scientists and social scientists. Rarely do "hard" scientists take the time to write analogous critiques of the social sciences or humanities, and rarely, these days, do social scientists critique the humanities as insufficiently scientific. This asymmetry suggests there is a strong tendency toward rearguard action stemming from a perceived loss of power, desire for enhanced status, and intellectual insecurity among social scientists and humanists. It has been called "science envy."

"Science envy" can stunt examination of academic texts in two seemingly opposite ways. The prestige of science sometimes results in only scientific texts' appearing to be worth studying; this form of "science envy" can limit our understanding of academic practices because humanists and social scientists stand to gain from monitoring their own practices. On the other hand, to debunk the knowledge-making possibilities of scientific texts may obscure significant differences between scientific and humanistic texts. "Science envy"—along with debunking and the trope of irony—ought not to dominate our new interest in scrutinizing the discourse of the academy. Within rhetoric and composition studies especially, our attention should not be so fixed on the fallibility of knowledge claims or the influence of extratextual social contexts that we fail to attend to the work that texts do in creating different kinds of knowledge.

My approach, then, resembles that of Charles Bazerman, who, in his study of scientific writing, has suggested that there be less emphasis on "the competitive struggle played out through scientific texts" and more on cooperative efforts that allow a scientific community to move forward with its knowledge making and the ways that texts may embody and reflect cooperative processes ("Natural Philosophers" 13).

A second alternative to seeing academic writing as a form of knowledge making comes from rhetoricians' suggestions that some professional academic writing is better characterized as epideictic than as knowledge-making. Epideictic rhetoric, as Perelman and Olbrechts-Tyteca have characterized it, is oriented toward celebration and preservation, toward "increasing adherence to the values it lauds" (50). Fahnestock and Secor have found a sample of literature articles to be epideictic—that is, functioning to celebrate the complexity of literature, affirm the shared values of a community, and keep alive a traditional set of texts ("Rhetoric of Literary Criticism").[8] And there are suggestions of epideictic functions elsewhere in academic writing (D. Sullivan, Carter). I will explore such possibilities further, particularly in the case of academic literary writing (chapters 5 and 7).

These arguments are useful, as I see it, not so much for denying that academic knowledge making exists or for reasserting the importance of categories derived from classical rhetoric. They are useful, instead, for emphasizing the differences of purpose that may exist in academic writing and the effects those purposes may have on textual outcomes. The categorization of "epideictic" is useful, then, not to describe a closed category or genre, but to describe variations in purpose that will help us understand differences in textual language, emphasis, citation, or organization.[9]

Other descriptions of intellectual tensions within the academy suggest analogous differences in purpose. Graff's depiction of the tension between "generalists" and "investigators" in literature departments at the turn of the century, for instance, suggests that literary critics have often not been preoccupied by "investigation"—or knowledge making, as I will call it. Similarly, the distinction between interpretive and explanatory (e.g., Geertz) is related (though imperfectly) to the distinction between generalist and investigator or epideictic and knowledge making. I discuss the origins and effects of such differences in purpose but rely primarily on the term "knowledge making," using the adjective "epistemic" to refer to language that is self-consciously directed toward serving the knowledge-making purposes of a disciplinary community.

If some academic writing may serve to celebrate or blame, more than to create knowledge, one way to examine that difference is to examine writing from different parts of the academy as if it were concerned to create knowledge. Through comparison, differences in textual features will help to reveal differences in intention. Rather than begin, then, with a system of classification that separates two or more discrete genres of academic writing (such as epistemic and epideictic) from each other, I prefer to begin with the model of a continuum, asking the question "If academic writing is a form of knowledge making, then what are the ways in which knowledge making occurs in particular texts?"

To begin with such a question allows us to acknowledge both common tendencies and differences while exploring disciplinary variation—differences that exist on a continuum, rather than as discrete categories. At the professional level with which I am concerned here, academics share a common focus on new knowledge (see Kaufer and Geisler), an obligation to situate work within a discourse community, and an obligation to give reasons for claims, all of which will enter into my discussion. These three generic features are not, however, distinguishing features of either novels or business memos.

If genres are not a priori formal classes but pragmatically evolving ways of doing work in different social contexts, as Carolyn Miller has suggested, we should expect academic texts to display common features resulting from the academy's focus on learning and knowing. We should also expect to find variations resulting from the differentiated goals and subjects of different parts of the academy. By focusing on the most typical purpose of academic writing—knowledge making—we can distinguish between generic features common to all academic writing and discipline-specific features.

The distinction between discrete genres and continuous classification systems allows us to avoid further problems. If we see classes of academic writing as discrete, then any overlapping or "blurring" (as Geertz has claimed in *Local Knowledge*) appears to demonstrate either that the classifications were erroneous to begin with or that boundaries are being surmounted. If we see classifications as continuous, then overlapping and blurring need not be evidence that invalidates the classifications.

As a model for exploration, then, I will assume that the academy generally aims at making knowledge and has, for that purpose, evolved epistemic language and epistemic practices that are perhaps most obvious and most unalloyed at the end of the continuum where we have ranged the sciences. The degree to which similar goals exist in the social sciences and humanities will be part of my subject here, along with the degree to which epistemic goals are foregrounded in texts. To posit, initially, that academic disciplines may be roughly ranged on a continuum by the degree to which their knowledge-making goals and practices are in the foreground is not to deny that there may be other goals in the social sciences and humanities, but it serves as a focal point for exploring the differences among the disciplines.

Disciplinary Communities

The rough consensus that has moved toward social construction has elevated a disciplinary community's decision making to a place of greater importance. With the conviction that knowledge claims are not decided by resort to either self-evident truths or infallible algorithms, Anglo-American philosophers such as Kuhn, Toulmin, or Rorty, and Continental philosophers in the hermeneutic tradition, have shifted the focus of what is defined as rationality.[10] Instead of emphasizing abstract logicality or the substance of ideas, their focus shifts to process and community—the process whereby a community of practitioners gives reasons for its choices, carries on negotiation and persuasion within the community, and selects some problems and solutions as superior to others on the basis of shared disciplinary understandings. This focus on community enables us to understand situational variations in academic writing more clearly, but only if we identify cohesive discourse communities. I use case studies of subfields in the social sciences and humanities to examine ways of describing their written discourse fully and contextually.

Case studies of discrete disciplinary subfields are particularly useful for several reasons. First, they increase the possibility of locating a working discourse community, rather than merely an abstract "community" that may have no consistent patterns of common communication. Disciplinary subfields allow us to isolate discourse communities of writers who read, cite, and are influenced by each other's work; citation patterns illustrate the patterns of communication.[11]

The distinction between a working discourse community and an abstract discourse community is helpful because the recent emphasis on discourse communities has also led to debate about how to identify such communities. Joseph Harris has argued that the notion of discourse community draws upon two different notions: an abstract "interpretive community" such as that described by Stanley Fish or "an actual group of speakers living in a particular place and time" as in the notion of a "speech community" described by Dell Hymes (Harris 14).

The distinction is helpful both for identifying discursive practices among professional academicians and for thinking about how and whether one wishes to "initiate" or "socialize" novices into disciplinary communities. To attempt to describe the discursive practices of literary academics, for instance, could appear a hopeless task if everything written about literature were included as possible items created by the same community. Graff's account of the historical succession of unresolved conflicts within literary studies offers ample evidence that there are multiple discourses within a discipline, and Peter Elbow's account of the 1987 English Coalition Conference suggests that English is a "grab-bag, garbage-pail, everything-but-the-kitchen-sink discipline" (*What Is English?* 110). Among the two notions of community, therefore, I have chosen the "speech community" version, emphasizing actual communication and influence among identifiable participants (though not necessarily the face-to-face communication of an oral community). For that reason, I have chosen small subfields—for example, Renaissance New Historicists—in which participants define their own disciplinary affiliations by what they call themselves, what forums they publish in, and whom they cite. Not all Shakespeareans identify with this particular subfield, but those I have included in my sample do so; they cite each other and cite the same extradisciplinary sources (e.g., Foucault).

The more localized "speech community" concept of discourse communities also helps us think about the issue of socializing novices. My examination here is restricted to professional academic writing (except for some comments in chapter 7), so I will scarcely touch on questions about whether or how to attempt to socialize students into academic communities or conventions. Nevertheless, I want to emphasize that the issue of socialization could be dealt with more effectively by separating questions about what professional academic writing does from questions about how, when, and whether to socialize novices.

The localized "speech community" concept of disciplinary discourse allows us to distinguish among the effects disciplinary practices have upon different participants—professional colleagues, graduate students, undergraduates, majors and nonmajors. Attachment researchers or Renaissance New Historicists constitute discourse communities because they know each others' ideas, attend the same conferences, and possibly talk to each other by phone or read each others' manuscripts before they are published. The same cannot be said about their students. So even for someone who wants to initiate students into the ways of thinking and writing in a particular discipline, it is important to realize that such initiation will necessarily involve something other than the kind of disciplinary community professionals may share.

I have chosen clearly identifiable disciplinary subfields for my sample, then, in order to be able to examine how actual clusterings of academics work together through their texts to negotiate knowledge claims. Studies of subfields allow examination of concrete, local discursive practices that may be specific to subfields but differ from practices elsewhere within the same discipline. Disciplinary subfields are not self-enclosed; they join in larger disciplinary groupings and overlap with other clusters. The subfields in my study are not necessarily representative of their disciplines, but my approach to textual analysis is intended to be useful as a method of examining other disciplinary subfields and to help answer questions about the homogeneity or heterogeneity of practices within and between disciplines.

The subfields I explore are studies of attachment as a subfield of developmental psychology, studies of New England colonial migration and inheritance patterns as a subfield of social history, and Renaissance New Historicism as a subfield of literary studies. (See Appendix.) In each case, I have tried to choose a field that is still current in that it provokes debate or new research and seems relevant to the frontiers of knowledge in the discipline. I attempt to contextualize the ongoing discussion within these fields by considering some of their subdisciplinary antecedents over the last twenty years, but my focus is primarily upon journal articles of the 1980s. I have focused on American writers and American journals for much the same reason that I have focused only on professional journal writing: in order to explore a working discourse community and have as few confounding categorical variables as possible. Discursive practices in British journals, for instance, cannot be assumed to be the same as those for journals published in the United States. Similarly, my focus is on academic writing written in English, and my findings of disciplinary differences in sentence subjects and clause structure (chapter 6) are not intended to be generalizable beyond academic writing in the English language. In each case, my choices have been made with an eye to producing comparable samples from the three disciplines so that my analysis is not undercut by categorical variables.

The Professional Level

To focus on knowledge-making texts and identifiable subdisciplinary communities leads logically to a focus on professional academic writing. Only at the professional level can academic writing be consistently characterized as knowledge making; students' texts are typically written to demonstrate knowledge or to aid students' thinking and learning, but not to create new knowledge or negotiate knowledge claims with a group of other experts. And, as I have already explained, it is only among professional academics that we can locate actual disciplinary communities of people who influence and are influenced by each other.

But there is a further advantage to focusing only on professional academic writing: along with increased interest in rhetoric and texts has come an increased interest in the social and ethical consequences of professional writing. Professionals in any field usually assume the responsibility for monitoring their own practices. Two kinds of monitoring are particularly relevant to my study here: monitoring of the communicative effectiveness of writing in a field and monitoring of the ethics entailed. This will not be a study of such effects, but I hope to begin establishing a descriptive basis for such studies. With more close descriptive work on academic writing, for instance, we will be better able to identify issues clearly. Currently, questions like "What constitutes efficient knowledge making within a disciplinary field?" are sometimes not distinguished from questions like "What constitutes effective communication from professional to layperson?" It is possible that some academic practices are dysfunctional both for lay and professional audiences; it is equally possible that some practices function well for one audience and not another. We need more close scrutiny of academic texts in order to help address such questions.

There are also ethical or political issues that we can better address if we have more thorough explorations of academic practices. Recent debates in rhetoric and composition about whether to initiate students into disciplinary practices or "resist" current practices have frequently been framed in terms of "accommodation" versus "resistance," but they may be framed too simplistically or in a misleading way. Patricia Bizzell, for instance, has framed the question as if we already fully understand what academic writing is and does: "A crucial question is whether academic writing can be turned against itself, to call into question the political and economic status quo the academy officially supports" (228). Elaine Maimon makes different assumptions in her account of the development of writing across the curriculum:

> Our goal was to map a course that would prepare students to move gracefully and fluently from one setting to another, understanding differences, learning intellectual tact. Such tact, we thought, had the best chance of developing in students the confidence to question conventions and to challenge rules. Generic approaches to freshman composition depend on understanding this paradox: rebels are people who know the landscape and who can move easily through it. Those who would keep students ignorant of the academic landscape in the name of helping them find their own rebellious voice do not understand much about guerilla warfare. (xi–xii)

I am suggesting, first, that we scarcely can articulate what the academic landscape is and, second, that these may be destructive dichotomies for us to be working with. Though Maimon here takes the accommodationist position within the debate, she either accepts—or is forced by the false dichotomy into accepting—the assumption that we should be trying to produce rebels. The "resistance" position may entail a number of arguable assumptions: that the status quo is unjust, that academic writing supports the status quo, that academic practices are monolithic, that we know what our own practices are, that we are able to initiate students into those practices, and so on. Any of these assumptions could be judged premature or simplistic, given the lack of close rhetorical and linguistic scrutiny we have spent on describing the nature, variation, or effects of textual practices in the humanities and social sciences.

The accommodation versus resistance debate has most often been framed in relation to undergraduates (e.g., Chase). But important ethical issues arise about how textual practices within a disciplinary community affect members of that community. Feminists are among those beginning to ask such questions. For instance, Olivia Frey has argued that professional writing about literature contains too many examples of the "adversary mode" to be feminist. Such a claim is worth exploring seriously, but to do so should involve further close descriptive work and debate about alternatives. For example, Frey objects to the sense of "argument" in which "writers get nasty and say things that hurt other writers' feelings" (511). She finds adversarial statements like "Critics to date have ignored . . ." or "Critical opinion about . . . differs considerably, betraying how badly . . . has been misunderstood." But before we can know whether such statements are frequently made and in what disciplines or subdisciplinary fields they are made, we need further descriptive work on varying practices within the academy.

Furthermore, a statement like "Critics to date have ignored" is not necessarily adversarial. Would it be more adversarial or less so to ignore opposing opinions altogether? The same examples might be used to argue that no matter how inclined academics are to ignore criticism they disagree with, they nevertheless act responsibly in calling attention to possible counterarguments. The possibility that some academic writing—literary criticism, for instance—may be less epistemic than epideictic is worth considering in relation to Frey's argument. If a discourse community's epistemic practices result in frequent statements like "Critics to date have ignored," then we can understand such statements in the context of larger epistemic and rhetorical goals. If, however, a community's rhetoric serves epideictic purposes such as celebration or self-display, then not referring to critics and counterarguments may be either self-aggrandizing or solipsistic. Graff has advocated more explicit confrontation or negotiation among conflicting points of view as the most likely way of overcoming "the dynamic of patterned isolation" (225) he sees as haunting the academy.

There is need for critiques of how efficient academics are in their search for knowledge, as well as whether they act in ways that are nonegalitarian, self-serving, adversarial, etc. But such critiques must be anchored to close descriptive studies that take account of disciplinary variation and that also involve full and complex understanding of the multiple contexts in which any academic writing occurs. I hope that this study will increase understanding of professional academic texts in the humanities and social sciences by offering more detailed descriptions of sample disciplinary discourse and by adding to our repertoire of tools for analyzing such writing. From this descriptive base, I hope we will be able to monitor and reassess our own practices, not only because they affect our students, but because they affect us as members of differing academic communities.

The Plan of This Book

Chapter 2 begins to describe key features of knowledge-making texts and provides the context for the ensuing chapters. It focuses on four patterns of variation in textual knowledge making that may be placed along a continuum extending from the sciences through the social sciences to the humanities. The four patterns I discuss are variations in (1) disciplinary compactness and problem definition, (2) explanatory or interpretive goals, (3) conceptually driven or text-driven inquiry, and (4) degrees of explicit epistemic accounting. I review arguments in the philosophy of science as well as empirical studies that warrant our assuming there are patterned variations in disciplinary writing related to the degree of particularism in academic subjects of inquiry. I illustrate the problematics of interpretive variation in text-driven inquiry with examples from New Critical literary interpretations.

In chapter 3, I use the case of attachment research in psychology to examine how attachment researchers have developed and pursued their disciplinary problem. Over a period of twenty years, articles in attachment research exhibit the continuity of their disciplinary problem and an ability to compact findings and elaborate on conceptual distinctions. I examine the development of attachment research in seminal articles and discuss its conceptually driven relation between generalization and data.

In chapter 4, I examine historians' arguments about narrative and analysis over the last twenty years in relation to the evolution of the subfield of Colonial New England social history. I consider the relation between particularism and abstraction in history, historians' comments on the lack of cumulative progress or synthesis in the subfield of Colonial New England social history, history's attempts to move toward the social sciences and yet its counteracting affinity with more typically or traditionally humanistic tendencies.

In chapter 5, I discuss problem definition and presentation in older Shakespearean criticism and recent New Historicist studies of Shakespeare. I distinguish between the epistemic problem presentation typical of most academic writing and the more anecdotal or narrative style favored by some New Historicists—exploring, in the process, the narrative and particularistic tendencies, deferred point making, and lack of epistemic warranting distinctive to some New Historicist work. Chapter 5 concludes with discussion of the issue of whether writing about literature, in this sample field, may be considered epideictic.

In chapter 6, I turn from text-level features to the sentence-level features that reflect and create text-level differences. To analyze how writers in my sample subfields vary in their use of abstractions or the degree to which they write "epistemic" prose, I examine their sentence subjects. Articles in the psychology sample most often employ epistemic sentence subjects and avoid particularistic ones. Articles in the literary sample use sentence subjects that are least epistemic and most particularistic. The history articles occupy a middle position between the psychology and literary samples. The empirical and linguistic analysis in chapter 6 is intended to complement the more global and rhetorical analysis of chapters 3, 4, and 5 so that approaching the same issues with different modes of analysis tells us something more than if only one mode of analysis were to be used.

In chapter 7, I conclude with some of the consequences of sentence-level variations in academic writing both for academic writers and for their students. I discuss how epistemic and nominal style may be useful for professional knowledge making and what its characteristic drawbacks may be. I attempt to clarify some misconceptions (as I see it) about academic writing, but also discuss the direction critiques of academic writing might take. Very briefly, I touch on ways in which this kind of descriptive study of academic writing can help us address issues about whether, when, and how to try to initiate novices into the practices of the academy.

CHAPTER TWO

Patterns in
Disciplinary Variation

If academic writing is a form of knowledge making, then differences in knowledge problems or ways of addressing such problems should account for much of the variation among the disciplines. This chapter will focus on four patterns of variation that are discernible if academic disciplines are placed, roughly, on a continuum in which scientific and humanistic fields lie at opposite ends of the continuum, with the social sciences in between. The image of a continuum is useful as a way of exploring both relation and difference from one field to another, without needing to imply that there are discrete genres or rigidly demarcated classifications. These are rough, approximate mappings, and the myriad subdisciplinary fields that constitute actual knowledge-making discourse communities do not fall neatly into the three designations of science, social science, or humanities.[1] Nevertheless, along this continuum, we may see four patterns of variation in the ways academics approach their knowledge problems: (1) variations from compactness to diffuseness, (2) variations in explanatory versus interpretive goals, (3) variations from conceptually driven to text driven in the relation between generalization and particular, and (4) variations in the degrees of epistemic self-consciousness that are explicit in texts.

These patterns are the subject of this chapter. I begin with models from the philosophy of science because they offer a way to explore variations in academic knowledge making. With a broad outline of what a model of scientific problem solving might involve, we are in a better position to examine how fields in the humanities and social sciences approach their knowledge problems differently.

Compact and Diffuse Disciplinary Problems

As arenas for knowledge making, disciplinary fields may be ranged roughly on a continuum from compact to diffuse in the ways they define, present, and attempt to solve problems. The terms here—"compact" and "diffuse"—are from Stephen Toulmin, but the distinction involved may be found in a variety of work on academic knowledge making. Kuhn has suggested that agreed-upon problems define the work of normal science, and Toulmin has suggested that there is a continuum from well-defined to diffusely defined problems. Toulmin sees compact scientific fields as characterized by a "sufficiently agreed goal or ideal, in terms of which common outstanding problems can be identified" (364). Diffuse and would-be disciplines, on the other hand, are the type found in the social sciences and humanities, characterized by their "absence of a clearly defined, generally agreed reservoir of disciplinary problems, so that conceptual innovations within them face no consistent critical tests and lack any continuing rational direction" (380).

Scientists' focus on clearly defined problems is illustrated in Gilbert and Mulkay's extensive sociological study of how scientists within the field of bioenergetics over the course of three decades worked to explain the mechanism of oxidative phosphorylation. Their study reveals much that might be considered extrascientific (personal rivalries, blindness about new ideas, self-justification), but no matter how the bioenergeticists differed in their solutions to the problem, they agreed for thirty years upon the crucial problem of their field—explaining how adenosine triphosphate was formed.

Any number of similar examples might be found. For instance, Bazerman's account of the research area in which Arthur Holly Compton worked shows how a field may be focused on a commonly perceived problem—for example, puzzling properties of X rays—despite scientists' having competing explanations of the phenomenon (*Shaping* chapter 7). Laudan, emphasizing the centrality of problem solving in science, would refer to this as an empirical problem in that it attempts to explain something about the natural world that strikes us as needing explanation. Compton, as Bazerman illustrates, began with explanations from classical electromagnetic theory but moved to quantum theory without shifting the nature of the problem area he worked on. Bazerman's account illustrates how a research area may be created or united more by its problem than by the proposed theories or solutions in the field; until one explanatory theory gains ascendancy, scientists working within a research area need not necessarily agree upon their theories even though they agree on their problem.[2]

To characterize academic writing as problem solving is not to imply that problems always result in clear solutions or that there are no extrascientific factors involved in knowledge making. It implies only that disciplinary or subdisciplinary fields are identified by the kinds of knowledge-making tasks they engage in and that these tasks may be characterized, loosely, as "problems"—puzzles within the discipline or goals toward which disciplinary work is oriented. As I have noted in chapter 1, some disciplinary writing may involve epideictic celebration as much as, or more than, it involves knowledge making, but to posit, initially, that professional academic writing is a form of knowledge making allows that hypothesis to be used for exploring how and why knowledge making differs from one discipline to another.

Beyond the academy, writing does not characteristically attempt to solve knowledge problems: the purpose of writing personal letters, for instance, may be to maintain emotional contact or to tell about an experience of interest to the letter's recipient. The purpose of writing newspaper reports is to tell the news. "Telling" in these cases is informative, rather than problem solving, aimed more at communicating information than at creating new knowledge or attempting to confront knowledge problems.[3] In business and technical fields, there is a more formally coded genre of problem solving that deals with specific problems (e.g., how to solve environmental or engineering problems in a community or a business) and offers specific solutions to be acted on. But academic problem solving, as I am defining it, involves a type of knowledge making, rather than a type of action in the world or a conventionalized genre offering "solutions." Academic writing involves problem solving insofar as it attempts to fill in pieces of a knowledge puzzle or problem considered important within a disciplinary discourse.

An academic discourse community is constituted largely by its sense of what still needs to be known or what kinds of questions should be asked about a particular subject of inquiry. Consequently, academic subfields are loose and frequently shifting, informal groupings held together by the problems they define. It is to problem definition, more than to either topics or problem solutions, that we must look, initially, in exploring how work in smaller disciplinary subfields may vary. Although disciplines and departments seem permanently fixed on the map of the academy, the actual working discourse communities in which academics produce new knowledge are less stable and more ad hoc in their dependence on what appears to need to be known or inquired into. In this way, knowledge problems shape the map of discourse communities, and discourse communities shape the map of knowledge problems.

The continuum from compact to diffuse and the link Toulmin posits between disciplinary compactness and kinds of disciplinary problems are supported by empirical work on disciplinary differences. Tony Becher finds that "hard" knowledge (as in the sciences) shows relatively steady cumulative growth, a process of accretion rather than recursive or reiterative development (Becher 13). In "soft" fields, on the other hand, he finds a more "laissez-faire manner in which new issues are selected and taken up" as a result of less well-marked or more permeable boundaries (14). As one aspect of this territorial metaphor, Becher distinguishes between "urban" and "rural" people-to-problem ratios; "urban" fields have a small number of discrete, separable problems and a large number of people working on them, while "rural" fields have many possible topics with problems "not sharply demarcated or delineated" and with fewer people working on a problem (79). Colonial New England social history and Renaissance New Historicism, as we shall see, are much more "rural" in these senses than is the psychological research on attachment.

The relatively greater number of problems in "rural" fields is connected to the relatively greater particularism in the humanities. Charles Bazerman's case study of articles in science, social science, and literature suggests a greater particularism in the writing about literature, and Becher, citing Bazerman's work (*Shaping*) and his own, contrasts the particularism of the soft disciplines to the greater "scope for patterning and reproducibility" in the more compact, hard disciplines: "scientific knowledge is concerned predominantly with universals; non-scientific knowledge tends to be focused on particulars" (14).

The greater scope for patterning in the sciences and, consequently, the relative compactness of its problem solving are indicated also in citation studies. Derek de Solla Price has studied how disciplines vary in percentages of references to archival versus recent research. Price predicted that fields like science that grow from the "skin" of the research front will have a high percentage of references to very recent work, whereas fields that grow from the "body" will have a high portion of archival references:

> With a low index one has a humanistic type of metabolism in which the scholar has to digest all that has gone before, let it mature gently in the cellar of his wisdom, and then distill forth new words of wisdom about the same sorts of questions. In hard science the positiveness of the knowledge and its short term permanence enable one to move through the packed down past while still a student and then to emerge at the research front where interaction with one's peers is as important as the storehouse of conventional wisdom. (15)

Price found, in his samples from the 1950s and 1960s, that journals in physics and biochemistry had indexes of 60 to 70 percent recent references (i.e., from the previous five years), while social science journals clustered around 40 percent, and some of the humanities journals dipped below 10 percent.[4] Price's characterization of the humanities as involving a slow digestion of everything that has gone before may no longer be accurate, as my chapters 4 and 5 will suggest. At this point, however, I am interested in his characterization of the "packed down past" of work in science. A high percentage of references to recent work would coincide with a compacting process in which researchers work on well-defined problems, with relatively clear criteria or an evolving consensus about what would constitute progress on those problems and would, therefore, no longer need to be cited. In such an enterprise, researchers can build progressively upon the work of their most immediate predecessors.

Similarly, in a study of communication activities in the physical and social sciences, Garvey, Lin, and Nelson found greater lags in the process of information flow in the social sciences—for example, lags between writing and publication and higher rejection rates in the social sciences. These lags may indicate that the social sciences have less clearly defined and demarcated problems than the sciences and therefore less clearly defined criteria for what constitutes good problem solving. When criteria are less clearly defined, interpretative variation increases. This is not to suggest that interpretation does not enter into the sciences or that the social sciences and humanities are inferior, but that the kinds of knowledge making involved in different disciplines may entail a number of consequences. The lags Garvey, Lin, and Nelson describe indicate that the sciences may be placed at an extreme on the continuum of compact problem solving; we may, by extension, suspect that the humanities are further along the continuum than the social sciences, in the direction opposite the sciences.

With so many indications of differences in disciplinary compact-ness, it is difficult to see how such differences could be explained solely by the individual preferences of academics or the accidents of tradition. Individual dispositions may be involved insofar as individu-als choose to enter disciplines that fit their individual learning styles; David Kolb, for instance, has found two styles that correspond roughly to the humanities and the sciences: (1) divergers, who prefer concrete experience and reflective observation, tend to be found in the humani-ties; and (2) assimilators, who create theoretical models and assimilate disparate observations into integrated explanations, tend to be found in the sciences (Kolb 238). Kolb's findings support other indications that the disciplines differ, but they do not offer a definitive causal explanation; there is no reason to believe that the differences between the sciences and the humanities (to use the two extremes) arise exclu-sively or even primarily from the differences in their practitioners. There appear to be further causes more firmly rooted in the subject matter of the disciplines, the kinds of knowledge problems connected to that subject matter, and the epistemic traditions that have evolved within the disciplinary conversation.

One explanation of the tendency toward particularism in the humanities is that the kind of compacting that makes sense in science simply would not be as fruitful given the subject matter of the humani-ties. Richard Ohmann has argued, for instance, that because science is arranged in a hierarchy of theories linked to central questions, specialists may work upon very small parts of those problems for the sake of improving the generality and economy of theories. Theory, in science, "is a device for reducing phenomena to their underlying

similarities, for doing away with them as unique and special cases.
. . . The intellectual holdings of a field are constantly being put in
better order, subjected to more inclusive theories" (Ohmann 9). Literary research, Ohmann argued, works on different principles because
there is no system of central principles by which to order and condense
phenomena—nor would literary scholars want to do away with the
complexity or uniqueness of literary works (13).

Ohmann was writing in 1976, before the impact of Continental
theory on the field of literary studies. The relation between particulars
and theory has been altered under that impact, with theory assuming
a far greater importance. Yet surely, even now, the Shakespearean
(whether New Historicist, textual scholar, or New Critic) does not
wish to do away with Shakespeare after having arrived at some kind
of generalities about Shakespeare or his social milieu. The social
historian of Colonial New England, as we shall see, may be either
reluctant or unable to reduce phenomena to underlying regularities.
The relative lack of disciplinary compacting in the humanities, then,
may be connected to the relative particularism of the phenomena
under study.

*The Connection between Compact Problems
and "Progress"*

To understand how some disciplinary problems may lead to
greater compacting involves invoking two notions that have become
suspect from their connections to an older foundationalist view of
knowledge—the notions of rationality and progress. Even in a non-
foundationalist, constructionist view of inquiry, however, there is
room for a more modest, contingent, relative view of both rationality
and progress.

The compacting of knowledge about a disciplinary problem occurs through the operation of communal decision making. Decision
making within a discourse community is influenced, of course, by a
wide range of cultural or contextual variables that are beyond the
scope of my examination here. I will be concerned with the part of
the process that appears in texts: persuasion, adjudication, reason
giving, citation, use of authority, and clear delineation of method. To
attempt to make good decisions within a disciplinary framework may
be called "rational" in the sense that it involves conscious attempts

to address and make progress on disciplinary problems within the disciplinary framework. This part of communal decision making is necessarily influenced by the number of other academics who are writing on the same problem and the degree to which the problem itself is generalizable. Becher's distinction between urban and rural helps explain why decision making might work differently in rural fields than in urban fields where many people concentrate on relatively few problems and there are fewer constraints on reducing phenomena to patterns.

Rational decision making involves the interplay between disciplinary community and individual practitioner and may occur in either (1) the social evolution of discipline-specific standards or practices of reasoning and theory-choice within a research tradition; or (2) an individual writer's use of those practices to persuade others who agree to the importance of the same standards, standards which have historical and social roots within a discipline, rather than roots in some transhistorical logic. By this argument, individual writers within any discipline become part of an ongoing conversation within that discipline, using its standards to represent their own role in the ongoing conversation and to convince others of the value of their individual contribution.

This rather limited definition of rational decision making is important because social constructionist models in varying ways have insisted on the fallibility of scientific reasoning. Kuhn's distinction between normal and revolutionary sciences, in *The Structure of Scientific Revolutions*, raised important questions about the rationality of paradigm shifts in scientific research, particularly in his argument that research paradigms are incommensurable. His argument that revolutionary developments in science were not the result of slow accretion within a research tradition but of breaks with the tradition— paradigm shifts—raised doubts about whether science worked in the objective, progressive way that many had formerly assumed. But at the same time, Kuhn insisted on what may be termed rational progress within normal science—the episodes of steady development between revolutionary paradigm shifts. If one were primarily concerned to explain paradigm change, then questions of incommensurability, anomaly, and crisis would be paramount; but if one is primarily concerned to examine the everyday workings of the academy, as I am, then the workings of normal science become more important. Although Kuhn's depiction of scientific revolution drew more attention than his depiction of normal science, for my purposes his description of normal science is more interesting because his characterization of it as "puzzle-solving" helps locate disciplinary variation in the way that a discourse community defines and works on its problems. The model of normal science that may be derived from a reading of Kuhn, then, emphasizes rationality and community, with progress occurring as the result of the operation of rational puzzle- or problem-solving within the disciplinary community of scientists.[5]

Rational decision making in a disciplinary community, then, entails a notion of possible progress on disciplinary problems. Though the notion of progress has been out of favor at least since Kuhn, there are many indications that a kind of progress occurs in science more consistently than it does in the social sciences or the humanities. It is useful, then, to consider what might, optimally, constitute progress on a disciplinary problem in a scientific community. Interestingly, both Kuhn and Toulmin explain their notions of rational progress by analogy to Darwin's concept of natural selection. Kuhn distinguishes between two competing notions of progress: evolving progress *toward* a goal and evolving progression *from* whatever preceded it (e.g., Kuhn 172). The former is a teleological notion and implies that science (in this case) is moving toward a closer fit with something like "truth." From the standpoint of the history of science, there are obvious problems with such a notion, and any sociological study of science can turn up instances of self-interested behavior on the part of scientists, behavior that casts doubt on the rationality or truth seeking of individuals. So the idea of progress has tended to be discredited, rather than simply this particular notion of progress.

Even more emphatically for Toulmin, Darwinian natural selection offers a model for examining the mechanism of "progress" without having to adopt some of the philosophical or teleological baggage discredited in the other idea of progress. In natural selection, changes in organisms occur randomly, rather than because they are goal-directed, but afterwards environmental constraints operate in such a way that some changes are adaptive and some are not. On the whole, the adaptive changes survive (or are "selected")—not because they are better in any absolute sense, but because they fit better within the environmental constraints. The mechanism of change is thus separate from the mechanism of selection.

Applied to scientific knowledge making, this model permits a distinction between the individual decisions of members of the community and the long-term selection processes operating in the community. Individuals may make irrational decisions that survive within the community, but in the long run, if enough individuals are involved, rational selections will occur; ideas and research findings that fit disciplinary paradigms or solve disciplinary problems most effectively will be chosen. Rationality, in this process, is defined not in relation to a priori truths but in relation to the tasks a particular academic discourse community sets for itself. The model suggests the importance of examining how particular academic discourse communities display their selection processes within their discourse.

If the disciplinary community is not only the source of ideas and problem solutions, but also the ultimate arbiter of their value, then the more academics working on the same problem, the more opportunities for both discovery and negotiation. Because of the influence of Continental theory in the humanities and some social sciences—for example, Foucault's "What Is an Author?"—emphasis has shifted, recently, to the individual's lack of importance as the source of new ideas: individuals are seen not as standing apart from communities but as socialized within communities. This notion of the community's importance in generating ideas is consistent with my explorations here, as will be seen, but it is perhaps more important to stress the role of community as arbiter, rather than community as generator. If some kinds of disciplinary discourse are less distinguished than others by the kind of progress this model of science describes, then we must look partly to the processes by which academic discourse communities monitor and arbitrate the work of the community.

From a variety of work in the history, sociology, and philosophy of science, then, we have a model of scientific communities as both generically like other communities and yet in important ways distinctive, as a species of community, from other academic communities. It is important not to adopt an either/or position but to see both the kinship and the difference. In kinship with other communities, scientific communities are subject to historical influences operating on them as upon other communities, not simply operating by some transhistorical logic. But sometimes this point has kept us from exploring the ramifications of the other point—that scientific communities are also different, even from other academic communities.

One aspect of this difference, according to Kuhn (164), is the comparative insulation of the discourse community in science; the community's insulation from extraprofessional concerns allows its discourse to develop without too much turmoil from competing viewpoints. Toulmin elaborates upon this point by saying that scientific communities require a protected "forum of competition"—like the local niche of Darwinian biology that allows a species to develop variations distinct from those of other species (e.g., the birds of the Galapagos Islands). Toulmin argues,

> Failing this professional isolation, and the critical control exercised by professional reference-groups, it will be much harder for novel ideas to stake out precise claims, and so establish their place in a well-founded body of knowledge. Instead they will be lost in a welter of speculative debates and polemical objections, in which their characteristic virtues and implications can no longer be identified and explored. And, once the essential balance on which conceptual evolution depends is destroyed, there will be no stable equilibrium short of intellectual conformism or conceptual anarchy. (*Understanding* 295)

A lack of limited, cohesive disciplinary understandings, in this scenario, prevents good conceptual innovation from gaining power and yet allows insufficient control over proliferating innovations.

By contrast to the "compact" disciplinary community Toulmin sees in science, fields in the humanities have some of the characteristics of the "conceptual anarchy" he describes. Kuhn's distinction about pre-paradigmatic, normal, and revolutionary scientific fields and Toulmin's distinctions about compact, diffuse, and would-be disciplines may seem to suggest that accident is involved in whether a particular field of research has arrived at well-defined problems and rational communal procedures. Perhaps, one could argue, some nonparadigmatic disciplines are merely latecomers in the academy and will eventually reach paradigmatic conditions like their elder siblings in physics. But we also need to look carefully at fundamental constraints on the degree of compactness disciplinary problems may reach. In the humanities, constraints may arise from the kinds of phenomena taken as the subject matter of a disciplinary enterprise. Additional constraints may have been shaped through the traditions and practices of the community's discourse, but in either case such constraints are likely to be more powerful than the individual wills of disciplinary practitioners. They affect how members of the community relate to each others' written texts, offer evidence, cite sources, and so forth and, therefore, affect the degree to which problems may be well defined or progress may be made on them.

Explanatory versus Interpretive Goals

Indications of how some disciplinary fields lend themselves to compacting less readily than others may be found in both history and literary studies. One article in my sample of New England Colonial history begins with a lament about the lack of cumulative synthesis in the field:

> During the last twenty-five years scholars of colonial New England, particularly its seventeenth century, have presented interpretations of such variation and complexity as to almost defy synthesis and to raise doubts as to whether "New England" is a meaningful category. Several superb, yet discrete, studies have examined a wide range of subjects from the dynamics of specific communities to variations of the New England mind, from the transfer of local institutions to the experiences of women and children. [Here the author footnotes "essays reviewing the nature and issues of recent New England studies" in Greene and Pole.][6] Together, these studies have sensitized us to the diversity of human experience in early New England. Yet, in general, the parts remain parts, their relationships uncertain. (Archer 477)

This complaint was published in 1990, but it was not the first in its field. In 1977, Michael Zuckerman wrote that New England historians had fallen into two camps, one emphasizing "the ascendancy of individualism" and the other "the sway of community." "Such studies," Zuckerman wrote, "constitute, collectively, an advancing embarrassment" (183). In 1978, Thomas Bender made the same complaint about the "community breakdown thesis" (51).

It is significant that we find such complaints in history recurring over the space of a decade—significant, also, that they occur in social history—for history is a field poised between the social sciences and humanities and torn frequently between the goal of resembling the "compact" disciplines in their ability to push forward with synthetic generalizations and, on the other hand, the goal of rendering the experience of the past as the humanities have more traditionally done. Social history, in particular, has aspired to render the experience of people whose lives did not appear in the traditional narratives of kings, politics, and battles. Archer's and Zuckerman's comments show the perplexity with which academics sometimes view the differing uses of generalization and particularism in academic writing.

These historians' comments indicate not a flaw in the subfield of colonial history but a characteristic tension in humanistic inquiry. The comparatively greater particularism of the humanities has a number of textual and epistemological consequences. What is at issue, however, may be articulated in different ways. It may be seen as a tension between particularism and generalization or between interpretation and explanation. Clifford Geertz, in his frequently cited "Blurred Genres," has argued that "many social scientists have turned away from a laws and instances ideal of explanation toward a cases and interpretations one, looking less for the sort of thing that connects planets and pendulums and more for the sort that connects chrysanthemums and swords" (*Local Knowledge* 19). His argument is worth examining since it has been widely accepted among humanists and "interpretive" social scientists. Geertz argued that social scientists have "just freed themselves, and then only partially, from dreams of social physics—covering laws, unified science, operationalism, and all that," so social scientists need to "develop systems of analysis in which such conceptions as following a rule, constructing a representation, expressing an attitude, or forming an intention are going to play central roles—rather than such conceptions as isolating a cause, determining a variable, measuring a force, or defining a function" (*Local Knowledge* 23).

I will argue that Geertz is partially right, but that his account is misleading. The "covering law" model of social science is indeed dead, and its death has helped fields like history address their own disciplinary distinctness more clearly (see chapter 4). But social scientists like the attachment researchers I will discuss are still committed to explanation—not to simplistic, reductionistic explanations of the billiard-ball-hits-billiard-ball type, but to explanation nevertheless. Two features of accounts like Geertz's are striking: first, the assumption that humanistic interpretation is preferable to modes of inquiry traditional to the social scientists. This hints of partisan turf battles conducted without trying to understand the reasons for differing modes of inquiry in different fields.

Secondly, such accounts often occur in hyperbolic language, as in the case of Rabinow and Sullivan's introduction to their 1979 volume, *Interpretive Social Science*:

> As long as there has been a social science, the expectation has been that it would turn from its humanistic infancy to the maturity of hard science, thereby leaving behind its dependence on value, judgment,

and individual insight. The dream of modern Western man to be freed from his passions, his unconscious, his history, and his traditions through the liberating use of reason has been the deepest theme of contemporary social science thought. Perhaps the deepest theme of the twentieth century, however, has been the shattering of the triumphalist view of history bequeathed to us by the nineteenth. What Comte saw as the inevitable achievement of man, positive reason, Weber saw as an iron cage. (1)

Such hyperbolic accounts of the death of an explanatory social science have been greatly exaggerated.

The phenomenon Geertz described might more accurately be characterized as a growing realization, in some social sciences at least, that there is room for interpretive as well as explanatory modes and that the explanatory mode involves more complexity than in earlier positivist assumptions about logical explanation. Whether the explanatory mode is disappearing is far more dubious. By foregoing apocalyptic fervor and academic turf wars and attempting to develop a more tempered, descriptive, and tolerant understanding of the varieties of academic discourse, we will find, I suggest, both explanatory and interpretive modes. We will learn, furthermore, to make two kinds of distinctions that tend to be neglected whenever hyperbole and turf wars enter in. We will learn to distinguish between good and poor work in either knowledge-making mode, and we will learn how to talk about whether some subjects of inquiry lend themselves better to one mode than to another.[7]

Rabinow and Sullivan's assumptions, like Geertz's, privileged "culture" over "nature" in a way that tended to preclude discussion of whether there are some subjects—even in the "human sciences"—that involve more generalizable processes than others. Attachment researchers have found enough evidence of the phenomenon of attachment in all cultures to justify the explanatory attempt to identify variables affecting attachment or to generalize about which kinds of attachment will result in problems later in life. To inquire, for instance, into the relationship between attachment and early maltreatment is not to privilege covering-law or billiard-ball models of causality. It is at least possible that human infants are born with a tendency to be attracted to the stimulation we label as "affection" and that abuse is experienced as aversive by infants cross-culturally. By being situated close to or past a blurred boundary between "culture" and "nature," then, early infant attachment may lend itself to explanatory—though not positivistic—methods of research more readily, for instance, than literary texts. Conversely, since literary texts are clearly in the realm of "culture," interpretive modes seem more appropriate than explanatory ones.

Geertz's emphasis on localized variations is congruent with Ohmann's account of how, in the humanities, value may be placed upon particulars apart from their ability to be subsumed under higher-level generalizations. Like literary scholars who may not want to do away with individual works of literature in the service of higher-level generalizations, New England social historians may be reluctant to move altogether away from individual experiences of seventeenth-century New Englanders toward generalizations about that experience. There are at least two possible reasons for such reluctance. First, generalizations may efface important patterns of variation in the same way that statistical averages may efface patterns of individual difference. But generalizations about individual experience tend to efface that experience in a second way also, because such generalizations frequently involve aggregate or quantitative presentation that distances the reader from the feel of everyday life in the past. A historian may prefer not to efface that experience.

On the other hand, a historian might be inclined toward uncovering patterns of experience in order to compare them, for instance, with analogous patterns in other times and places—social patterns in seventeenth-and eighteenth-century Virginia or Pennsylvania history, for instance, may be contrasted to the New England pattern. To discern such patterns, a historian might need to move away from rendering individual particulars and use the quantitative methods of the social sciences in order to generalize and categorize. But these competing historical projects exist in tension with each other. Although much of the social history of Colonial New England contains quantification, many articles display an uneasy feeling that the field is having difficulty progressing toward better generalizations.

This complicated issue is not easily addressed by either/or choices or by judging one kind of academic inquiry superior to another. Two kinds of differences in tandem make fields in the humanities distinctive from more "compact" fields like attachment research: (1) the humanities tend to be rooted in phenomena, data, or texts which are potentially worth knowing about for their own sake, not simply as the necessary first step toward generalization; and (2) the humanities tend to involve more intermediary representations—such as literary texts—between raw phenomena and generalization, thereby creating more phenomenal layers. For example, if Shakespeare's plays are viewed as a realistic mirror of life in general or even the life of his time, then they present a single layer for understanding. But with that assumption largely abandoned, interpreting Shakespeare involves more questions than just what lens Shakespeare looked through and what lenses we, in turn, look through. We may ask how he represented Elizabethan life and may examine his representations for signs of internal inconsistencies, preoccupations, or exclusions that he may not have intended or been aware of. We may ask whether and how his representations may have constituted ways of acting indirectly on his world, rather than realistic reflections of that world, and so on. Geertz's discussion of "thick description" (*Interpretation*) is one way of describing the density of layers with which interpretation must deal.

The humanities tend to be concerned with phenomena, then, that are richly layered in their phenomenal representation. The social sciences, like psychology, are perhaps differently layered. In chapter 3, I will discuss how attachment research moved forward over a period of two decades partly through increasing complexity or elaboration at a theoretical level.

Conceptually Driven versus Text-Driven Generalization

Both the humanities and social sciences range from the top to the bottom of the ladder of abstraction. They both contain particulars and generalizations, but they differ in the use or direction of their generalizations. I will describe the characteristic mode of knowledge making in the humanities as interpretive and its use of generalizations as relatively particularistic. Compact knowledge making typical of the social sciences and sciences, on the other hand, I will describe as "conceptually driven" in that conceptual questions generate inquiry. The metaphoric "driven" (as in rear- or front-wheel drive) is useful for describing something about the direction and impetus within these fields, without having to imply that one field is abstract and the other concrete.

A typical interpretive academic enterprise, as in the case of literature, may begin with a text and then move upward in interpretation from particulars of the text toward higher levels of abstraction. Although the given material of literature is textual, in other areas of the humanities the given material may be films, historical documents, or works of art. When humanistic interpretation is "driven" by phenomenal material such as texts, it may be called "text driven" as a way of emphasizing its difference from, for instance, attachment research that begins with a conceptual question.

To suggest that literary study is often "text driven"—particularly in the New Critical mode—is not meant to deny the kind of insights that reader-response theories have allowed us to see; certainly readers bring attitudes, memories, and cultural influences to texts in ways that help determine our readings, and certainly readers are active constructors of meaning. To describe literary interpretation as text driven is to suggest, first, that a reader or interpreter of a literary text begins in some way with the text, a given that exists prior to interpretation and drives the development of interpretive abstractions based on it. Though the interpreter will bring preconceptions to the text, the text brings the preconceptions into play. The preconceptions do not drive the interpreter to approach the text.

By contrast, scientists are likely to set up studies (whether case studies, for instance, or experimental studies) in order to make progress toward answering specific conceptual questions. Evidence of conceptually driven work may be seen in Gilbert and Mulkay's interviews with biochemists, as in the following account from "Leman's" interview:

> When I arrived here, I thought that the clearest way of demonstrating that energy input served to promote ATP dissociation from the enzyme rather than the formation of a covalent bond, would be to show a change of binding affinity for the ATP upon energisation. Everything up to that point had been kinetic evidence . . . and I felt some nice good thermodynamic data would help. (Gilbert and Mulkay 48)

This statement suggests that Leman began wanting to demonstrate that "energy input served to promote ATP dissociation" and felt convinced that the best way to prove or demonstrate his hypothesis would be to look at one sort of data rather than another. Gilbert and Mulkay conclude, from this statement, that "Leman does not describe himself as testing the model or trying to disprove it. Rather he portrays his actions in terms of looking for new kinds of evidence to furnish additional support" (48). This, I suggest, is one form that rational, conceptually driven work will take: looking for support for a conceptual explanation. Gilbert and Mulkay's interviews suggest, furthermore, that "when there are two or more competing 'theories' available in a given area of investigation, each will usually lead to the design of quite distinctive experiments" (63). If a theory is a proposed solution to a disciplinary problem, then designing an experiment specifically to prove a theory should constitute normal practice within a conceptually driven field of knowledge making. In chapter 3, I will examine how attachment researchers move from conceptual problems—for example, how healthy attachment occurs—to observing specific cases. The cases they choose or the experiments they devise are constructed in the service of a conceptual question.

To say that literary interpretation tends to be text driven by the impulse to explain a text (or set of texts), not conceptually driven by a disciplinary problem external to the text, is to oversimplify because it does not account for changes of emphasis since the New Criticism. Current cultural critics may be said to have more conceptually driven modes of interpretation, but if so, they may also be said to work more like social scientists. It is easier to sort out the kinds of complexities I am concerned with here by beginning with a relatively simple model and concentrating on unblurred examples before investigating possible blurrings. For that reason, my examples of paradigmatically "text-driven" academic work come from literary interpretations that may be called "close readings." These "close readings" are likely to be considered old-fashioned by vanguard critics and theoreticians, but they continue as a staple of classroom discourse and are also useful in exploring some of the differing points on the continuum of academic writing.

To say that social science discourse is more conceptually driven and converging in its generalizations than literary interpretation is not to invoke either of two seemingly related binary oppositions: the subject/object or the inductive/deductive opposition. I do not mean to imply that one type of academic writing is either more subjective or more objective than another. Recent literary criticism as well as the philosophy and sociology of science have suggested that neither literary texts nor scientific data are perceived without the mediation of preconceptions the reader or investigator holds. Such work has also suggested that there is no such thing as pure induction—generalization based solely on lower-level instances without higher-level preconceptions of some sort. The "hermeneutic circle" provides a model of how abstract preconceptions may guide interpretation of particulars and how interpretation of particulars may, in turn, help form abstractions. If inductive reasoning is from the bottom up and deductive reasoning is from the top down, probably most or all academic work involves a continual interplay between bottom-up and top-down reasoning.

But the opposition I wish to explore is not between preconception and something else or between bottom-up and top-down reasoning; rather, it involves two different ways in which the generalizations and particular instances of a field stand in relation to each other. This model is to serve as a tool of analysis rather than a rigid taxonomic ordering—as a model of continuous, rather than discrete categories. The continuum in this case involves differing relations between higher-level abstractions and lower-level textual or other particulars (using the metaphor of the "ladder of abstraction" on which abstractions are "high" and particulars are "low"). I will initially describe cases distinctly separated from each other on the continuum, rather than the middle ground between them (where subfields of history tend to lie), hoping, thereby, to identify major tendencies that would otherwise be obscured—tendencies with far-reaching implications for writers.

Particularism in New Critical Literary Interpretation

New Criticism, defined broadly as a type of literary interpretation that focuses on close readings of texts, still affects the way literature is taught and the way literary texts are read, though as a method of interpretation it is now in disfavor at the higher levels of the profession.[8] Both attachment research and Colonial New England social history have a continuous history since the sixties, with key works from the sixties still regularly cited and used as models for current research. By contrast, literary studies in the past twenty years has distanced itself from the New Criticism dominant through the 1960s, and current critics tend either not to refer to predecessors from that decade or to refer to them oppositionally—as employing a mode of interpretation that current critics oppose. Perhaps this difference is a matter of accident: perhaps the subfields I examine from psychology and history simply happened to spring up in the sixties, and twenty years from now literary studies will show a similarly continuous line of scholarly descent starting in the 1980s. One could argue that psychology and history made the transition from preparadigmatic to paradigmatic in the sixties and that literary studies made its transition in the eighties. But it seems equally likely that the discontinuities in literary study over the last two decades reflect a greater difficulty in arriving at consensual paradigms than exists in fields within or closer to the social sciences.

To understand this discontinuity in literary studies is, in part, to understand the particularistic tendencies of the humanities. New Critical writing about literature gives a sense of what more recent literary studies evolved from (or against) and shows especially clearly some of the ramifications of particularism. New Critical interpretive writing—with its close readings of texts and reluctance to look to extraliterary biographical, social, or historical influences—may be characterized as particularistic in that its genesis lay in particular textual details. The text(s) in question might exhibit seeming incongruities, unusual juxtapositions, or repeated motifs that could be construed as interpretive "problems." From these textual particulars, interpreters construct more abstract categorizations or classifications of some part(s) of the text.

In the process of moving upward toward more abstract classification, terms and/or concepts could become increasingly divergent among different interpreters. This means not that interpreters worked purely inductively without preconceptions, but that they could choose abstract categories relatively unconstrained by any prior professional or disciplinary agreements about one set of preferred terms or about disciplinary problems to be solved. Over the last two decades, by contrast, attachment researchers have focused on a set of common and predictable disciplinary questions about attachment, but no such common starting point could be said to drive New Critical interpretation. The relationship between particular and abstract conceptualization in literary interpretation and attachment research could be diagrammed as, respectively, an inverted triangle and a triangle. In literature, any particular part of the text to be explained could lead upward to a broadening set of abstract conceptualizations (the inverted triangle) of the text while in psychology the top-level conceptualization has been the point of origin for an increasingly elaborated set of concepts and applications as attachment researchers move down the ladder of abstraction from concept to particular data.

In New Critical literary interpretation, with the text a given, the interpreter built interpretive abstractions of the sort that Fahnestock and Secor (*Rhetoric*) have called categorical propositions; when given a text or a piece of a text, intepretation involved telling what the text—or part of the text—was *about*. Often a repeated textual image was chosen—for example, windows in *Wuthering Heights* (see Van Ghent)—and the image was then classified as being *about* something else, an instance of some theme that could be abstracted from the text. Interpreting a text or part of a text as an instance of a more abstract categorization involves establishing criteria by which to do so, but it is possible to have different criteria and therefore to generate different systems of categorization. These differing categorizations, I suggest, account for much of the variation in New Critical literary interpretation and, therefore, for a tendency toward noncompact disciplinary development.

We see an example of how categorizations of textual items may vary in Elizabeth Gaskell's novel *Cranford* (1853; rev. 1864). A novel firmly within the realist tradition, *Cranford* depicts a group of unmarried, provincial, Victorian ladies whose lives are characterized by their social customs, the kind of hats or caps they wear, and a set of letters exchanged by the main character's parents. To construct an abstract interpretation of these concrete textual data—such as the letters from the parents of the main character, Matty—involves choosing abstract terms relatively unconstrained either by Gaskell's text or by disciplinary conversation about it. The letters could be interpreted, for instance, as signifying the father's tendency toward idealism and the mother's toward pragmatism. What is interesting, for my discussion here, is how underdetermined that particular abstract categorization is. The abstract categories might just as easily be worded differently—the letters still seen as Gaskell's means of contrasting male and female, but perhaps described as male concern for justice versus female concern for love instead of male idealism versus female pragmatism.

The reader-response theorist could undoubtedly say a great deal about this kind of variance among individual readers or about how interpretations vary over time. Current interest in gender, for instance, enables readers to see gendered categories in Gaskell's text. I am concerned here, however, with the disciplinary or professional implications of the variation and its consequences for writers in the discipline. Since Gaskell's text does not require any particular reader to choose one set of terms for an abstraction rather than another, as a type of text-driven discourse it will tend toward divergent abstractions and therefore divergent language in the absence of a disciplinary problem that requires sustained negotiation about the meaning of the letters. Even if all readers agree that the letters in *Cranford* are salient items for literary interpretation, they still may not agree on what category the letters fall into—that is, whether they represent a difference between idealistic and pragmatic characters or between characters preoccupied with justice and those preoccupied with emotion. Then even among those who agree on the first of these two categories, some might choose different language to describe the same category. Someone might legitimately prefer "formal" to "idealistic," and someone else might prefer "practical" to "pragmatic." In fact if we substitute "formal versus practical" for "idealistic versus pragmatic," it is hard to know whether we are still talking about the same categories. These abstractions are "upward diverging" in that as interpretations move upward on a ladder of abstraction, they are increasingly likely to diverge from each other in language and possibly in meaning. Only sustained attention to interpretive problems in Gaskell by a cohesive, working discourse community would lend compacting pressures to this otherwise "rural" academic discourse.

Interpretive disagreements may occur at different levels on the ladder of abstraction. An example of disagreement at a relatively high level may be seen in interpretations of George Eliot's *Middlemarch*. Even among feminist readers, some have seen the novel as realistic in showing that a nineteenth-century woman like Dorothea Brooke would marry and not pursue a career while others have criticized Eliot for undermining her own ideals; they have seen her as too fearful of public opinion or too handicapped by her own condition to be able to allow Dorothea to live with the freedom Eliot achieved in her own life (e.g., Edwards). This kind of interpretive disagreement involves evaluation rather than categorization. Both sets of readers have agreed on their categorization of what Dorothea's marriage means and what *Middlemarch* is about; they have simply disagreed on their evaluations thereof.

Sometimes an entire text can produce basic categorization problems. The categorization problem in Anthony Trollope's *Mr. Scarborough's Family* (1883) is unusually striking in that critics scarcely agree on what the novel is *about*. In Fahnestock and Secor's terms, the categorical proposition about the novel is in question (*Rhetoric*). The differences of opinion about *Mr. Scarborough's Family* are far more basic than those about *Middlemarch*. The character of Mr. Scarborough has been considered by some to be heroic (Kincaid), by others megalomaniacal (Cockshut). Some describe Scarborough's actions as successful, some as not successful. Some think the novel itself advocates moral relativism; some think it demonstrates the dangers of moral relativism. The patterns are so inconsistent that the following interpretations have been possible: (1) that Scarborough is heroic but not successful, and the novel supports moral relativism, (2) that Scarborough is heroic and successful and the novel supports moral relativism, or (3) that Scarborough is megalomaniacal but not successful, with the novel showing the dangers of relativism, and so forth through a number of critical permutations. The novel has been described as "about" a variety of abstract issues: "honesty" (Cockshut 235), "individual freedom in a moral society" (Polhemus 241), "primogeniture and the laws that support it" (apRoberts 155), "the problem of trust" (Slakey 318), and the disappointment of old age (MacDonald 107–10).[9]

In the case of Gaskell and Trollope, the variation in text-driven interpretation derives partly from the multivocality of texts and signs. In the case of Eliot, ideological preferences enter into differences in evaluation. But in each case there are also socially situated disciplinary influences operating. Particularly with a novelist like Trollope, there are relatively few critics at work on a large body of literature, so that Trollope criticism offers a fairly extreme example of a "rural" field (Becher) in which few critics address a potentially large number of problems, thereby reducing the opportunity for disciplinary negotiation on each particular claim.

Particularism in Shakespeare Criticism

Although Shakespeare has received far more sustained critical attention than Gaskell or Trollope, some of the same interpretive divergence may be found in text-driven readings of Shakespeare. In 1979 Richard Levin published a critique of the "new readings" of Renaissance drama still being produced under the influence of New Criticism then, even though the influence of Continental theorists like Derrida was already being felt in literary studies at the theoretical level. Levin characterized these new readings as, to use my own terms, particularistic and text driven. He summarized what fourteen readings of Jonson's *Volpone* since 1937 had produced in the way of disparate "central themes" when critics moved upward in abstraction from the particulars of the drama to a "central theme." As in the case of *Mr. Scarborough's Family*, there was wide variance in the abstractions chosen to characterize what *Volpone* was about:

1. avarice
2. money and the power it confers
3. lust and greed
4. immoderate desire
5. disorder
6. disinheritance
7. disease and cure
8. the unnaturalness of sin
9. the folly of worldliness
10. the false estimation of reality
11. the idea of "playing"
12. corrupted creativity
13. the comic spirit itself
14. the centrifugal personality

(*New Readings* 14)

In the case of thematic readings of Shakespeare, Levin found the connection between particular and abstraction to be troubling because critics tended to find either the same theme for different works or different themes for the same work, as in these samples he quoted:

> *A Midsummer Night's Dream* can . . . be reasonably regarded as a sustained meditation on reality and illusion.

> [*A Midsummer Night's Dream* is] Shakespeare's first attempt to explore and justify the distinctive qualities of his art as a way to knowledge.

> *Much Ado about Nothing* . . . must take its place in Shakespeare's incessant debate about the conflict between appearance and reality. (*New Readings* 12)

As Levin saw it, to claim that both *A Midsummer Night's Dream* and *Much Ado* are about illusion and reality was to negate the differences in character and plot action that make them different plays at the particular level. To find conflicting claims about the central theme of a play such as *A Midsummer Night's Dream* demonstrated to Levin that there was something amiss in the workings of literary studies. Part of what he described confirms the phenomenon I have pointed to with Trollope and Gaskell—that the particulars of literary texts are complex enough to enable divergent abstractions to be built upon them. Some kinds of literature—morality plays, for instance—might not promote the same degree of divergence because they would point toward only one abstraction or one conceptual generalization. But Shakespeare, Gaskell, and Trollope all offer their readers (or audience) richly complex human stories from which divergent abstractions may be drawn.

Part of the uneasy relation between particular and abstraction may come, then, from literature's standing in a different relation to abstraction than does, for instance, attachment research. To theorize that the attachment between parent and child has a primary importance in the child's life is not to assert that other factors (e.g., good nutrition, cognitive stimulation, cultural practices, genetic inheritance) are unimportant. But attachment researchers have been able to abstract "attachment" from the complexity of phenomena in order to examine its role.

In the case of Renaissance drama, however, as Levin saw it in 1979, there were two problems making the relation between abstract and particular problematic. The first of these was his sense that the "central themes" identified for Renaissance plays were the wrong kind of abstraction:

> The thematists, we saw, assume that the play is not about what it appears to be about—the particular actions of particular characters— because it is really about a general idea. Consequently, the characters and events are no longer significant in their own right, but as exemplars of the idea, which is supposed to be the object of our response. And since in the abstractness of that idea the specific structure or physiognomy of the play is inevitably lost, the tendency of this approach is to lead us away from our actual dramatic experience. (*New Readings* 200)

Recent New Historicists, as I will discuss in chapter 5, focus on different kinds of abstractions than their New Critical predecessors, abstractions not likely to be posed as universal or ahistorical themes (whether the New Historicists' abstractions lead away from the actual dramatic experience or not is a separate matter). Levin argued, in part, that New Critical literary abstractions rose too high on the ladder of abstraction. The particulars of *A Midsummer Night's Dream* would not be disregarded if we described it as a play in which young lovers become confused about which person they are in love with. But to make the leap upward in abstraction from a play about the irrationality of young love to a play about reality and illusion is to lose some anchoring in the particulars of the drama. Levin saw the "new readings" as relying on thematic leaps that were arbitrary in two ways. First, "the choice of the general class is wholly arbitrary since any character or event belongs to many different classes and subclasses" (26). This I take to be as true of Gaskell and Trollope as of Shakespeare: signs and meanings are multivalent or multivocal by their nature, and so the choice of general class will diverge with different interpreters.

But Levin argued, secondly, that "there is no reason why [characters] should be regarded as the representatives of any class at all" (26). The "thematic leapers . . . operate upon the major figures, which include some of the most highly individuated characters in our literature. But this individuation must inevitably be diminished to the extent that we view them as class-representatives, for they will then possess only those traits shared by all members of the class" (26). This second criticism points to a historical phenomenon in literary criticism, a tendency to essentialize or universalize present in older criticism and frequently criticized by current New Historicists.

Levin was critical not just of the kinds of abstraction present in close readings but also of the role of the scholarly community. He argued that there were no controls from within the discourse community on the kinds of interpretations being published. He saw publish-or-perish pressures on academics as forcing critics to churn out more readings; to be published the readings needed to be novel, and so the "my-theme-can-lick-your-theme gambit" resulted (196–97). Shakespearean criticism in the academy (then as now) proceeds without the real-world exigencies involved in, for instance, attachment researchers' decisions to look at the reasons for infants' successful and unsuccessful attachment to their parents. For attachment researchers, external problems like World War II orphans or abused children have lent a sense of exigency to the field's research problems, but such exigencies are lacking in Renaissance literature. Literary critics by the 1970s were presented with a shrinking job market, a still-expanding pool of job candidates, exponentially increasing publication, continued pressure to publish or perish—and no expansion at all in the territory Shakespeare represented for them to inhabit.[10]

As a result of the general laissez-faire critical atmosphere, critics could create novelty by means of the "my-theme-can-lick-your-theme gambit," with individual critics outflanking other critics' themes by going either above or below them on the ladder of abstraction. Whenever critics went upward to outflank each other, they contributed to the "escalation of inclusiveness" (38). The problems Levin saw in New Critical readings of Renaissance drama as of 1979, then, were of two sorts: (1) the problematic relation between particular and abstraction, and (2) the failure of the discourse community to monitor its productions rationally.

Levin's solution to the problem focused on the relation between community and rationality. He pointed to the community's failure to adjudicate rival interpretations (203), to overcome the "attitude of cynical laissez-faire" born out of implicit recognition of the publish-or-perish pressure (206), or to arrange the review process so that "rational conversation" could be encouraged (207).

These, then, may be seen as potential liabilities of a text-driven enterprise like the New Criticism: that laissez-faire community practices would allow the movement from particular to abstraction to be made without any rational controls on the diverging results, that the community would lack either well-defined problems to address or well-defined criteria for adjudicating contributions to the field, and that, in consequence, staking out "new" interpretative positions would fill the vacuum where rational negotiation or communal problem solving might conceivably operate.

Variations in Epistemic Self-Consciousness

Much of the preceding discussion has been only indirectly connected to actual textual presentation, but it has been necessary to lay out the larger patterns of variation that affect seemly local features of academic articles. Introductions in compact disciplinary work, for instance, reveal each of the patterns I have discussed: compact disciplinary problems, explanatory goals, and conceptually driven generalization.

In attachment research, for instance, it is characteristic, to find immediate statement of the problem addressed in the article. Three traits of initial problem definition or presentation in psychology articles are particularly worth noting: (1) there is no attempting to hook the reader (as students in the humanities are often taught), but instead an immediate, getting-down-to-business focus on the professional problem; (2) the focus is not on the phenomenon under study—child development, in this case—but on the state of knowledge and argument current in the research field; and (3) the key conceptual terms are standard to writers in the field.[11] Sroufe, Fox, and Pancake (1983), for instance, begin as follows:

> The concepts of dependency and attachment have received a great amount of attention from developmental psychologists. Historically, three stages in the history of these concepts may be discerned: (1) the rise to prominence of the dependency concept (e.g., Sears, Maccoby, & Levin, 1957), (2) assimilation of the ethological concept of attachment to the dominant dependency paradigm and interchangeable use of the terms (Gewirtz, 1972; Maccoby & Masters, 1970), and (3) the separation of the two concepts, with a concurrent ascendancy of attachment (Ainsworth, 1969, 1972; Ainsworth, Blehar, Waters, & Wall, 1978; Bowlby, 1969; Maccoby, 1980; Sroufe & Waters, 1977). A new and fruitful interrelating of these concepts, now distinguished, remains to be accomplished. (1615)

The position the writers take toward the substance of psychological research here is typical. The initial focus is on the professional problem, rather than on the phenomenon under study or the findings themselves, because the first step is to validate the importance of the approach—that is, to characterize the state of attachment research as regards some particular part of the disciplinary enterprise and therefore to locate one's own contribution therein. Particular findings, in this way, are closely connected to the state of knowledge in the field.

But if we turn to a brief sampling of academic writing at the other end of the continuum of problem definition and presentation, we can find a very different kind of problem presentation in current literary studies. It is not my intention to discuss Renaissance New Historicism fully in this chapter but to begin outlining, through contrast, some patterns of variation. In Renaissance New Historicism, one can find two differing approaches to initial problem presentation. The introduction of the article may fill roughly the same professional role I have described in psychology—that of framing the current argument in its relation to previous arguments in the field. This kind of introduction is epistemic in its focus on the knowledge-making processes of the field. For instance, Jean Howard's first paragraph in "Renaissance Antitheatricality and the Politics of Gender and Rank in *Much Ado About Nothing*" directly addresses previous work on Shakespeare in four out of its nine sentences and distinguishes her own position in three of the nine. She characterizes the failures of earlier criticism: "Much of this criticism aspires to articulate an unchanging or universal meaning for the play—a task both impossible and impossibly idealist" (163). And she concludes the introductory paragraph by articulating her own position:

> In contradistinction to a criticism committed to the drama's place "above ideology" and to its aesthetic and thematic unity, a political criticism of Renaissance drama will focus precisely on the silences and contradictions which reveal the constructed—and interested—nature of dramatic representations and on the ideological functions served by the plays as produced and read at specific historical junctures and through the mediation of specific theatrical and critical practices. (Howard 164)

The progressive, line-of-descent account offered in Sroufe, Fox, and Pancake depicts attachment research as slowly building on its foundations and gaining the power to differentiate between competing explanations so as to choose more powerful ones. Despite its emphasis on progressive conceptual change and the shortcomings of the dependency perspective, the account is, nevertheless, one of continuity within the field of attachment research. By contrast, Howard's account is one of rupture—a fairly common kind of account in literary studies. Rather than accounts of continuity, James Battersby finds a kind of conventionalized scapegoating in the attitudes of current critics toward earlier critics: "[Theorists] are always distinguished from traditionalist critics—those mostly mythical beings, usually invoked for purposes of invidious comparison, who truculently persist in crediting the discredited" (51).

Despite Howard's emphasis on rupture, her account may nevertheless be called epistemic in that, like the psychology articles, it explicitly characterizes the state of professional discourse in relation to the work Howard undertakes. However, Howard's introduction is epistemic in a different way than Sroufe, Fox, and Pancake's. Her problem presentation is more oppositional and less preoccupied with subtly accounting for degrees of progress in current research in her field. Her first paragraph contains only two footnotes to other criticism (a study from 1961 and one from 1981) while the comparable first paragraph in psychology refers to nine works in the field of attachment research and is able to show some continuity and progress on a communal knowledge problem.

A second kind of introduction may also be found in Renaissance New Historicism, a nonepistemic, anecdotal or narrative introduction. The introduction from Stephen Greenblatt's "Invisible Bullets: Renaissance Authority and Its Subversion" focuses on Renaissance writers and anecdotes, rather than on the state of Renaissance study, and does not explicitly *present* a communally defined problem at all. In chapter 5, I discuss this particular example and the anecdotal style typical of much New Historicism. I am not, in this chapter, trying to account for why some Renaissance New Historicists have turned toward anecdote rather than epistemic accounting, nor am I considering how nonepistemic writing might be viewed on its own terms. But I am trying to indicate what kinds of differences in disciplinary problem presentation need to be explored.

The differences in mode of initial problem presentation may suggest that mode of textual presentation of problems may vary independently of the nature of disciplinary problem definition. But more often the two are connected: certain types of disciplinary problems are likely to be presented succinctly and at the beginning of an article, and fields in which writers tend not to give succinct, communal problem definitions are likely to be fields in which problems take one sort of shape rather than another. Despite this interconnection, though, it is useful to keep the distinction between problem definition and problem presentation in mind, especially later when we look at the Renaissance New Historicists' modes of presentation.

In this chapter, I have focused primarily on patterns of variation as a context for looking more closely at the differences in actual texts. The very small sample of Renaissance New Historicism I have referred to already indicates some of the differences to be found among academic disciplines and thereby indicates questions we may ask about academic problem definition. I now turn to case studies of three subdisciplinary fields.

Case Studies in
Three Subfields

CHAPTER THREE

Attachment Research
Compact Problem Definition in a Conceptually Driven Field

Attachment research has developed over the last twenty to thirty years as a subfield of developmental psychology. Within the larger discipline of psychology, developmentalists focus on understanding infancy and childhood. Within that subfield, there are further subfields; developmentalists more interested in cognition focus their research on the development of thinking and reasoning while those interested in social behavior focus on emotions, attachment, peer relations, and personality. Attachment research is a readily identifiable subfield among those focusing on social development. The field's boundaries are permeable in that developmental researchers with other primary interests might look to attachment research for possible explanations of the origins of child abuse or which kindergarteners are most popular among their peers. But despite this permeability, attachment research remains an identifiable field because of the clarity and continuity of its problem definition.

I begin with a historical account of the growth of attachment research in order to trace the continuity, development, and compacting of its problem definition. I then discuss the relation between generalization and particulars in this conceptually driven, explanatory field.

Progress and Compacting in Attachment's Problem Definition

The abstract from a 1983 psychology article in my sample of attachment research will serve both to introduce some aspects of compact problem definition and to describe typical concerns in attachment research:

> In the past 15 years, a major advance in the study of early social development has been the conceptual distinction between attachment (the relationship between infant and caregiver) and dependency (the reliance of the child on adults for nurturance, attention, or assistance). Having made this distinction, it is possible to ask questions anew concerning the relationship between infant-caregiver relations and later overdependency of the child. In this study such a tie was examined by assessing children with varying attachment histories in a preschool setting. It was found that groups of children classified at 12 and 18 months as avoidant (Ainsworth Group A) and resistant (Ainsworth Group C) both were highly dependent in the preschool, based on teacher ratings, rankings and Q sorts, observed physical contact seeking, and observed guidance and discipline received from teachers. Children who had been securely attached (Group B) were significantly lower on all these measures and significantly higher on "seeking attention in positive ways." The high dependency of both anxiously attached groups, despite their differences in manifest behavior in the attachment assessments, suggests that the roots of overdependency lie in the quality of the early infant-caregiver relationship. (Sroufe, Fox, and Pancake 1615)

This abstract displays a number of traits of compact disciplinary work, beginning with its representation of disciplinary progress. Writing in 1983, Sroufe, Fox, and Pancake were able to represent their field as having fifteen years of cumulative work. Their term "advance" implied that the field was making progress on the problems it had chosen to focus on, as did their statement "Having made this distinction, it is possible to ask questions anew." Even if this was merely an overly neat narrative imposed upon a messy body of research over time, it is still significant that practitioners in the field could convincingly represent the field to each other as having progressed—that kind of narrative of the research field, as we will see, is either difficult to tell in history and literature or else does not seem valuable to tell.

The kind of concepts foregrounded by Sroufe, Fox, and Pancake offer further signs of a compact discourse. The choice between "attachment" and "dependency" in the first sentence of the abstract foregrounded the conceptual and disciplinary focus, rather than the phenomena themselves: what was at stake was causal explanation within their disciplinary discourse. By the 1980s, attachment researchers, according to Sroufe, Fox, and Pancake, had come to separate the two concepts of "dependency" and "attachment." Earlier learning theories had associated the two concepts because both "emphasized early caregiver-infant contact and because most of the same behaviors (crying, clinging, proximity seeking) underlay both constructs" (1615–16). When assumptions underlying the dependency concept were discredited, attachment also fell into disfavor, according to this account. Sroufe, Fox, and Pancake undertook in this article to "disentangle" the two concepts and "reexamine the relationship of dependency to attachment" (1616). The terms "attachment" and "dependency" were communal and stable in the sense that they were understood and used in the same ways by researchers in child development whether they were advocates of attachment theory or not. The conceptual point of the article could be made succinctly because both concepts were frequently used in an ongoing literature and represented clearly differentiated causal explanations.

The three classifications of avoidant (A), secure (B), and resistant (C) attachment that Sroufe, Fox, and Pancake mentioned had similar compacting effects: they grew out of lengthy collaboration and negotiation within the field, allowing researchers to replicate, refine, or extend each others' work. The classification categories were developed through collaboration, with common origins in the Strange Situation procedure devised by Ainsworth and Wittig (1969). The Strange Situation procedure has continued for two decades to be a standardizing—and therefore compacting—procedure for the field. In this procedure, children in a room with their mothers are briefly separated from their mothers (by her leaving the room) and then observed. Children who respond to the mother's leaving and reappearance without becoming upset but also without seeking contact on her reappearance are classified, under the procedure, as Avoidant (A). Those who respond by becoming upset and not calming down on her return, possibly becoming angry and hostile toward their mothers, are classified as Resistant (C). Those classified as Secure (B) are those who become moderately upset upon mother's leaving but seek proximity on her return and are fairly easily quieted.

If progress is seen as a moving from, rather than a teleological moving toward, then it can be seen as a narrative of continuity tracing intellectual descent. In the narrative that follows, I do not attempt to cover all work in attachment research or to suggest that alternative narratives could not be told; I do suggest, however, that from the point of view of participants in the field, what follows would look like a reasonable narrative of the progress by which the field of attachment research moved forward over the last two decades.

The progress within attachment research can be seen as occurring in five stages. The stages are continuous, rather than discrete—not clearly demarcated, linear, or rigid—but they nevertheless suggest an evolution through these five phases: (1) initial theory formation; (2) development of a procedure allowing better observation, description, and eventually quantification; (3) classifications of behavior and refinement of those classifications; (4) differentiations, elaboration, and refinements at the conceptual level, with the top-level concepts still in place, but with further development of layering at slightly lower conceptual levels; and (5) increasing applications of attachment research to related problems. The last two stages occur simultaneously, but by discussing each of these stages separately, I hope to differentiate the ingredients that have gone into the process by which attachment research has been able to move along and grow in importance.

Stage One:
Initial Theory Formation

John Bowlby's first volume of *Attachment and Loss* was published in 1969. It read, in its first sections, like an example of Kuhn's revolutionary science in that before even introducing what he had to say about attachment, Bowlby spent a great deal of time explaining his shift away from the then-dominant Freudian model. Bowlby presented himself as initially faced with a problem and with data that could not be well explained by the reigning paradigms. In the Preface, he explained that in 1950 the World Health Organization asked him "to advise on the mental health of homeless children" and that he began with the principle that "What is believed to be essential for mental health is that the infant and young child should experience a warm, intimate and continuous relationship with his mother (or permanent mother-substitute)" (xi–xii). Reviewers of his 1951 study, however, pointed out how little was known "about the processes whereby these ill effects are brought into being" (xii), and so began Bowlby's problem-solving project of explaining attachment.

In Bowlby's second chapter, he explained another kind of external exigency:

> Apart from a few early references, some of them by Freud, no series of observations of how infants and young children behave when separated from mother was on record until the early 1940s. Then the first observations, made in the Hampstead Nurseries during the Second World War, were reported by Dorothy Burlingham and Anna Freud (1942, 1944). . . . The second series of observations are those made by Rene Spitz and Katherine Wolf on about one hundred infants of unmarried mothers who were cared for in a penal institution (Spitz and Wolf, 1946). (Bowlby 24)

These two kinds of external exigency—the request from the World Health Organization and the empirical observations beginning in the 1940s—are worth noting as more likely to occur in a field like psychology than in the humanities. One can scarcely imagine the same kind of external exigency leading to new frontiers in Shakespeare scholarship, though claims of exigency of a literary kind are nevertheless made.[1] Like the problem of drug-addicted babies today, problems arising from separation became especially noticeable under particular historical circumstances, that is, during the war with its attendant dislocations. So, in the case of attachment research, the academic problem of explaining infant attachment was generated partly by a practical external problem suggesting a need for better understanding.

Despite the urgency of the problems of attachment that Bowlby's work was intended to address, however, the author spent relatively little time on them at the outset, just the brief mentions in the preface and chapter two. He devoted far more space and effort to disciplinary issues, justifying his departure from the Freudian model of mother/infant relations. The first half of his first volume, *Attachment*, is devoted not to attachment but to justifying and explaining what Kuhn might call a paradigm shift, a turning away from Freud and toward an ethological and adaptationist theory. Since Bowlby was trained as a psychoanalyst, his lengthy (175-page) justification of the new adaptationist model is striking—a long and rather laborious route to what has since become attachment theory, but a laborious route that Bowlby's successors have not had to repeat. Once done, it has remained done, and his successors have been able to start at a point much further along the route, taking much more for granted.

Bowlby began by offering an alternative to the energy model of drives that Freud held, a model derived from the influence of nineteenth-century physics. Instead of drives that are like entities, building up, overflowing, subsiding, and building up again, Bowlby turned to animal behavior from the Continental ethological tradition (Lorenz, Tinbergen) and evolutionary biology of a more British version (a line of descent from Darwin to one of Bowlby's mentors, Robert Hinde). In this perspective, the attachment between mother and infant is the product of natural selection over the course of human evolution. In times of danger, it is adaptive for an infant to be close to the mother, and therefore complex behavioral systems have evolved in which infants and their mothers (or primary caretakers) interact in ways that increase proximity or contact when it seems needed.

What is particularly noteworthy about Bowlby's lengthy replacement of the Freudian model is that, on the one hand, he is careful at the outset to show how Freud might have approved of this new direction and how Bowlby's own work might be seen as a legitimate development from Freud. On the other hand, he spends far more time explaining and justifying the importance of the adaptationist perspective, as if hesitant to adopt this position of apostasy without the most thorough justification.

As Kuhn suggested, the reigning paradigm in a period of normal science does not automatically solve all the problems within the field; instead it helps identify problems and directions for research to take. Bowlby, in 1969, described four "classes of problem to be solved" (331):

a. What, descriptively, is the range of variation in attachment behaviour at any particular age, and in terms of what dimensions are variations best described?
b. What antecedent conditions influence the development of each variety of pattern?

c. How stable is each pattern at each age?

d. How is each pattern related to subsequent personality development and mental health? (331)

These have, in fact, been the problems attachment research has dealt with for the last two decades—not because of the authority of Bowlby, but because these are the kinds of problems developmental psychologists consider important, the kinds of problems that constitute the disciplinary identity of psychology.

Stage Two:
Development of a Procedure Allowing Observation,
Description, and (Eventually) Quantification

Although Bowlby laid out the theory of attachment, the next step in the development of the field is associated with Mary Ainsworth, who was a member of Bowlby's research unit in London from 1950 to 1954 (Bretherton and Waters ix). Ainsworth, with coworkers, devised a procedure for empirical examination of infant attachment. The procedure—the Strange Situation (Ainsworth and Wittig, 1969)—allowed observation of infants under conditions more stressful than in their own homes and thereby allowed researchers to observe how attachment behavior was evoked by stress. Initially, the procedure allowed Ainsworth and her coworkers to compare different children in the same situation, and eventually the Strange Situation procedure allowed large-scale study of infant attachment of a standardizable sort.[2] The procedure is still used as the primary method of studying attachment. It consists of eight episodes in which mother and infant are joined in a room by an observer, mother leaves the room, mother reenters, mother leaves again, and mother reenters a second time (Ainsworth and Wittig 114–16). The infant's reaction to the mother's departure and reentry are observed and later analyzed.

Stage Three:
Development and Refinement of Classifications

As a stage in the progression initiated by Bowlby's work, the Strange Situation procedure had the virtue of allowing the move from description and observation to classification. The Ainsworth and

Wittig article that first described the Strange Situation differs from most of the later attachment research in containing brief case studies or case histories of individual infants. The authors described the distinctive individual responses of six of the fourteen infants in the sample, referring to them by name, describing their reactions to mother's leaving the room, and describing some of the family interactions in the background. For instance, this is part of the case study of Karen, who was classified in group C (resistant attachment):

> For her first six months Karen was kept most of the time in her own room with the door closed. Her mother's policy was not to pick her up if she merely cried, but only if she screamed. But her screaming tended to be muffled by the distance and by the closed door. Moreover, her mother could tune her out, either not hearing her crying at all, or believing that she heard happy, singing noises. Karen would announce that she was hungry by screaming, but even after her mother acknowledged that it was time to feed her, there was often a long delay while she readied her food, and dealt with the interruptions provided by the other children [Karen's four siblings]. (Ainsworth and Wittig 133)

The brief information on Karen's history clearly helped point to the article's concluding generalizations about what "variables of mother-infant interaction . . . seem to foster the growth of healthy attachment, while at the same time fostering the growth of competence" (136).

Ainsworth and Wittig identified five variables as common in the securely attached infants: (1) the mother's using "frequent and sustained physical contact" to sooth the baby in distress; (2) "the mother's sensitivity to the baby's signals" and ability to adjust her interventions to the baby's rhythms; (3) "an environment which is so regulated that the baby can derive a sense of the consequences of his own actions, and come to feel that what he does can have some consistent and hence predictable effect on what happens to him"; (4) freedom to explore visually and through locomotion; and (5) "mutual delight the mother and baby take in their transactions with each other" (136).

The model of a compact discipline that I have described would predict that as a field of research progresses some things can be dropped or taken for granted. The kind of individualized case history seen in the passage about Karen tends to drop out of the literature.

As I will explain in in chapter 6, there are no instances of sentences about individual babies like Karen in my sample of current articles on attachment.[3] It appears that Ainsworth and Wittig initially worked by looking closely at individual examples and generalizing from them. Then as research progressed, both through an increase of data studies and through conceptual refinement, the individual cases became no longer necessary as a point of focus in articles. Compared to case studies as a vehicle for moving the field forward after the point reached by 1969, the generalizations made possible by classification must have seemed more reliable than any particulars about particular children and more capable of being refined to pinpoint the differences between pattern and individual variation.

The relation between generalization and particular evolved over the course of attachment research. Perhaps the most important step toward generalizations that could benefit the field occurred only marginally in the 1969 Ainsworth and Wittig article and was relegated largely to a footnote. The authors noted that the fourteen infants in the sample appeared to fall into three groups, though the groups were not yet named (i.e., avoidant, secure, and resistant) and not foregrounded as they were later to be.

By the time Ainsworth, Blehar, Waters, and Wall published *Patterns of Attachment: A Psychological Study of the Strange Situation* in 1978, they had introduced and developed a substantial body of research on a classification system to make sense of the results found with the Strange Situation. They described three categories of attachment—avoidant (A), secure (B), and resistant (C), naming the three groups that Ainsworth and Wittig had described in 1969, but assigning far more importance to the categorizations and formalizing them to a greater degree.

It is indicative of epistemic self-consciousness and of disciplinary compacting that the authors of *Patterns of Attachment* could discuss explicitly the drawbacks and virtues of classification and could advocate their classification system as contributing to progress within their research field—a "first step toward grasping the organization of complex behavioral data" (56). They explained that they developed a classification system, not because of "a belief in a more or less rigid typological concept of the way in which human behavior is organized," but because "one must first describe and classify when one sets out to study natural phenomena" (56). They then quoted Robert Hinde

(1974): "Description and classification may not seem very difficult tasks, but their neglect hampered many aspects of psychology for half a century. . . . This descriptive phase, essential in the development of every science, was bypassed by those experimental psychologists who attempted to model their strategies on classical physics" (Hinde 5, quoted in Ainsworth et al. 56).

The virtue of the three categories of attachment explained in *Patterns of Attachment* was that differences in instances of behavior such as crying or clinging could be seen to fall into three overall patterns, rather than as a large number of discrete behaviors. On the whole, the avoidant infants (category A) did not seem worried when their mother left the room, and they avoided contact with her when she returned. The secure infants (category B) were upset by the mother's absence but greeted her on her return and calmed down quickly. The resistant or ambivalent infants (category C) were upset when the mother left but did not calm down when she returned. They seemed to want contact, but when she made overtures on her return, they might react with aggression.

These larger patterns are not determined by individual items of behavior, such as crying, because the individual items have different meanings in different contexts. Crying may, for instance, be a sign either of proximity seeking or of anger. One infant might lift her arms to encourage her mother to pick her up, while another might crawl toward the mother with the same goal in mind. Thus individual items of behavior had to be lumped together in larger categories such as "proximity seeking" or "contact resisting," and then the overall patterns of proximity seeking and so forth had to be described.

In the generalizations that resulted, infants in attachment classification A are low in "proximity seeking" while those in both classifications B and C are high. On "contact resisting," however, infants in classifications A and B react the same way (low on contact resisting) while those in classification C react differently. If one simply took "contact resisting" in isolation—without considering where it came in the Strange Situation sequence—then the A and B groups could not be differentiated. To lump all behaviors together without looking at the patterns, then, would produce a seeming mishmash. The classification system overcame that problem, and so once the classifications were in place, more researchers began using both the procedure and the classifications.

Stage Four:
Differentiations and Refinements at Conceptual Levels

By 1978, then, an increasingly complex ability to differentiate meanings in context had allowed attachment research to move forward in several ways—to explain data, refine the initial theory, and preserve its conceptual focus in the face of critiques by researchers with rival explanations. Since then, journal articles on attachment have taken several forms: refinement and elaboration of the classification system, theoretical articles refining conceptual elements in response to critiques, and applications of attachment research to situations such as day care, child abuse, later relations with peers, learning in school, and so forth.

The theoretical articles refining conceptual elements and refuting opposing constructs are especially worth looking at in relation to the model of progressive accumulation in science. Four such articles in particular stand out as milestones: (1) one by Sroufe and Waters (1977) distinguishing between trait theories and the theory of attachment, (2) the one by Sroufe, Fox, and Pancake (1983) discussed above, distinguishing between the concept of dependency and that of attachment, (3) one by Sroufe (1985) defending the concept of attachment as something that cannot be reduced merely to differences in temperament, and (4) one published in 1992 by eight well-known attachment researchers (Vaughn et al.) attempting to reconcile the relational and the temperament perspectives. From this list alone, several aspects of the research community are visible: Sroufe's importance as a theorist, the continuity within the field, the communal interactions (Waters was coauthor of *Patterns* with Ainsworth, coauthor of the 1977 theoretical article with Sroufe, one of eight coauthors of the 1992 article), and the importance of refining and differentiating concepts.

In "Attachment as an Organizational Construct" (1977) Sroufe and Waters distinguished between organizational and trait constructs, the former defining attachment research and the latter belonging to its challengers. They presented the problem in their first paragraph:

> Assumptions concerning the nature of constructs underlying developmental research are often only implicit, yet they guide data collection and interpretation of results. For example, a number of researchers have provided data concerning intercorrelations among behaviors pre-

sumed to be indices of attachment (e.g., Coates, Anderson, & Hartup 1972; Maccoby & Feldman 1972). Noting that such "index" behaviors do not intercorrelate highly, do not show temporal stability, and are strongly influenced by context, critics have concluded that the attachment *construct* itself is wanting, that concepts such as attachment relationship and affective bond are superfluous, and that varying patterns of attachment behavior among infants are of little consequence (Cairns 1972; Gewirtz 1972a, 1972b; Masters & Wellman 1974; Rosenthal 1973; Weinraub, Brooks, & Lewis 1977). It has been suggested that individual differences be disregarded (e.g., Masters & Wellman 1974) and that research on attachment be reduced to study of contingencies within the contemporary interaction of caregiver-infant dyads (e.g., Cairns 1972; Gewirtz 1972a, 1972b; Rosenthal 1973). (Sroufe and Waters 1184)

Several aspects of this problem presentation are important as signs of the conceptual activity and epistemic self-consciousness in the field. The amount of activity, to begin with, is evident from Sroufe and Waters' ability to list thirteen other researchers whose work has indirectly or directly challenged attachment theory. Those challenges, together with the amount of work supporting attachment theory, represent a great deal of sustained focus on this one disciplinary problem. The first sentence showed that Sroufe and Waters had developed an important conceptual tool for arguing with their critics, rather than merely ignoring them. By not simply pointing to data or evidence to answer their critics, they avoided the charge of naive positivism; they did not argue that the evidence spoke for itself. And they recognized that constructs guide interpretation of data. Interestingly, they used that theoretical insight to enhance their own arguments; that is, they argued that their critics were interpreting data through the wrong lens and therefore failed to see the import of attachment theory. They thereby undermined their critics' argument that the data did not support the claims of attachment research, and they demonstrated the conceptually driven nature of their argument.

Their ability to refer economically, in their first paragraph, to eight articles representing the opposing position was a sign that psychologists of competing perspectives were nevertheless able to address each other's findings, talk each other's language, and standardize their accounts of research findings in their field.[4] That is, whether or not they agreed with each other, developmental psychologists still found it important to argue explicitly about their differences (something that literary critics are not inclined to do in quite the same manner). Sroufe and Waters represented the field of attachment research as one involving progress with a continuous line of descent from Bowlby. They discussed Bowlby's views not in order to distance themselves from him, as some Renaissance New Historicists do with their predecessors from the 1960s, but to indicate the direction in which the field was moving—that is, being elaborated, refined, and further differentiated.

We see here that research constructs of the sort found in attachment research are layered; at the top level of the hierarchy is a general concept of the importance of the child's relationship with the primary caregiver(s).[5] There are not simply two layers—the concept and the data—but also intermediary layers with further differentiations. In the following passage on Bowlby, we see Sroufe and Waters creating or defining such intermediary layers:

> Bowlby's (1969) conceptualization is the starting point for an organizational view of attachment and remains the definitive work on the topic. By casting attachment in systems theory terms of set goals, goal correction, and function, he removed the construct from encumbrance by drive reduction and causal trait concepts. . . . Significant as Bowlby's classic work has been, his control systems model (as distinguished from his broader theoretical perspective) requires elaboration to yield a truly viable developmental construct which can serve a vital integrative function in the study of infancy. Bowlby discarded drive reduction in his working model of attachment at the expense of motivational and affective components, which are central to the organizational view presented here and which are not tied to drive reduction theories, except by tradition . . . (Sroufe and Waters 1185)

At the same time as this Sroufe and Waters article, the authors of *Patterns of Attachment* (including Waters) were arguing that "index behaviors," particular behaviors such as crying, should be seen not as discrete items of behavior, but as parts of patterned behavior. Through arguing for an "organizational" approach—emphasizing the relationship between caretaker and infant, rather than merely items of the infant's behavior—Sroufe and Waters could marshal theoretical constructs to interpret the data in different ways from those who argued by means of trait constructs.

The same kind of issue emerged again in relation to a different set of opposing arguments in Sroufe, Fox, and Pancake's "Attachment and Dependency in Developmental Perspective" (1983). This article made the point that attachment and dependency were initially linked, but that the linking was "unfortunate": "When assumptions underlying trait theory (cross-time and cross-situational generality, intercorrelated indexes, etc.) were challenged, both concepts fell into disfavor" (1616). Distinguishing between dependency and attachment allowed Sroufe, Fox, and Pancake to hypothesize that although dependency is the norm in infant attachment behavior (as seen in infants' contact seeking, interaction with, and being nurtured by the caregiver) secure attachment in infancy would lead to later autonomy, rather than to later dependency (1617). By contrast, children who are later found to be overly dependent, they hypothesized, would be likely not to have been securely attached in infancy. The data from their study in a preschool setting, along with other data, thereby fit the attachment hypothesis. The concept of dependency, by contrast, seemed unlikely to explain the apparent instability over time in which securely attached infants showed dependency as infants and autonomy later on but avoidant and resistant infants later showed dependency. From the standpoint of the psychologist's disciplinary interest in stability over time and in the antecedents and consequences of behavior, attachment research, therefore, appeared to offer better explanations than did older views of dependency.[6]

In the third of these theoretical articles, "Attachment Classification from the Perspective of Infant-Caregiver Relationships and Infant Temperament" (1985), Sroufe replied to another set of critiques surrounding the same kind of issue: whether the patterns of differences in attachment are simply manifestations of temperamental differences in the infant or caregiver. Kagan and others had argued that differences in attachment classification did not reflect differences in parental interactions with the child so much as inborn variations in the temperament of the child. Sroufe argued, again, that attachment is a relational (or organizational) construct—the index of a relationship, rather than something inherent in a person. Temperament was therefore inadequate, Sroufe argued, for conceptualizing attachment because temperament is the characteristic of an individual.

The fourth of these articles by Vaughn, Stevenson-Hinde, Waters, Kotsaftis, Lefever, Shouldice, Trudel, and Belsky (1992) was the collaborative effort of eight authors from seven institutions in the United States, Canada, and England, entitled "Attachment Security and Temperament in Infancy and Early Childhood: Some Conceptual Clarifications." The "conceptual clarifications" they offered were to help resolve the difference between the relational perspective (e.g., Sroufe) in attachment research and the temperament perspective. As they characterized it, the "core dispute in this controversy is whether factors regulating the expression of affect are intrinsic to the child (temperament) or are emergent properties of the child-adult relationship (attachment)" (463).

What is interesting about the article, from my perspective here, is not just their conclusion that "the strong versions of both the temperament and the attachment positions are flawed" (464) but the extent of collaboration involved and the evidence such collaboration affords of the disciplinary compacting within attachment research. The compacting is evident in the authors' ability to draw on six different sets of data, a variety of measures of temperament and attachment, and a highly developed set of discriminations for negotiating the claims of the two opposed arguments. Such compacting can only result from lengthy, sustained attention to the same problems by an extensive group of researchers who collect data in the same conceptually driven manner and build on, refine, and dispute each others' work.

Whether Sroufe's relational argument is vindicated or modified by the opposing argument of the temperament research, the alternation of proposed conceptual model, critique, redefinition and refinement in attachment research has moved along in a way that may be described as progress, at least within the framework of attachment research itself. If, ultimately, the temperament researchers convince attachment researchers to modify their concept of what causes differences in attachment classification, perhaps both sides will feel that they know more about child development than they did before the process of refining descriptions and explanations of infant attachment began.

Stage Five:
Applications of Attachment Research

Concurrent with the theoretical refinements I have described above, attachment researchers have extended the uses of attachment theory and the Strange Situation procedure to explore such subjects as children's later relationships with parents and peers, social popularity, and aggression. The research base within the field of attachment has, in effect, burgeoned into an academic industry, with applications spreading in many directions beyond the core of attachment theory that has been present since Bowlby. Though there are periodic theoretical treatments that concentrate solely on theoretical argument without new data (e.g., Sroufe's 1985 article), most articles in the field remain rooted in empirical studies, even when their primary contribution appears to lie in conceptual refinement. At the same time, the uses of attachment research have spread to connect with more issues within developmental psychology. The more the applications, the clearer the need or directions for conceptual refinement.

The dual process of conceptual refinement and extended application is apparent, for instance, among the sample articles whose language I analyze in chapter 6. Egeland and Sroufe (1981) examined the connections between attachment and early maltreatment; and Carlson, Cicchetti, Barnett, and Braunwald (1989) examined the usefulness of a fourth attachment classification (Type D for disorganized/disoriented) in studying maltreated infants. Belsky and Rovine (1988) examined the correlations between nonmaternal care and security of infant-parent attachment. Cohn (1990) examined associations between attachment and peer social competence of six-year-olds.

These extended applications also involved conceptual progress. In addition to their insights into the connections between attachment and maltreatment, the Egeland and Sroufe article helped clarify the difference between Type A and C attachment, and the Carlson et al. article (1989) not only helped develop the Type D categorization but also used that category to help understand the mechanisms of insecure attachment. Both the Belsky and Rovine and the Carlson et al. studies found gender effects indicating that boys are at greater risk with extensive nonmaternal care (Belsky and Rovine) or in the absence of a male partner in the home (Carlson et al.). The complexity of these effects could scarcely have been discovered or examined if fewer researchers had been at work on attachment research for a shorter period of time because in each case these studies rely on a base of well-developed and established insights as building blocks for further conceptual clarification.

Attachment research has become a powerful explanatory field within developmental psychology partly because its conceptual refinement has not occurred in a vacuum. These studies are highly specific in that distinctions are attended to carefully—for example, the distinction between abusing and neglecting a child, between a child's rejecting or ignoring a parent, between girls' and boys' reactions to father absence, between socioeconomic variables, between individual differences in temperament. But the attention to specifics is not attention to anomalous particulars so much as to classifiable differences. Contextual variables are accorded full attention, but the conceptually driven character of the knowledge-making enterprise provides a continual framework for understanding particulars.

How Attachment Research Is Conceptually Driven

On the continuum of academic discourse between interpretation and explanation or text driven and conceptually driven, attachment research may be considered explanatory and conceptually driven. Despite the importance of data, attachment researchers resemble most social scientists in that they do not typically *start* by looking at data without a hypothesis first directing the questions they ask, and their hypotheses tend to be communally defined within the disciplinary subfield. Someone may read or watch Shakespearean drama without a purpose, but the child developmentalist does not ordinarily, in a professional capacity, observe children's behavior without some hypothetical proposition involving a conceptualization such as attachment. The conceptualization is collaboratively developed and may involve explanatory prediction about patterns in other data.[7] An attachment researcher who begins research by setting up a strange situation procedure to study abused children's relations to their parents has already chosen a conceptual lens in the way a critic of Shakespeare or Trollope under the New Criticism did not do prior to approaching the text.

Attachment theory was conceptually driven from its inception in that Bowlby's understanding of evolutionary theory allowed him to see ways in which other interpretations might be wrong. He argued that the phenomenon he termed "attachment" had been wrongly explained earlier by secondary drive theory. In the latter, a limited number of drives were postulated, and then other behavior was assumed to be learned by association. By this logic, for instance, "liking to be with other members of the species is a result of being fed by them" (Bowlby 210–11). Bowlby used concepts from evolutionary theory to ask questions about what sort of data would discredit secondary drive theory. For instance, Lorenz's work on imprinting showed attachment behavior could develop without the young receiving food or other conventional rewards (Bowlby 211). If attachment occurs independently of the posited drive for food, then it must be the result of an independent behavioral system.

Conceptually driven arguments were still necessary for Ainsworth, Blehar, Waters, and Wall in *Patterns of Attachment* (1978) to sort out the explanatory potential of attachment theory as compared to social learning theory. Whereas Bowlby had used evolutionary theory to argue against both Freudian and behaviorist explanations, by this later period the arguments occurred within the discipline of psychology and between somewhat closely related alternative theories; some disciplinary compacting, in other words, had occurred, with both Freudian and behaviorist views fairly well discredited. Through a decade of argumentation and research, attachment researchers had essentially won the conceptual battle and defined the conceptual starting point from which child developmentalists would view attachment. This disciplinary compacting stands in obvious contrast to the laissez-faire, my-theme-can-lick-your-theme approach Levin perceived in literary criticism of the same period.

The way in which this conceptual compacting occurred was not mysterious: it involved criteria drawn from the conceptual layers of the disciplinary discussion. Attachment researchers won their battle through persuading an increasing number of developmental psychologists that the conceptual lens they looked through had more explanatory power than its competitors. The battle was won not by data, but by a more convincing fit between data and attachment theory than between data and social learning theory.

The way that criteria drawn from the concept of attachment were evoked to sort out better explanations was illustrated in *Patterns* when Ainsworth, Blehar, Waters, and Wall discussed a review by Maccoby and Masters (1970) which "attempted to rework attachment theory so that it is in harmony with the earlier dependency paradigm" (285). Because Maccoby and Masters viewed attachment as a trait (rather than an organizational construct, in Sroufe and Waters's terms), they considered *strength* of attachment particularly important. As Ainsworth and her colleagues wrote, "They suggested 10 possible measures of behavior strength, including the number of persons toward which the behavior is shown—a criterion obviously at variance with evolutionary-ethological attachment theory . . ." (286).

This "variance" lay in the incompatibility of attachment occurring toward a number of people. A key element of the evolutionary interpretation is that attachment evolved among primates as a way of keeping the child close to the caretaker while the child was still too helpless to defend him- or herself from predators. From that theoretical perspective, it would be nonsense for a child to be indiscriminate about which person to show attachment toward, and a child would be expected not to show strong attachment to most adults. So Maccoby and Masters's three criteria to support a trait hypothesis were deemed "largely irrelevant" by Ainsworth et al.:

> We can see no theoretical basis for expecting all attachment behaviors to be positively correlated—in other words, that a baby who cries much, for example, should also smile, vocalize, approach, and cuddle in when picked up significantly more often than others. This is not to say that we view the ways in which a baby mediates his attachment to his mother as unrelated to one another; but we view their intercorrelations as complexly patterned rather than in any simple, unidimensional relationship implying strength of attachment. (287)

In other words, if each of these infant behaviors were viewed separately and the strength of each calculated, an infant who cried a lot and an infant who smiled or cuddled a lot might be considered to have equally "strong" attachment, but "strength" on individual items of behavior was not a sensible way to consider the complex relationship between baby and mother.

The use of conceptual criteria here illustrates not just progress and compacting through increasing ability to make close discriminations, but also how the field is conceptually driven. The criteria for deciding what counts as evidence, for classifying behavior or attachment patterns, and for accepting or refuting other researchers' explanations are all driven by the top-level theories in the field.

It is not surprising to us—post-Kuhn—to find that theories drive decisions about what counts as evidence, but such an insight need not be treated as a dirty secret that scientists try to conceal. Ainsworth and her collaborators—like Sroufe and Waters in their 1977 article— were quite aware of the ways in which theories drive consideration of data (Ainsworth et al. referred several times to Kuhn in order to depict attachment research as a paradigm shift). They pointed to this phenomenon explicitly as a positive, not negative, aspect of their endeavor. Evolutionary theory helped them, they might argue, to derive criteria for acting rationally as members of a research community.

As more or less the result of having explicit criteria for making choices about evidence and classification, the generalizations within attachment research have become more complex over the last two decades, while the criteria and the relation between generalization and particular have also evolved. In Ainsworth and Wittig's 1969 article, generalizations took the form—at least in part—of induction, with various particulars about the behavior of children in their sample leading toward generalizations about patterns of attachment. But the relation between them was complex. As a tentative generalization, for instance, the researchers posited that Karen was insecure partly from having gained no sense that her wishes would receive response. The evidence of Karen's crying in episodes 4 and 6 of the procedure (mother's leaving the room) did not by itself set her apart from most of the rest of the babies. The violence of her crying, however, and the mother's seeming insensitivity in episode 8 when she reentered the room and then put Karen down again, suggested a qualitative difference from the behavior of, for instance, Brian (Group B) who did not cry so hard in episodes 4 and 6 and who clung to his mother in episode 8, with mother cuddling him in response (Ainsworth and Wittig 126–28, 132–34).

The generalizations necessary to differentiate Karen, for instance, from Brian must have seemed somewhat precarious in the 1969 Ainsworth and Wittig study, with a sample of only fourteen infants and no accumulated body of research on the subject. Working with a trait construct—as Sroufe and Waters defined it in 1977—one might simply examine particular instances of behavior (e.g., crying, cuddling) and therefore find Brian and Karen similar or dissimilar by virtue of their crying, but Ainsworth and Wittig saw patterns of difference by looking at patterns of interaction, not at individual items of behavior.

The relation between individual instances of behavior and interpretation was again discussed by Waters in 1978 when he critiqued "operational" definitions:

> When discrete behaviors are used to define attachment operationally, all instances of looking, or vocalizing, or approaching are summed, on the assumption that all instances of phenotypically similar behaviors are equivalent. This assumption is consistent with the atheoretical orientation from which operational definitions often proceed. (Waters 492)

Instead of this atheoretical assumption, ethological theory pointed to ways of seeing patterns in the data. The interpretation of data was, in this way, conceptually driven.

By 1978 in *Patterns of Attachment* Ainsworth and her colleagues had decided that the second reentry (episode 8) in the Strange Situation was most telling; that decision arose, it appears, from something like ethnographic observation, with observations of many infants and repeated studies leading the researchers to a growing conviction of what the salient patterns were. This was not research by algorithm; nor was it deductive reasoning. It involved something like induction through immersion in particular data. It may not, intially, have been very different from the process whereby a reader of Trollope comes to have a feel for the kinds of motivation in Trollope's novels, or the reader of Shakespeare comes to have convictions about motivation in Shakespeare's plays. But attachment researchers had a conceptual frame to refer to in questions of interpretation. That frame allowed them to dismiss some kinds of interpretations and ask questions about others.

As these examples indicate, attachment researchers and New Critical literary scholars have used differing ways of relating particulars to concepts and pursuing their initial insights. The conceptually driven process in attachment research and the text-driven process I have described in literary interpretation differed because the process in psychology involved the research community's repeated focus on the same phenomena, through the same lens. This continuity of focus allowed a progressive development of criteria that served to keep the generalizations about data from becoming as divergent as they might in literary studies.

In sum, three aspects of the relation between particular and conceptual are involved in differentiating the compact field of attachment research from the more diffuse field of literary criticism I have so far described. Something like ethnographic immersion is involved in both fields at some point, with researchers deriving intuitions from immersion in their data. But in attachment research the sustained focus through the conceptual lens of attachment theory meant that the research community defined its problems communally and approached its data through that focal point. The field's conceptually driven criteria allowed it to make decisions in consistent ways—ways that might be described as "rational" if we understand rationality to involve the disciplinary community's process of selecting what counts as a good contribution to disciplinary knowledge.

CHAPTER FOUR

Colonial New England Social History

*The Problematics of
Contemporary History Writing*

The discipline of history illustrates some of the tensions between
the knowledge-making modes of the humanities and the social sciences. On the continuum from particularistic, text-driven, interpretive discourse to conceptually driven, explanatory discourse, writing
in history shows forces pulling in both directions. These tensions are
often implied in comments by historians about the state of knowledge
in a subfield, for example, Archer's and Zuckerman's complaints about
the lack of synthesis in New England colonial history. And they are
revealed in what historians say about neighboring disciplines or what
neighboring disciplinary practitioners say about history.

In a discussion of the difference between history and sociology,
Peter Burke points out history's greater tendency to use a variety of
terms for what sociologists might view as one type of phenomenon.
Burke writes that political historians have generalized about institutional changes in European history by coining phrases such as "the
state as a work of art," "the new monarchies," "the Tudor revolution
in government," "the rise of absolutism," and "the nineteenth-century
revolution in government" (Burke 70). "To a sociologist," Burke
writes, "all these changes will look like local examples of stages of

transition from one major type of government to another, from what Max Weber called a 'patrimonial' to what he called a 'bureaucratic' system. Weber's typology is one of the most important contributions to the theory of political organization since the Greeks distinguished monarchy, aristocracy and democracy" (70–71).

The sociological enterprise Burke describes is conceptually driven in its assumption that a set of transhistorical structural concepts such as patrimony and bureaucracy may provide a unified language and a focal point to begin analysis. For the sociologist, the structural concept as an abstraction exists prior to the examination of particular local circumstances, whereas the historians' varied and less abstract terms ("the Tudor revolution in government," etc.) originate in interpretation of particular phenomena.

The historian, then, may be torn between the desire to elucidate local particulars and the desire to generalize about historical processes. An example of this kind of tension may be seen in comments by a social anthropologist, P. C. Lloyd, in *Africa in Social Change* (1967). He began with a number of questions revealing how conceptual issues could drive the need for analysis of phenomena—questions about "the impact of the processes of modernization upon the traditional societies" such as "How far are the patterns of Western industrial society, and in particular the stratification of society into social classes, being reproduced in West Africa?" (13). This question would not necessarily arise for someone interested primarily in the particulars of African history. For instance, if there were an African society with no stratification, the historian beginning with phenomena to interpret would not be likely to raise questions about stratification. But a social scientist beginning with conceptual questions about stratification (especially stratification in the West) might be likely to use models of stratification to ask why an African society does or does not have a particular kind of stratification. The question is conceptually driven, and terms like stratification or modernization are likely to be standardized among writers in the field.

Lloyd raised the question of local versus generalizable knowledge in his Introduction:

> Continually we find apparent paradoxes. Modernization often seems to result in an intensification of tribal relations rather than in their decay; or, it seems to be the society with the less highly developed political structure which accepts change more readily. Many of these

paradoxes are, however, resolved when one studies individual societies in detail. And so one is caught between the need for detailed studies of small areas or individual problems, and the urge to generalize. . . . In abstracting, from the diverse and complex patterns of West African society, the principal variables, we may construct theoretical models which are illustrative of contemporary changes. It is with such models that we might, subject to the availability of relevant data, make our predictions of political revolution, of economic advance or stagnation. (Lloyd 13–14)

Lloyd's use of terms like "principal variables," "models," and "predictions" are signs of an affinity for the conceptually driven enterprise of a social scientist. Though his mention of abstracting from the data makes his enterprise sound analogous to the text-driven interpreting of a Gaskell novel, his focus on a generalizable model that could be used to predict social change puts him in the social science part of the continuum.

In the light of current suggestions that interpretation is replacing explanation in the social sciences (e.g., Geertz; Rabinow and Sullivan), Lloyd's 1967 statement may seem overly sanguine about the possibilities of finding "principal variables," "theoretical models," or predictive ability. But these were hopes found in the social sciences in the 1960s and in the comments of historians who aspired to increase the synthetic power of historical work—the sort of hope forming the background for Zuckerman's and Archer's dismay about the progress of Colonial New England social history.

If attachment research over the last two decades gained increasing explanatory power from continued focus on attachment theory, the last two decades of work in the subfield of Colonial New England social history examined here might better be described as one of accumulation, rather than progression, with practitioners in the field periodically expressing worries about the difference between accumulation and progression.

By the 1960s, the importance of generalizing or synthesizing had been impressed on historians both because of the prestige of the social sciences and the influence of philosophy of history. At the same time, the importance of particulars was felt because of two other, divergent influences: the traditional historical concern with facts and the new interest in social history. Traditional history had periodically announced its allegiance to telling it, as Leopold von Ranke advocated, "wie es eigentlich gewesen" (as it really was).[1]

But at the same time, the 1960s saw an increased interest in social history, and historians began to show a different, nontraditional concern for some of the less dramatic details of the past. Social history, according to Peter Novick, became "*the* growth industry within the profession," with a quadrupling in the percentage of all dissertations in history between 1958 and 1978 (440). Novick's definition of social history is useful: the study of "the everyday experience of popular classes, whether in cities, factories, or the home; regardless of the race or gender of those studied: it thus includes much (though not all) of what are sometimes separately designated as urban, labor, family, black, and women's history" (440).[2]

With its interest in history from the bottom up, social history quite naturally was concerned with particulars about mundane lives, rather than large-scale political events and heroes. Yet those who helped quadruple the number of emerging social historians were also, often, influenced by the generalizing proclivities of the social sciences. According to Novick, two groups finding a home in social history were those influenced by Parsonian sociology and young Marxists—both of whom were likely to be influenced by conceptually driven modes of knowledge making. In this chapter I will look at two places where a tension between the particularistic, interpretive, text-driven tendencies and the conceptually driven, generalizing tendencies in contemporary history writing may be seen: first, in the discussions of narrative versus analysis threaded through historiographic discussion in the last two decades and, second, in the sample subfield of Colonial New England social history.

Views of Narrative and Analysis

Since historians frequently describe their discipline as concerned with "change over time," the rhetorical organization most appropriate for conveying change over time might seem to be narration.[3] Yet narrative has become problematic for the historian, and over the last two decades discussions of the problems of writing history have returned repeatedly to the issue of narrative versus analysis. Narrative, by this period, had come to be viewed as perhaps not a form of knowledge making or, to put it differently, not the sort of knowledge making for which cousin disciplines like sociology awarded respect. Though historians have framed and analyzed the issue in different ways, their discussions center on whether there is still a place for narrative in writing history and how current developments in analyzing historical phenomena may or may not be compatible with the writing of narrative.

From a rhetorician's point of view, the ongoing historiographic discussion of narrative is particularly interesting because historians use the word "narrative" differently from rhetoricians. In historians' comments, narrative emerges, alternately, as a way to order texts or a way to analyze phenomena, the historian finding it difficult to talk of narrative without becoming immersed in discussion of historical interpretation and causal explanation.

To discuss the role of narrative in history requires, first, recognizing a basic terminological difficulty that reflects important problematics in the field. The same word "history" can refer to (1) past phenomena, (2) the interpretation the historian constructs, and (3) the text the historian writes. My concern is with the texts historians write. Most historians today probably agree on distinguishing between the first and second of the three meanings: that is, they agree that the past is something other than the interpretations historians construct. They are likely to hold different views of the amount of objectivity or subjectivity involved in interpretation, but they might at least agree that the past has not formed itself into a coherent sequence of events without the aid of human minds sifting, hypothesizing, connecting, and analyzing.

The second set of distinctions—between history as interpretation and history as text—is less frequently acknowledged to be important, probably because discussions of objectivity so often emphasize the importance of the first set of distinctions. More often than rhetoricians, historians elide the distinction between thoughts or interpretations on the one hand and their textual representation on the other. Many historians, perhaps the majority, have a healthy respect for good writing, agree that there is no "history" (in the second or third senses of the term) without writing, and can name historians they consider good as opposed to bad writers.

Nevertheless, the distinction between interpretation and text is often elided. When historians talk of "social history" or "political history," for instance, they refer both to interpretive stances and textual results. When upper division courses in "historical methods" are taught, they may focus on strategies for finding or interpreting data. There is a tendency, in short, for historians to view "writing history" as the relatively unproblematic offshoot of the hard work of probing, analyzing, discovering, and explaining—a tendency to think good writing is separable from good history, a matter of merely superficial style. J. H. Hexter, perhaps something of an exception among historians in his 1971 *Doing History*, distinguished between the second and third senses of "history" and criticized historians like H. L. Marrou who claimed that "a completely elaborated history already exists in the mind of the historian before he has begun writing a word of it" (quoted in Hexter 154).

The referential or terminological problem surrounding "history" reflects a deeper split in allegiance and focus for many historians, a split between knowing *what* and knowing *why* that occurs elsewhere in the humanities. In his 1979 "The Revival of Narrative," Lawrence Stone argued that about fifty years ago, historians abandoned a two-thousand-year-old tradition of narrative because they recognized that "answering the *what* and the *how* questions in a chronological fashion, even if directed by a central argument, does not in fact go very far towards answering the *why* questions" (4–5). Knowing *what* the American Revolution was, for instance, has usually been important to American historians and Americans in general. Interpretations of the Revolution, however, involve *why* questions—why it occurred, why its results were what they were. The *why* questions are almost impossible to phrase without addressing the *what* questions, but the reverse may be less true. One can know, learn, or tell the *what* without invoking the *why*, though doing so is far more problematic than it first appears.

The distinction between the *what* and the *why* of historical phenomena has been embodied in the distinction historians often make between narrative and analysis or between description and analysis.[4] History-writing of the last twenty or thirty years may be seen as retaining, in different degrees, a fundamental commitment to phenomenal particulars—the *what* of history—while at the same time working out ways of dealing with *why* questions. History may be seen as a discipline in search of its own voice, fundamentally committed to its own *what* questions and yet, at times, intellectually either too insecure or too courageous to ignore the challenges from prestigious or systematic "scientific" disciplines. Historian Carl Schorske has described historians as "conceptual parasites" adopting concepts from other fields and undergoing an "identity crisis" (408, 417). In a variety of ways, trends in recent history writing may be seen as exploring whether there is some knowledge, form of reasoning, or rhetoric distinctive to history as a discipline or whether history is, in effect, an interdisciplinary field with no content or logic or its own, needing to borrow concepts and modes of explanation from other disciplines.

I begin my account of the ongoing discussion as the influence of logical positivism on history was in its death throes around twenty years ago. We need not enter into much detail about logical positivism to see the problem it posed for historical narrative. Carl Hempel in 1942 had published an article titled "The Function of General Laws in History" disputing the traditional idea that history is—or should be—concerned with the particular, rather than with general laws. He proposed to show "that general laws have quite analogous functions in history and in the natural sciences, that they form an indispensable instrument of historical research" (231). The function of general laws, according to Hempel, was explanation and prediction:

> The explanation of the occurrence of an event of some specific kind E at a certain place and time consists, as it is usually expressed, in indicating the causes or determining factors of E. Now the assertion that a set of events—say, of the kinds C_1, C_2, . . . , C_n—have caused the event to be explained, amounts to the statement that, according to certain general laws a set of events of the kinds mentioned is regularly accompanied by an event of kind E. Thus, the scientific explanation of the event in question consists of
> (1) a set of statements asserting the occurrence of certain events C_1, . . . C_n at certain times and places,
> (2) a set of universal hypotheses, such that
> (a) the statements of both groups are reasonably well confirmed by empirical evidence,
> (b) from the two groups of statements the sentence asserting the occurrence of event E can be logically deduced. (232)

Hempel's first "illustration" of this logic concerns "the cracking of an automobile radiator during a cold night" (232). His talk of initial and boundary conditions and empirical laws may, from our vantage point, seem hopelessly irrelevant to the complexities and indeterminacies of historical events. Conscious of critiques from within philosophy—for example, Toulmin, Rorty—of the focus on formal and logical explanation, we can see ample reason for historians to have ignored the kind of reasoning Hempel presented, but Peter Novick suggests that even more important in their rejection of philosophy was historians' sense that their own disciplinary autonomy was at stake (399–400).

By the end of the 1960s, there had been attacks on the general law model (or the "covering law model" as William Dray termed it) from both philosophers and historians. Dray (1959) had distinguished between explanations of what and explanations of why or how, only explanations of "why" involving the kind of covering law Hempel was concerned with. The philosopher W. B. Gallie (1964, 1968) argued that history had its own rhetoric of explanation associated with narrative and distinctive from the rhetoric of the sciences. In history, Gallie wrote, "an incident or action cries out for historical investigation primarily because it is memorable, story-worthy, and because it embodies one of those failures or achievements, opportunities lost or taken, which we want to know about . . . " (2).

The historian J. H. Hexter, writing in 1971, made a strong case for two claims that are still under discussion twenty years later. The claims are related, yet separable: (1) that the rhetoric of history writing is distinct in kind from the logic or rhetoric of the sciences and (2) that the historian's role is to convey the *what* of history. Hexter saw narrative as the appropriate rhetoric of history, though he did not see narrative and analysis as mutually exclusive (*Doing* 40). As part of his critique of general law explanations from philosophers of science, for instance, Hexter offered several competing versions of why the Giants won the World Series in 1951. He argued that a version conforming to the general law model would explain nothing of interest to someone motivated by the question "How did it come about that . . . ?" or "Tell me more about . . ." Such questions, Hexter argued, arise not from a desire for fuller explanation but for a "confrontation with the riches of the event itself" (*Doing* 42–43).

One hears little of logical positivism in the seventies and eighties, critiques like Hexter's apparently having succeeded. But if we see Hexter as situated at a crossroads in historiography, we may see him as proposing a path that historians have not pursued, that is, fully exploring the rhetorical possibilities available through narrative. Megill and McCloskey point to Hayden White's not referring to Hexter in White's *Metahistory* (1973) as a sign that "a general conversation had not yet developed" ("Rhetoric of History" 224). Instead, historians have pursued "analysis"—not with the rigidity of the logical positivists but nevertheless with some holdover of their sense that social science explanations might aspire to a generalizability lacking in traditional history.

Perhaps what happened was that two intellectual currents with possible relevance to historians met in the 1960s and in one sense muted each other. On the one hand, the logical positivists overstated their case in a way that might have led historians to take the opposite tack of developing a full rhetoric of narrative and reaffirming their commitment to *what* explanations typical of the humanities. On the other hand, the growing interest in social history—including family history and demographics—was leading historians to see the explanatory power of concepts from the social sciences. This current, which I return to in my discussion of Colonial New England social history, usually led historians away from narrative and toward analysis and quantification. The tension between *what* and *why* explanations was, thus, unresolved.

In the 1970s and 1980s, the discussion of narrative and analysis continued, joined with recurring questions about whether the influence of social science—particularly sociology and anthropology—was leading history astray. The ongoing discussion can be traced through successive articles by Lawrence Stone, Bernard Bailyn, Joyce Appleby, and Allan Megill. All four began their arguments by explaining what the social sciences contributed to historians' explanatory power. Appleby, for instance, traced the influence of complex models from Weber through Geertz. But each of the four found the influence of the social sciences to be at least partly detrimental to the writing of history. Their analyses varied somewhat but clustered around two issues: (1) coherence and intelligibility and (2) the distinctive disciplinary purposes of history.

Stone's 1979 explanation of the "revival of narrative" discussed the issue of intelligibility and accessibility to the reading public, but his argument shifted uneasily in what it presented as admirable about narrative. At times, Stone described narrative as easier to follow or remember than non-narrative history; at other times, he presented narrative as having substantive content—an alternative to "economic and demographic determinism" (19). His description of historians' "new" narratives (as of 1979) conveyed little sense of what the rhetorician finds at the heart of narrative—ordering over time. Stone described five ways in which "new" historians' retreat from some of their earlier positions nevertheless distinguished them from traditional narrative historians:

First, they are almost without exception concerned with the lives and feelings and behaviour of the poor and obscure, rather than the great and powerful. Secondly, analysis remains as essential to their methodology as description. . . . Thirdly, they are opening up new sources. . . . Fourthly, they often tell their stories in a different way from that of Homer, or Dickens, or Balzac. Under the influence of the modern novel and of Freudian ideas, they gingerly explore the subconscious rather than sticking to the plain facts. And under the influence of the anthropologists, they try to use behaviour to reveal symbolic meaning. Fifthly, they tell the story of a person, a trial or a dramatic episode, not for its own sake, but in order to throw light upon the internal workings of a past culture and society. (19)

In Stone's account, "narrative" only very tangentially involved chronological sequencing. His lumping together of Homer, Dickens, and Balzac suggested little awareness of how Dickens and Balzac depicted the lives of the obscure and went beyond "plain facts" to explore subconscious or symbolic meaning. In Stone's rather tentative praise for narrative, then, we see an image of narrative that a rhetorician, Balzac, or J.H. Hexter (to name a few) might see as somewhat impoverished—a notion of narrative as something rather close to "the plain facts." Above all, Stone showed little explicit sense of narratives as texts; he made no distinction between the nature of historians' interpretations and the kinds of texts they write. He tended to equate narrative with the historians of *mentalité* in the Annales tradition in France (e.g., Fernand Braudel or Le Roy Ladurie). The Annales influence with its talk of "total" history and "history without events" would perhaps have been better seen as a return to "description" rather than "narration" but the longstanding historical dichotomy between narration and analysis apparently kept the distinctions between narration and description from seeming important; both were concerned with the *what* of history.

Consistent with his nontextual notion of narrative, Stone saw "analysis" as having succeeded traditional narrative because of economic and/or demographic determinism (7), and so he saw a "revival of narrative" resulting from "disillusionment with the economic determinist model" of explanation (8). A new interest in the culture of the group and the will of the individual made both group and individual more important agents of change than if impersonal forces such as demographic growth determined change. This recognition of more independent variables, Stone argued, coincided with increased interest in social history—what it was like to live in the past, how the common people lived, as opposed to kings and nobles. Together these new interests were leading to a revival of narrative, he argued. And finally, almost as an afterthought, Stone concluded that "a desire to make their findings accessible" to an intelligent reading public made dry, quantitative, jargon-ridden prose less enticing than narrative. Stone's tentative endorsement of narrative drew attention, but he cannot be said to have gone into questions about the rhetoric of narrative as fully as Hexter had earlier.

In a 1981 presidential address to the American Historical Association, Bernard Bailyn also raised the issue of access or coherence but came closer than Stone to separating trends in interpretation or analysis from trends in textual representation. Bailyn saw three trends as altering the way history is written. He first distinguished between manifest and latent history, with manifest roughly equaling the *what* and latent equaling the *why* of history. Traditional history writing, Bailyn argued, was largely manifest history—"the story of events that contemporaries were clearly aware of, that were matters of conscious concern, were consciously struggled over, were, so to speak, headline events in their own time even if their causes and their underlying determinants were buried below the level of contemporaries' understanding" (9). More recent historical work, on the other hand, drew on quantitative studies of demographic and other data to illuminate latent history—"events that contemporaries were not fully or clearly aware of, at times were not aware of at all, events that they did not consciously struggle over, however much they might have been forced unwittingly to grapple with their consequences, and events that were not recorded as events in the documentation of the time" (10).

The second trend Bailyn saw was increasing "outlines of systems of filiation and derivation among phenomena that once were discussed in isolation from each other" (18–19). If an older, event-centered history could focus on specific events in their own time and place—the Armada, for instance, or the American Revolution—the social sciences had raised the possibility that generalizable processes link phenomena in different times and places. Bailyn did not quite state it as I have—as an incursion of the generalizing social sciences on the traditionally particularizing discipline of history—but each of the three trends he described was stimulated by the increasing importance of social theory among historians.

One of his examples was family history, a subject first developed by the French, then picked up by the English, and from there spreading to the United States (as in the case of Colonial New England history). In family history, we can see how social science approaches to history might push history from a particularized, interpretive enterprise toward a more conceptually driven one. If, for instance, the events of the Armada are particular to its time and place, then the historian of the Armada need not be acquainted with scholarship on the American Revolution. But in the field of family history, if scarce resources are believed to affect fertility or decisions about family size, then there are reasons for a historian of Colonial New England to look at scholarship on fourteenth-century French peasants to explore possible interrelations between scarce resources, for instance, and fertility. The possibilities for conceptual coherence may entice, even as the possibilities for narrative coherence may recede.

The third trend Bailyn described was an "intensifying effort to relate the world of interior, subjective experiences to the course of external events" (19). This trend might, presumably, open up the possibility of narrative because fictional narrative has a rich history of relating subjective experience to the course of events. As we will see, however, both historians of *mentalité* and historians preoccupied with nonelite groups in history have, for different reasons, not seized on narrative as the ideal mode for relating subjective experience to event.

Altogether, then, Bailyn saw "history" (in its second sense of interpretation) as becoming more complex, including more strands and more layers. He ended by writing:

> The greatest challenge . . . is not how to deepen and further sophisticate . . . but how to put the story together again, now with a complexity and an analytic dimension never envisioned before; how to draw together the information available . . . into readable accounts of major developments. . . . In the end, however, historians must be, not analysts of isolated technical problems abstracted from the past, but narrators of worlds in motion. . . . (23–24)

In this way, Bailyn advocated the new narrative without describing how it might take shape. Coherence becomes more problematic if there are more levels of analysis going on simultaneously—even more problematic if multiple strands of analysis must also be ordered to convey change over time. Bailyn advocated narrative not so much because he thought current trends in historiography had made narrative more feasible, but because current trends had made the "story" of the past less coherent, and he hoped for increased coherence, increased public appreciation for history. By his own account, then, there was likely to be an increasing gulf between professional history and coherent narrative. In this way Bailyn may be said to number among those historians who separate the second and third senses of "history"—history as interpretation and history as textual representation—with style assumed to be the inessential dress of thought.

Joyce Appleby, writing in 1984 about "Value and Society" in Colonial American historiography, began by discussing how contemporary social theory from sociology and anthropology allowed historians to dispense with the dichotomy between "morals" and "ideas" and instead probe "values" in complex relation to society:

> Belief in the dominance of social reality has led to the abandonment of the old liberal story of individual endeavors, but like the Whig interpretation of old, the new models have structured the historians' imagination. The use of value as an organizing theme has shifted the attention of scholars from a progressive sequence of events to the patterned reception of those events in a multilayered society. (298)

This "shift" away from "progressive sequence" hints at trouble in constructing narrative. And unlike Stone and Bailyn writing earlier, Appleby saw narrative not just as a mode for producing coherence but also as a way of representing change. She saw some incompatibility between history as a discipline concerned with change over time and the concepts social science introduced into history.

Arguing that historians "may be paying too high an interest rate on our debts to the social sciences" (307), Appleby first pointed to the concern for general laws in the social science lexicon: abstract nouns such as "process, pattern, system, organization, and structure" suggest permanence and consistency while obscuring diversity in place and time; and conceptual nouns such as "peasant, community, and network" appear to have concrete referents but are "abstractions firmly attached to a theoretical literature" (307). The generalized conceptual lexicon of social science is, then, at odds with history's focus on change over time. Here, we see how deep the tension between particularizing and generalizing may go; the social science lexicon is not simply a "dress of thought" that could be altered without producing a change in historical knowledge making. Instead, the language constitutes the knowledge making, and the static generalizations of social science represent a fundamental shift in thinking about historical processes.

According to Appleby, "The one borrowing historians should return immediately" was the "belief that change can best be accounted for as the transformation of social forms—feudalism to capitalism, traditional to modern" (307). The problem lay in "invoking the immobile structural analysis to move," but the difficulty of "get[ting] this particular story going" has been caused by seeing society as a "system of systems established to achieve stability": "The normative quality given continuity and persistence then leads to an interpretation of change as the promoter of tensions, fear, anxiety, and guilt" (307–8). By seeing society as system and thereby seeing change and fluidity as abnormal, in other words, social science not only has distorted its interpretation of historical flux but has also constrained coherent narrative representation of the past.

Like Appleby, Allan Megill writing in 1989 also problematized history's borrowings from the social sciences. He began by arguing that there is a profound bias in contemporary history writing in favor of *why* accounts, rather than *what* accounts. He discussed "metaphors of verticality" in which the observable is less important than the "hidden," "underlying," or "fundamental"—rather like Bailyn's distinction between manifest and latent, except that Bailyn appeared to applaud historians' increasing ability to probe latent causes while Megill saw it as privileging the explanatory project (631).

This bias for "explanation" Megill saw as having arisen from the prestige of the physical sciences—their success with causal explanation—and the logical positivists in philosophy whose philosophy of science led to denigration of the *what* accounts historians wrote. Megill quoted, for instance, the Social Science Research Council's 1954 "Bulletin 64," which said "The truly scientific function begins where the descriptive function stops" (632). He saw the explanatory bias as deriving from the "prejudice for universality" in that explanation seems universalizable while description is "merely particular" (632).

Megill distinguished between description and narration by seeing description—or his preferred term, "recounting"—as answering a *what* question, while narration "blends recounting and explanation" (638). Nevertheless, narrative's "alleged revival"—his reference to Stone—is "shadowed by deeply held prejudices" derived from the bias for explanation (638). Megill did not identify narrative with chronology, seeing chronology as only one of the elements of narrative.

Megill's article appeared in an issue of the *American Historical Review* containing several other historiographical essays along with an "*AHR* Forum" section of five essays from a 1988 American Historical Association session aimed at "examining some of the current intellectual cleavages in the American historical profession" (654). Views of narrative found in these pieces suggest that Megill's view is by no means widely accepted; narrative is more often considered as a function of interpretation or ideology, rather than of rhetoric. Megill's piece may be seen as a development of his and others' work on the rhetoric of inquiry, but the contrast between his view of narrative and views in the same *AHR* issue shows how little progressive development or compacting has occurred in the history profession over the last twenty years in connection with the issue of narrative.

In the *AHR* issue, for instance, social historians Lawrence Levine and Joan Wallach Scott praised the historical profession's increased concern with nonelite groups as "actors in their own right" (673). Yet while the idea of "actors" in history might, conceivably, suggest possibilities for narrative, Levine concluded:

> If we tell people continually that history is invariably narrative storytelling about those whose power, position, and influence are palpable, then that is precisely what they will expect from us. But this is only one form of history, and it is incumbent upon us to inform the public, by deed and word, that there is no exclusive preferred form for the writing of history and that no single group in history and no one aspect of the past—the social, the political, the cultural, the economic—is inherently more important, or more essential, or more relevant than others. (679)

Levine, then, considered narrative history to be a form suitable only for telling the history of elites and large political events. For him, valuing diversity would mean resisting narrative history, and narration could be neither a vehicle for valuing nonelite experience nor a form of organizing historical material that could be neutral in its political import.

Joan Wallach Scott also equated narrative with a particular ideology about historical interpretation: "I think that engagement in a democratized historical practice calls into question orthodox notions of objective mastery by fragmenting historical vision into conflicting accounts of what happened in the past. . . . It is finally the plurality of stories and of the subjects of those stories, as well as the lack of any single central narrative that conservatives find intolerable because it undermines the legitimation of their quest for dominance" ("Crisis" 691). Narrative, once again, was equated with a particular ideology. Scott assumed that "narrative" implied a single story.

At the other end of the political spectrum in the "*AHR* Forum," Gertrude Himmelfarb—without explicitly addressing the question of narrative—argued that social history of the sort Scott endorsed created incoherence in history writing. How, asked Himmelfarb, "can all these groups ['women, blacks, Chicanos, etc.'], each cherishing its uniqueness and its claim to sovereign attention, be mainstreamed into a single, coherent, integrated history?" (664). Despite their difference in politics, Levine, Scott, and Himmelfarb were united, in 1989, in assuming that narrative history would have to involve a single kind of coherence and that narrative was incompatible with attention to the lives of the powerless.

If Hexter's 1971 work provides a starting date in the ongoing debate over narrative, at least two decades of the debate appear to have witnessed no progress toward consensus. The debate permits at least five generalizations about the discipline of history:

1. Disciplinary compactness and progression of the type I have described in attachment research is not occurring within this particular discussion. There is no progressive sorting out of problems or arriving at greater clarity in defining the area of disagreement. Instead, writers like Levine and Scott, on the one hand, and Himmelfarb, on the other, continue to take positions without attempting to negotiate with their opponents and without taking any explicit notice of the more rhetorically informed and sophisticated notions developed by Megill.

2. Many historians writing about narrative continue to view narrative as a matter of style resembling the superficial dress of thought, rather than constitutive of or inextricable from the kind of knowledge making involved.

3. Those who do not consider narrative to be a superficial style are likely, however, to equate narrative with one kind of ideology and to be oblivious to the full range of narrative possibilities. In a 1991 opinion piece in *The Chronicle of Higher Education*, for instance, Joan Scott argued against "prominent liberal historians" who warned that

multiculturalism might result in a "cult of ethnicity" or a "proliferation of separate histories of different racial and ethnic groups" (B1). Scott repeatedly connected the issue of multiculturalism to the issue of stories: "These historians insist that the story of America is that of individuals benefiting from democracy" or "Is this the one true story of America, or only a particular way of telling it?" (B2). These quotations demonstrate how several sets of oppositions may be conflated: the issue of multiplicity and contradiction versus homogeneity and consensus in the American experience is conflated with the issue of proliferating separate histories of different racial/ethnic groups versus sharing a common culture. In each case, Scott saw homogeneity and sharing a common culture as connected to writing narrative history. Coherence, which a rhetorician might consider as part of text making, becomes ideologically charged and removed from the domain of text making.

4. Somewhat lost in the debate, because of the narrow definition of narrative and the focus on ideology, is the issue of audience. Though Stone indirectly tried to raise the issue of readership in 1979 and Bailyn did so more explicitly in 1981, readership has remained at the periphery of the debate on narrative. In 1987, Megill and Donald McCloskey wrote that the growing split between professional historians and the wider public arises partly from a marked rise in the rigor of evidential demands among professional historians (232). Evidential demands and other epistemic concerns, as I will discuss below, are far more likely sources of the strain on narrative than ideology itself. If the purpose of writing history is to inform and incite the sympathy of a general audience, narrative may be a far more appropriate form of writing than if the purpose is to fill in the gaps in knowledge and to argue about competing causal explanations.

5. The debate surrounding the issue of narrative serves to confirm and extend the perception, seen in Bender, Zuckerman, and Archer, that history is not making progress. Taken together, the discussion of narrative and the discussion of progress in social history serve to confirm that there remain, in the discipline of history, fundamental tensions between affinities with the humanities and affinities with the social sciences. Arguing about competing causal explanations and conveying the nature of experience—of either nonelites or elites—are not mutually compatible kinds of knowledge making and text making. I will return to this observation in the discussion of Colonial New England social history below.

By way of commentary on the first four generalizations above, however, I would suggest that the tension involved in narrative versus analysis has little to do with whether narrative tells the story of the powerful or the powerless. Nineteenth-century novelists like Dickens and Balzac have demonstrated the power of narrative to render the plight of the obscure. Writers like Dickens and Balzac (or Tolstoy and Eliot) pushed the form of the novel beyond its picaresque or single-plotted forerunners because they wanted to tell narratives involving multiplicity, contradiction, and heterogeneity. Nothing in the nature of narrative prevents contemporary historians from doing the same. But narrative cannot, perhaps, so easily reconcile the opposing tensions of a professionalized, quantified, social science-minded history with the more populist aim of making history intelligible to nonacademics.

The tension between narrative and analysis is best explained as a tension between two incompatible goals: that of finding generalizable patterns in the past and that of interpreting or, in Megill's term, "rendering" the past. The former project pushes history in the direction of the social sciences, the latter in the direction of the humanities. The former will show a relatively greater taste for conceptually driven questions, the latter a greater taste for dealing with local particulars. The former will be concerned with causes and the latter with meaning. But within the former—the explanatory project—there is a further tension: between analyzing the causes of change over time in the way Appleby finds germane to history and analyzing social forces with the tools of social science. Within this latter set of oppositions, the tension between particular and general plays a key role.

"Progress" and "Compactness" in Social History

I have already quoted Archer and other historians who discuss their dissatisfaction with the state of progress in New England social history, but there is another side to the story also—a sense that historians know more than they did twenty or thirty years ago and that social history has by some criteria or other aided progress or opened up possibilities for increased understanding in the discipline of history. Writing in 1981 on "Family History in the 1980s: Past Achievements and Future Trends," Lawrence Stone was able to list, as generally agreed on, the following large-scale changes in the history of the western family:

1. declining external influence of kin on the nuclear family,
2. greater emotional bonding between spouses, with marriage based on affection,
3. abandonment of the concept of the child as an immature adult (whose labor might be exploited) and instead a growing child orientation,
4. growing specialization of women's activities in child care and education, and
5. the slow evolution of the concept of privacy, with value placed on affective individualism. ("Family History" 73–74)

Agreement on these processes might look like agreement on *what* questions, but the ability to abstract causal variables like influence of kin on the nuclear family and the linkage of these five processes begins to suggest at least the possibility of answering some *why* questions—that is, of using the variables Stone listed ("Family History") to look at specific historical particulars in context in order to see how the processes were or were not operative in a particular context.

Stone continued by describing some of the disagreement that remained:

> If one examines the theories of all those who have attempted a general overview of this question of the evolution of the modern family— Engels, Aries, Flandrin, deMause, myself, Shorter, Greven, and now Degler and Norton—it seems clear that there is fairly general agreement that the changes described took place sometime between 1680 and 1850. It is also agreed that they were highly class specific in origin. But there is no agreement in sight about which were the leading sectors in the change, nor when or why the changes occurred. (75)

Stone then detailed—for several pages—the lack of consensus about which were the leading sectors, when the changes occurred, and what causal explanations could be given. He concluded by suggesting an agenda for the 1980s: "The central, unresolved questions—the core program for the 1980s—are first, where, when, and in what classes did the new 'bourgeois' family type first emerge; and second, were the key independent variables attitudinal or economic, or both. What effect, in short, did modernization in the broadest sense of the word have on family life or family life upon modernization?" (83). Stone's use of the term "modernization," a term originally imported into history from sociology, indicated that family history had become, to some degree, conceptually driven. By comparison to the more cumulative and conceptually driven field of attachment research, the research Stone described showed both a lesser degree of consensual progress and a more diffuse conceptual focal point. However, as long as we avoid rigid taxonomies in describing academic writing, it is possible to see an important kinship between the kind of intellectual enterprise pursued in attachment research and the enterprise Stone described. Social history cannot display the same degree of compactness as attachment research because attachment is a more isolable phenomenon and is the subject of study of a far more discrete, self-contained group of researchers.

There are at least two ways to explain why attachment research is more compact than family history. Attachment research's standardized experimental paradigm allows manipulation of variables in ways that help isolate the phenomenon under scrutiny, and that identification of discrete variables allows for repeated examination of aspects of the phenomenon. But also the phenomenon of attachment may come closer, than family structure, to being a universal cross-cultural phenomenon. Cross-cultural studies of attachment have found attachment in all cultures, although the percentages of children falling into one attachment category rather than another differs from one culture to another (Lamb et al.; Sagi and Lewkowicz; van IJzendoorn and Kroonenberg). Moreover, only three (or perhaps four, see Main and Solomon) categories of attachment have been found cross-culturally— far fewer variables than exist when one turns to considerations of family structure within varying social and historical contexts. The cultural differences in attachment may lead to branching out within attachment research, to increasingly wider studies of cultural variables, but the originating theory that attachment represents a basic phenomenon in human and mammalian infancy enables research on attachment to branch out from such a compact initial focal point that the field itself experiences the effects of compactness.

Social history, by contrast, draws on a wider range of scholarship and may be studied in a wider range of contexts. The scholarship it draws on is multidisciplinary and multinational: for example, in France, the work of Aries, Duby, Ladurie; in England, the work of Laslett or Wrigley and Schofield; in the United States, Herlihy, Stone,

Hareven. Researchers and theorists may come from anthropology (e.g., Goody, MacFarlane), sociology (Tilly), history (Laslett, Stone, Natalie Zemon Davis). Laslett, for instance, refers to himself as a "historical sociologist" (*Family Life*).

American historians interested in this work might be said to have two or three academic allegiances or to belong to two or three overlapping discourse communities—(1) the subfield of specialists concerned with one region of the United States rather than another, (2) the larger subfield of historians who study American (as opposed to French or English or Roman) history, and (3) the subfield of historians, sociologists, anthropologists, and psychologists interested in family history. Compactness of the sort possible with attachment research is simply not possible when a historian studying a community in colonial Massachusetts also finds it helpful to read work on medieval French peasant families, to compare the differing family patterns of colonial Massachusetts to those of colonial Pennsylvania, or to account for the differences between family patterns in differing Massachusetts towns.

In my sample of Colonial New England social history, the most frequent references are to historians doing similar work on New England communities: for example, Philip Greven's 1970 work on Andover is consistently cited. But two other kinds of citations occur also: citations to family and demographic research not focused on New England (e.g., Laslett's work on England, Ladurie's work on France), and earlier American historians' influential interpretions of the American past (e.g., Frederick Jackson Turner and Louis Hartz).

To some extent, then, subdisciplinary compactness works against full and rich understanding of wide-ranging contextual variables. But a difference in degree of compactness is not necessarily the same as a difference in kind of academic enterprise. The conceptually driven tendencies within family history—its assumptions about the contribution of such variables as fertility rates, family structure, inheritance practices, or age at marriage—move it toward the social sciences in a way that, for instance, an account of the Armada or a rendering of the life of a peasant would not do. The difference between the enterprise in attachment research and the enterprise in family history that Stone described is partly a difference in degree, not in kind.

And yet claims about differences in kind are currently being made—usually framed as the incompatibility between hermeneutic interpretations in the humanities and nonhermeneutic explanations in the social sciences. Geertz's comments on "Blurred Genres" are perhaps the best known of this type of argument. It is partly from lingering distaste for logical positivism and the kind of hyperlogical "laws" Hempel believed in that writers like Geertz have depicted the social sciences as turning toward modes of explanation in the humanities. Geertz has argued: "[A] challenge is being mounted to some of the central assumptions of mainstream social science. The strict separation of theory and data, the 'brute fact' idea; the effort to create a formal vocabulary of analysis purged of all subjective reference, the 'ideal language' idea; and the claim to moral neutrality and the Olympian view, the 'God's truth' idea—none of these can prosper when explanation comes to be regarded as a matter of connecting action to its sense rather than behavior to its determinants" (*Local* 34).

Perhaps all Geertz meant by this was that social science should contain two kinds of explanatory models: one connecting behavior to its determinants, and another connecting action to its meaning. But if he meant that social science should not be or is, in fact, no longer interested in causal explanation, then he seems to have been privileging a kind of enterprise more typical of the humanities, while denigrating another kind of enterprise still thriving in the social sciences. The covering law model of Hempel may well be dismissed now, as may explanations of the sort described as "vulgar Marxism." But the activity that Geertz described as "mainstream social science" is a reductive version of the kind of view of science we have seen, for instance, in Alan Sroufe's theoretical writings on attachment and would preclude the kind of progress Lawrence Stone perceived as having occurred in the field of family history.

Colonial New England Social History

Work in Colonial New England Social History shows traces of at least three kinds of enterprises I have discussed. The first of these is showing how life looked to ordinary people of that period—rendering, describing, or narrating events in their lives in such a way that modern readers can perceive or feel how it was to have lived then. One such example is Robert Gross's *The Minutemen and Their World* (1976) which contains narrative elements and is not guilty of either the charges leveled at narrative by Joan Scott or those leveled at social history by Gertrude Himmelfarb. That is, Gross's narrative of obscure people in a particularized context brings the reader to a sense of the larger political connections by which small events and obscure lives were linked to the major event of the American Revolution. Accounts like Gross's that provide rich description or narration of the *what* of the American past are most likely to appear in book-length studies.

But if we focus on professional journal articles as the knowledge-making forum of the academy, the kind of academic enterprise Gross carries out is not the norm. Professional articles in the field, to be sure, contain much information useful for constructing a narrative or describing lives of the time, but articles are structured, typically, by two other principles corresponding to the particularistic interpretive mode of the humanities and the explanatory, conceptually driven mode of the social sciences.

The two strands are discernible, though often intertwined within a single article. Their intermingling reflects the dual importance of the *what* and the *why* foci within social history. The interpretive, *what* strand appears dedicated to providing information and to helping resolve interpretive questions about the traditionalism or modernity of New England settlers. But at the same time, a more conceptually driven, explanatory strand occurs—involving questions like those Stone suggests, drawing on concepts imported from the social sciences, and offering to contribute to some cumulative or synthetic understanding of processes in colonial or family history.

The interpretive strand traditional to the humanities is often present, for instance, in debates about the interpretive accuracy of earlier characterizations—e.g., Frederick Jackson Turner's frontier thesis or Louis Hartz's assumption that Americans were early characterized by liberal individualism. Turner or Hartz are frequently used as points of departure for arguing that previous historians have incorrectly interpreted the "mobility" or the "individualism" of seventeenth- or eighteenth-century Americans. This interpretive strand has some affinities with the ambiguities characteristic of textually driven literary interpretation. In historical analysis, a case can be made for interpreting the same historical phenomena as instances of either "individualism" or "traditionalism." "Mobility," as evidenced by migration, might in some circumstances be a sign of "individualism." But as Greven argued in his study of Andover, mobility might merely be the result of overpopulation, or as Patricia Tracy argued in her study of Northampton, Massachusetts, mobility might possibily be a device to keep the younger and potentially landless generation together in the same community with their parents. The interpretive strand has the liability of encouraging binary oppositions, and in a field dedicated to examining change over time, there are only so many times that change from one binary element to another can occur—only so many times, for instance, that traditionalism can be supplanted by individualism. The explanatory strand, however, has the liability of not explaining particular differences.

To examine how the interpretive and explanatory strands mingle and work against disciplinary compactness in New England Colonial social history, I begin with foundational work in the late 1960s—work roughly contemporaneous with the foundational work in attachment research—because the unfolding of work over two decades in this subfield of history differs from the more compact disciplinary progression over the same period in attachment research.

In the late 1960s, there was a sudden flurry of studies of the social history and demographics of Colonial New England towns. In 1970, for instance, three now well-known and frequently cited studies of Colonial Massachusetts towns appeared: Kenneth Lockridge's study of Dedham, John Demos's study of Plymouth, and Philip Greven's study of Andover. As Joyce Appleby described this congruence, "In 1970 communities studies [sic] burst upon the scholarly skyline like a meteor shower, leaving behind a trail of monographic meteorites" (303).

In perhaps the most frequently cited of these "meteorites," *Four Generations: Population, Land, and Family in Colonial Andover, Massachusetts*, Philip Greven commented on how the appearance of studies by younger historians sharing similar premises suggested a significant change in historians' study of the past, reflecting "the belief that historians must seek to explore the basic structure and character of society through close, detailed examinations of the experiences of individuals, families and groups in particular communities and localities" (vii–viii). His comments on the importance of other disciplines and quantifiable data revealed the explanatory strand in his work, with references to quantification and to structure showing the influence from social science in general, especially sociological studies of the family. At the same time, though, Greven's references to particular localities showed the bottom-up orientation of social history—its attempt to go beyond studying the elites of traditional historical work.

These two strands interacted with each other in Greven's work:

since common people usually leave different kinds of traces than do elites, they could not be easily glimpsed through the literary documents or famous events that inform us about elites in history. So to examine common people required some of the quantitative tools of demography. John Waters in his 1970 review of Greven, Demos, and Lockridge summarized both these interactive strands, derived from French and then English prototypes: "social history must be rewritten from the bottom up" and the "documents upon which these new works rest clearly distinguish them as a specific historical genre: family reconstitution forms, land division records, tax rolls, deeds, estate inventories, court cases, archaeological findings, and museum artifacts" (Waters "Review" 657). Among these were the kinds of data Greven would use.

Greven's "Preface" showed that this emerging field of historical study already involved cohesive, aggregate work—with historians at different institutions probing similar data in similar ways with similar questions in mind. He referred to the books by Lockridge and Demos, having read parts of their studies in article or dissertation form before their publication in book form.[5] In short, Greven's work as a young scholar in 1970 was already positioned in a cohesive field whose scholars were in contact with each other or were moving in similar directions, looking at similar material, asking similar questions.

In addition to resourceful use of archival material to reconstruct the lives of early Andover inhabitants, Greven's book was especially noteworthy for its following of twenty-eight Andover families and their descendants over four generations in order to discern how psychological attitudes toward family and the individual shifted along with shifts in fertility, longevity, and the availability of land. More so than Demos and Lockridge, Greven attempted to trace change over time. Appleby's later caution about the difficulty of accounting for change when using structural concepts from sociology may apply less to Greven than to others because his story, in Appleby's term, "moves."

Among his conclusions, Greven saw earlier historians as having overemphasized the disruption of traditional communal life in the new world; he pointed to recent work in English history (Laslett and Harrison) that had discovered an unexpected amount of mobility in English rural life and showed how the first two generations in Andover achieved the kind of order, stability, and close-knit community often thought to have been ruptured by the experience of immigration to

America. In emphasizing stability and community in Andover, Greven dissented from the work of earlier historians (e.g. Bailyn, Handlin) who had emphasized "declension"—"the falling away, often involuntarily, from the standards and the modes of behavior of earlier times and places" (264). He also dissented from Talcott Parsons's work positing a sociologist's version of the declension interpretation—that "industrialization and urbanization had made the older forms of extended family life impossible, and the nuclear family became the only viable form in our societies" (284).

Greven's final conclusions about the colonial American family were as follows:

> The process of change, though, is far more complex than we have generally assumed; it is not simply a long-term change from the extended family to the nuclear family, coinciding with industrialization or urbanization. Changes in family structure usually occur *within* definite periods, within particular places, whether rural or urban, and within particular societies, whether agrarian or industrial. (287–88)

Similar conclusions have been announced by a number of historians since Greven, but what is puzzling, by contrast to the compact subdisciplinary development seen in attachment research, is how frequent the seesawing has been between historians announcing conclusions like Greven's and those announcing conclusions unlike his. There appears to have been little incremental development of consensus.

Historians' laments about the lack of cumulative synthesis in colonial social history show the continuity, repetition, and yet tension within the historical conversation sustained on the subject of the family and community since Greven's work. The debate, typically, has been articulated as a choice between two binary opposites, with several versions of the binaries frequently occurring: community versus individualism, tradition versus modernization, extended family versus nuclear family, precapitalist versus capitalist, and rural versus urban. Greven, in the quotation above, explicitly pointed out the problem in positing change as the change from one period to another, and I have already noted Joyce Appleby's caution, issued in 1984, about the "belief that change can best be accounted for as the transformation of social forms" such as "traditional to modern" (307).

Michael Zuckerman in 1977 wrote that historians of the American character had fallen into two camps, one emphasizing "the ascendancy of individualism" and the other "the sway of community." These two groups "talk[ed] past one another" while a third group who saw community as giving way to individualism had "place[d] that passage in every generation from the founding of the colonies to the middle of the twentieth century" (183). "Such studies," Zuckerman wrote, "constitute, collectively, an advancing embarrassment" (183). The "embarrassment," for Zuckerman, lay in the binaries being misleading, as well as in their proponents' "setting those static characterizations in historical sequence" (183). Like Greven, Zuckerman criticized sociologists' concept of modernization as offering too sweeping an antithesis (the traditional community giving way to modernism); instead, Zuckerman theorized that modernization in the early American context could lead simultaneously to individualistic and communal concerns.

In a 1978 book, Thomas Bender took up the same point, referring to Zuckerman and expanding on the flaws in the "community breakdown thesis" (a version of the "declension" thesis Greven disputed). Bender cited a number of studies and wrote, "If these books are placed in serial order, they offer a picture of community breakdown repeating itself in the 1650s, 1690s, 1740s, 1780s, 1820s, 1850s, 1880s, and 1920s" (51). Bender explained this flaw in American historiography, in part, as deriving from sociologists' binaries: (1) Gemeinschaft versus Gesellschaft, (2) rural versus urban, and (3) traditional versus modern. He, too, criticized modernization theory as an "ahistorical logic of change" (23). He objected to the three dichotomies being used to characterize whole societies and objected to characterizing change in "totalistic terms" or viewing change as sequential. He objected, in other words, to the effects of a conceptually driven sociology on the study of history, but he did not want to abandon concepts: "However critical I have been of urban and modernization theory, I am not proposing that we abandon theory and concentrate entirely upon the concrete and particular. Rather, we must strive to cast our theory in terms that can accommodate the concreteness of context and the particularity of change over time . . ." (32–33). Again, this resembles the point made by Greven, Zuckerman, and Appleby and is a reminder of the possible tension between conceptually driven and more particularistic, interpretive, or text-driven work.

Tensions within the interpretive tradition are evident from James Henretta's frequently cited 1978 article "Families and Farms: *Mentalité* in Pre-Industrial America," which revisited the individualism versus community debate. Henretta argued against "entrepreneurial" interpretations in which colonial farmers were seen as liberal individualists. He concluded that "lineal values" in which family wealth was built up, conserved, and passed along for offspring mattered more than the individual. The emphasis on the welfare of the entire family "inhibited the emergence of individualism" in preindustrial northern America (26). Though Henretta critiqued others in the field, he did so more to dispute one pole of the binary interpretive tradition than to alter the basic binaries between which historical interpretation had been oscillating. In other words, his critique of interpretations which characterized the early colonists as "entrepreneurial" did not so much break out of a disciplinary discussion as continue it. The same set of oppositions between individualism and community still inform the central conceptual questions a decade later.

In the 1980s, the same issues were still under discussion, without dramatic further compacting of the issues. Darrett B. Rutman in a 1986 review article, "Assessing the Little Communities of Early America," raised questions about whether twenty (or more) years of community studies had collectively added up to new generalizations. However, he suggested there were some generalizations to be made, some discernible "central tendencies"—a term which showed the pull social science still exerted on history in 1986:

> The main thrust of the processes underway in the communities of early America—the central tendencies—seems clear enough after reading through the products of two decades of intense scrutiny: toward scarcity (from an early plenty) and, with scarcity, mobility; toward internal complexity; toward integration into the larger society. But it is always "toward," never "to." The processes glimpsed are necessarily incomplete at the end of the span with which we deal.
> Clear too, in the literature is the virtually unchanging milieu within which the processes were played out in our period: invariably small scale, face-to-face, neighborly; a population concerned in the main with the day-to-day and generation-to-generation, and connected only tenuously with the ideas and great events of a colonial capital or the far seat of empire itself. (178)

These are primarily descriptive generalizations that do not involve causal explanation. They show that some degree of compacting had occurred over roughly two decades, yet only of a very general and categorical sort, not going very far, if at all, beyond the causal general-izations possible from Greven's work in 1970. This difficulty in even arriving at descriptive generalizations raises the question of what keeps the field going, whether progress is being made toward greater communal understanding within the field, and, if not, what other knowledge-making functions may be involved. At this point, I turn to the articles in my sample of representative current work in the field.

A Sample of Current Articles in Context

Current professional articles in the field may be seen in the context of the two discussions above—the problematics of writing history and the unfolding subfield of the social history of Colonial New England. Three of the four sample articles come from 1989 or 1990 issues of journals and one from 1982.[6] One comes from the *Journal of Social History* and three from the *William and Mary Quarterly*. Each is a logical place for an article on social history in Colonial New England to appear, but the *William and Mary Quarterly* is particularly important because it has published perhaps the majority of articles in the field. Justification for describing the articles as belong-ing to the same discourse community may be found in their citations: all cite Greven, most cite Lockridge or Demos, the later articles usually cite the earlier articles in my sample, and all also cite key historians, sociologists, and so forth, working in the same theoretical areas though not focused on Colonial New England.

None of the articles might be called a narrative; none would serve—as would Robert Gross's *The Minutemen and their World*—to tell a story or bring together a coherent, accessible narrative in the sense that Stone and Bailyn saw as likely or desirable. The articles are all arranged topically, rather than chronologically; several of them, however, explicitly discuss change over time.

The first of the articles, John Waters' "Family, Inheritance, and Migration in Colonial New England: The Evidence from Guilford, Connecticut," may be typical of the social science strand within his-tory, though it shows connections to each of the three strands I have discussed. The social science strand predominates and is obvious in four interrelated components: quantification, figures and tables, distinctive causal variables, and references to social science research on the family done by researchers interested in other countries and periods. These references are a sign of subdisciplinary identification not only with the study of New England or the colonial period but also with the study of family structure.

The quantitative emphasis is evident in Waters' initially erecting his generalizations on large-scale, quantitative data, though he then illustrates the categories of households with case studies. He begins with a 1732 Guilford listing of 76 households containing 406 men, women, and children and finds that of his four household classifications, 68.42 percent were nuclear, while 15.79 percent were multiple lineal or stem families. These figures are conveyed in one of three tables, the other two giving quantitative data on "Male Heir Persistence" and "East Guilford Taxed Wealth Distribution."

Waters identifies four contextual variables: property holdings, marriages, residency patterns, and outmigration. His ability to identify these as distinctive variables shows the social science influence in his work, yet his embedding the discussion of these structural variables in four case studies of families shows the historian's emphasis on context.

Finally, the key conceptual issues he identifies show their social science roots. He first raises the issue of what early New England families were like, using a familiar opposition within historians' debates: whether the family was nuclear, mobile, and modern (as Demos suggested) or traditionally agrarian, extended, and stable as Waters (in his early work) and Henretta had suggested. Waters quickly moves beyond these binary oppositions, however, with the suggestion that historians' differing interpretations have been caused by their looking at different families. To shed light on the problem, he turns, first, to quantitative analysis and to an issue in family history occurring outside studies of New England and/or outside the discipline of history. He uses (1) the sociological analysis of Pierre LePlay for the categorical concepts of extended, stem, and nuclear families; (2) the demographic work of Peter Laslett and the Cambridge Group for the History of Population and Social Structure for methods of analyzing family types; and (3) the anthropological work of Meyer Fortes and Jack Goody, stressing the "flow of life experience through time" to generate Waters's own life-cycle analysis (Waters 68). In this way, he combines structural categories with change over time.

But lest this sound like a form of social science indistinguishable from work in sociology or anthropology, Waters frequently uses a paragraph style more characteristic of historians: that is, paragraphs containing abstract social science concepts but illustrated with details more particularistic than would be needed to argue the point. Here is one such paragraph:

> Our fourth family, the Meigses, formed a continuing parochial elite and maintained first-quintile wealth status and concomitant social position throughout the colonial period. They were not one of the Kentish founding families as were the Cruttendens, nor did they marry into Guilford land like Edward Lee, nor did they engage in trade like Thomas Blachley. Rather, John Meigs, their progenitor in Guilford, was recruited because of his skill as a tanner. In 1661, after a period of friction with his predominantly Kentish neighbors, this Somerset-shire man proved himself by his "speedy" warning of two of the Puritan regicides to flee from Charles II's agents who followed close on their trail. Meigs became Guilford's first local hero. He joined the church, mended his ways, and concluded his days as an established pater familias (see Figure I). Each of the next three generations supplied deacons to the service of the Lord, and the town fondly remembered one of these, Timothy Meigs, A.B. Yale 1732, as "Our Israel's sweet singer." Three members of the family represented Guilford at the General Court; two of these three also served as militia officers; and three others held military posts, the most famous being Phineas Meigs who died in the little known Guilford battle of 1782 "Contending for the Freedom of his Country in the 74th Year of his Age." His tombstone proclaims his heroic stature; the family plot in which it stands holds the remains of this elite clan of landed farmer-artisans whose life was dominated by family and rooted in their fields. Lovingly the Meigses spoke of this earth as the "land called the Maj[o]rs," the "jed Pierson Lot," the "Lot called the Felix [Meigs] lot," while in their deeds they wrote proudly that this soil had belonged to an "honoured Father" or had come to them from "our Honoured Grandfather." (Waters 74–75)

There are reminders of social science here: the reference to "quintiles" and to Figure I of the text, which is an abstract diagram of the John Meigs's household with triangles representing males, circles females, and interconnecting lines representing generational connections (Waters 69). But the above paragraph shows more detail than would be strictly necessary for supporting the generalizations involved. The Meigs progenitor need not have been named, and his occupation could have been generalized to "craftsman," rather than specified as "tanner." Such details as the "speedy" warning, Timothy Meigs's graduating in 1732, the quotation about Phineas, or the descriptions of fields do not so much substantiate or advance generalizations, as they give a feeling for the life of these otherwise obscure figures. In this fashion, in the midst of generalizing tendencies from the social sciences, Waters displays his historian's affinity for the particulars of historical context—particulars which lead not toward causal explanation but toward, as Megill terms it, "rendering" experience. In my linguistic analysis (see chapter 6), this affinity for particular details shows up as a clear difference between history and psychology, and I have already commented that there is not one sentence in my psychology sample comparable to, for instance, "Lovingly the Meigses spoke of . . ." in its focus on individual particulars.

The historians in my sample vary in the degree to which they incorporate particularistic detail beyond what is necessary for substantiating generalizations. Toby Ditz's article, "Ownership and Obligation: Inheritance and Patriarchal Households in Connecticut, 1750–1820," shares many of the characteristics of Waters's article but less of the particularized flavor that Waters includes to render something of the life of the colonial period. Ditz, like Waters, begins by disavowing the binary opposition created in earlier historical debates. She characterizes the debate as still containing vestiges of the older consensus, in which "Louis Hartz's liberals and Frederick Jackson Turner's democratic frontiersmen, the lucky heirs to a seventeenth-century natural rights tradition and America's material riches, created a middle-class society, at once egalitarian and individualist" (235). The opposite and more recent interpretation, as Ditz characterizes it, comes from Henretta and Waters, and emphasizes not liberal individualism but patrilinear values involving "conservation of ancestral homesteads and continuation of their family names on local land" (237). Ditz refines the latter interpretation by arguing that the mid-eighteenth-century Connecticut estate holders in her study felt the tension between keeping their estates intact in order to enhance the power of one heir and distributing their estates equally among heirs. The strategy she finds estate holders adopting might be described as a compromise in which they acted to establish as many new households as possible among their offspring, but without egalitarian beliefs about individualism.

Several aspects of Ditz's article stand out as typical of social science tendencies within social history. The introductory section of her article resembles a social science article in its epistemic focus on previous research and methods of analysis. There are references, as in Waters, to social scientists' and social historians' working on other regions or eras but contributing toward general concepts or methods of analysis. There is some quantification, as seen in two tables.

Most interesting, for my purposes here, is the form the generalizing tendencies take. In one sense, Ditz's enterprise involves local contextualizing in that she examines the interaction between family values and economics within two contrasted places (the more prosperous valley town of Wethersfield and four less prosperous upland towns) and two periods of time (the colonial period and the 1820s). In this way, Ditz avoids generalizing from one place to another or one period to another. But this local contextualizing is clearly not in the service of capturing the *what* of past particulars. Instead, hers is a study of general processes as they are affected by generalizable variables (such as fertile versus infertile land) found in particular local configurations. Wethersfield is not a subject for its own sake, as it might be in a local history written for a local historical society, but as a type of town that can illustrate some of the effects of fertile land and market access.[7]

Despite the historian's emphasis on historical and contextual variables, then, this type of history is concerned with aggregates. Human actors, not surprisingly, make their appearance, in Ditz's article, primarily in the aggregate. Although there are brief examples of the inheritance strategies of four colonial estate holders—Jehiel Rose, Henry Curtis, John Pierce, and Deacon John Chapman—each makes his appearance as an example of general tendencies. We are told none of the small, extraneous details Waters tells us about the Meigs family. The one-paragraph appearance of Henry Curtis, for instance, is sandwiched between generalizing statements and offered as illustration of the generalization:

> This study includes a few landed parents who did not leave wills; it shows that the daughters of these intestate parents almost always got some land. . . . For example, Henry Curtis. . . . Thus his daughters' shares of parental land became minute.
>
> As this example suggests, although a majority of daughters inherited some land, formidable gender inequality was still a feature of colonial practices. (Ditz 249)

This example is typical within my sample of professional articles in this field. But it is not the field itself, so much as the professional forum that seems to preclude further narrative treatment.

Robert Gross's *The Minutemen and Their World* emerges from the same field, same research sources and techniques but is intended for a different purpose, as Gross explains in the following passage:

> Many writers have told Concord's story. For the most part, theirs have been tales of great events and great men—of the "embattled farmers" and the distinguished writers who have brought fame to the town. It sets the Concord Fights, as it used to be known, in the context of the townspeople's ordinary lives, before and after April 19, 1775.
> . . .
> This study is part of the "new social history." It is based on a reconstruction of eighteenth-century Concord from such sources as vital records, genealogies, tax and assessment lists, wills, deeds, petitions, and the minutes of town meetings. . . . Unfortunately, quantitative social history can be dull and tedious work, and at times it requires technical knowledge and skills. In this book, I have chosen to relate Concord's response to revolution directly and simply, without flogging the evidence. The detailed support for my conclusions and the sometimes dry methodological issues of this research have been left to the notes. (Gross vii–viii)

It is not Gross's sources, then, nor his kind of analysis, that distinguishes his text from those found in professional journals. The differences, instead, derive from rhetorical considerations about what kind of text making best serves Gross's purpose:

> Social history, like any other branch of history, should be accessible to as wide an audience as possible, for it deals with everyday, fundamental experiences of human life. . . . It thereby provides us with our closest points of contact with men and women of the past. By seeing how earlier Americans have lived and struggled in their daily lives, we can come to recognize them as people like ourselves and gain a new understanding of our society and our heritage. (Gross viii)

The purpose Gross announces is not to make knowledge—to offer new analyses, correct former causal explanations—but to reach and engage a wide audience. In order to do so, he does not merely suppress "dry methodological issues" but also turns from aggregate to individual and places his individuals as actors both in history and in the syntactic structure of the text. I explore the connection between rhetorical purpose and sentence-level use of individuals as actors further in chapters 6 and 7, but Gross shows how narrative treatment of colonial social history might focus on individual actors. This passage occurs at a point of transition from discussing Colonel Barrett to discussing David Brown:

> When Colonel Barrett and his family went to town in 1775, they traveled the Groton Road, which passed near their home, winding southeasterly for nearly two miles to the North Bridge. Several hundred yards above the bridge, where the road bent to the left, a small red house stood with two adjacent barns on a twenty-acre lot. The colonel no doubt stopped by there often to discuss Concord's military preparations. It was the homestead of David Brown, the forty-two-year-old captain of a Minuteman company. Brown, too, had a son under his command, but, unlike Barrett, he could not assure the young man's future. Seventeen-year-old Purchase Brown had no place to go but down if he chose to spend his life in Concord. (Gross 83)

This transition from Barrett to Brown is made descriptive in a way that appeals to the reader's visual sense of place (already well mapped out earlier in *The Minutemen*), rather than the reader's sense of analytic categories. Brown is not simply introduced as another category of Concord resident, but as someone connected to Barrett by place (the bridge, the left-bending road, the small red house) and an agent who acts (discussing preparations with Barrett, commanding a company, worrying about his son's future).

The fact that *The Minutemen* is included in this academic subdisciplinary community (through citations and similar research, for instance) illustrates that this community recognizes the powers of narrative and differing purposes of writing for academic and lay audiences. I turn now to writing in a subdiscipline of literary studies where narrative has entered into writing in academic forums.

CHAPTER FIVE

Renaissance
New Historicism
Epistemic and Nonepistemic
Textual Patterns

The historians' lament —that work in New England social history has not yet produced agreed-upon synthetic generalizations— has a kindred lament in current writing about literature. Reflecting on the rapid rise of "New Historicism" in Renaissance studies over the last decade, Louis Montrose writes:

> "The New Historicism" has not yet begun to fade from the academic scene. . . . But neither has it become any clearer that "*The* New Historicism" designates any agreed upon intellectual and institutional program. There has been no coalescence of the various identifiably New Historicist practices into a systematic and authoritative paradigm for the interpretation of Renaissance texts; nor does the emergence of such a paradigm seem either likely or desirable. ("Professing" 18–19)

The word "desirable" is the only clue, here, that the problematics of writing contemporary literary criticism may differ from those of writing history. Though we have seen little reason, in chapter 4, to assume that historians are on the verge of compacting their disciplinary enterprise in the way attachment research is compact, nevertheless historians' laments show a strong sense that disciplinary progress might be desirable. In Montrose's statement about Renaissance New Historicism, however, "coalescence" into a paradigm may not even be desirable. This chapter explores why that should be so: how academic writing about literature in the subfield of Renaissance New Historicism differs from writing about history or psychology and how the absence of compactness and progressive work in Renaissance New Historicism shapes and is in turn shaped by the kinds of texts New Historicists write.

It is useful, initially, to contrast attachment research and literary studies in order to see the broad outlines of difference that help define the New Historical enterprise. In the subfield of attachment research, articles typically begin with a problem definition and presentation that emphasizes the disciplinary line-of-descent in which writers place themselves. The ability of a disciplinary community to use line-of-descent accounts in problem presentation requires, as I have discussed in chapter 2, some compacting of disciplinary problems and progressive work on them, progressive in the sense of moving forward and solving enough parts of the problem to leave parts of it behind. Toulmin, as we have seen, attributed disciplinary compactness partly to a community's insulation from extraprofessional concerns, without which new ideas "will be lost in a welter of speculative debates and polemical objections. . . . there will be no stable equilibrium short of intellectual conformism or conceptual anarchy" (Toulmin 295). Suggestions that literary studies may contain more conceptual anarchy than other disciplines come from a number of sources: Elbow suggests that "English" is "a profession that cannot define what it is" (*What Is English?* v), and Graff's historical account of the profession depicts a repetitive pattern in which conflicting aims are tolerated but not "brought into fruitful relation and opposition" (*Professing* 250).

To draw attention to the relative lack of disciplinary compacting in literary studies is to take the vantage point of the social sciences, looking at literary studies from the outside. To do so is unfair to the extent that it valorizes a particular view of academic work—or valorizes disciplinarity in a way some academics might contest. But such an initial vantage point allows us to see differences that we may then attempt to account for from *within* the disciplinary viewpoint of literary studies. The quotation above from Montrose is one sign that literary studies may not value compactness or that something about literary studies may entail practices that work against disciplinary compactness. In exploring these possibilities, I turn first, for contrast, to kinds of problem definition and presentation in older, historically oriented, but nevertheless text-driven studies of Shakespeare. I then discuss the problems typically defined for New Historicist work and, finally, look in some detail at the distinctively anecdotal textual presentation favored by some New Historicists.

Problem Definition in Earlier Criticism

Earlier Shakespeare criticism with a historical emphasis—as opposed to an exclusively textual emphasis—gives us a reference point from which to begin so that we are not merely comparing the textual focus of one era to the historical focus of another. The introductions of a 1965 article by Jonas Barish and a 1957 article by Paul Olson have three distinguishing traits relevant to my analysis here: (1) they define the problem immediately, (2) they represent their interpretive community as congenial but relatively unsituated, and (3) they focus on the text.[1]

The first sentence of Jonas Barish's article, "The Turning Away of Prince Hal," on Hal's rejection of Falstaff in *Henry IV*, introduced its problem immediately: "The rejection of Falstaff, like much else in Shakespeare, has tended to turn a searchlight on us, and make ourselves reveal ourselves either as moralists or as sentimentalists" (277). The problem—"the rejection of Falstaff"—was economically condensed for purposes of identification and then later redefined as "the turning away of Prince Hal". Though Barish soon cited a number of critics, he did not present the problem as a professional one with which the discipline had been struggling; nor did he focus on prior professional, disciplinary discussion. By implication, the problem was in the interaction between text and reader. The "searchlight on us" implied that Shakespeare's text appeals to a universal human dilemma that arises from different preferences rooted in human nature or "instincts" (Barish 277).

The two kinds of readers Barish postulated were distinguishable in that one kind preferred order and the other preferred freedom. These proclivities were presented as deriving from individual personality rather than professional training. The reader was part of an unsituated "we": "If we range ourselves naturally on the side of authority, with its promise of order and justice, we will tend to endorse the casting off of the embodiment of disorder, the enemy-in-chief of the Lord Chief Justice. . . . If, on the other hand, our instincts prompt us to range ourselves more strongly on the side of freedom and spontaneity, we may tend to remember the vitality in Falstaff more than his lawlessness . . ." (277). By the end of the first paragraph then, Barish had set up his problem and was ready to proceed. In the discussion that followed, he referred to the differing literary characteristics of the genres of comedy, tragedy, and history, as Shakespeare used them, to explain why "the exponents of order, however repressive, are felt to warrant our allegiance" (285).

Paul Olson's study, "A *Midsummer Night's Dream* and the Meaning of Court Marriage," began with reference to common opinion: "The opinion that A *Midsummer Night's Dream* is largely a shimmering fabric of 'moonlight, with a touch of moonshine' [Chute] has become stock among students of Shakespeare." Olson's second sentence conveyed some of the same sense to be found in Barish that differences in critical readings result either from readers' differing temperaments or from differences inherent in texts: "One rephrases habitual insights concerning gossamer and magic whenever one treats of the work" (95).

In his next sentences, however, Olson set up an opposition between the generic "one" and historical scholars: "The efforts of historical scholars to place this comedy in the setting of its dramatic tradition, to see it as '*sui generis*, a "symbolical" or masque-like play' [Brown, Chambers, Welsford, Sisson] suggest that we ought to revise our romantic preconceptions of its structure and theme." The generic reader, then, was guilty of "romantic preconceptions" and Olson took on the task of revising those preconceptions. The problem, therefore, had been defined by the fourth sentence.

It is significant that the "we" and the "our" Olson represented imply he embraced this romantic generic reader as a member of his own interpretive community, not a distant "they" who might be construed as adversarial. He offered no sense of radically oppositional readings among subgroups of Shakespearians, as current Renaissance New Historicists often do. Instead, he appeared to offer a congenial attempt within the interpretive community to correct itself and move toward better understandings.[2]

A third distinguishing trait of these older articles is their textual focus. Olson's focus, for instance, was on the Shakespearean text, despite his emphasis on historical scholarship. The history with which he was concerned was treated as unproblematic background useful for illuminating the text. New Historicists criticize their predecessors for just this treatment of history, in which history becomes the unproblematic reference point grounding discussion of the literary text (e.g., Howard, "The New Historicism," or Montrose, "Renaissance Literary Studies"). Olson's assertions about what the courtly audience would have thought of parts of the play were made with no account of resistance or heterogeneity in the audience.

In summary, Barish's and Olson's problem presentations and definitions were characterized by (1) immediate definition of the problem motivating the article, (2) representation of a relatively congenial but not highly specialized community of readers, and (3) textual focus.

Problem Definition in the New Historicism

Problem definition in Barish's and Olson's articles was text-driven by textually specific problems in interpreting Shakespeare's plays. The current New Historicism, by contrast, is more conceptually driven in that generic, conceptual problems are brought to the plays and then stimulate interpretation of specific plays. Louis Montrose has listed the following problems as those New Historicists typically address:

> Inhabiting the discursive spaces traversed by the term "New Historicism" are some of the most complex, persistent, and unsettling of the problems that professors of literature attempt variously to confront or to evade: Among them, the essential or historical bases upon which "literature" is to be distinguished from other discourses; the possible configurations of the relationship between cultural practices and social, political and economic processes; the consequences of post-structuralist theories of textuality for the practice of an historical or materialist criticism; the means by which subjectivity is socially constituted and constrained; the processes by which ideologies are produced and sustained, and by which they may be contested; the patterns of consonance and contradiction among the values and interests of a given individual, as these are actualized in the shifting conjunctures of various subject positions—as, for example, intellectual worker, academic professional, and gendered domestic, social, political and economic agent. ("Professing" 19)

Montrose offered this list of six problems as "inhabiting" New Historicism in general, not merely Renaissance New Historicism; so his list may already, in order to be inclusive, have generalized beyond some of the particularities of Renaissance New Historicist focuses. Nevertheless, the problems in Montrose's list reveal a rather striking degree of generality and a significant shift toward the conceptually driven, when compared to Barish's earlier article. The first kind of problem, for instance—"the essential or historical bases upon which 'literature' is to be distinguished from other discourses"—is conceptually driven in being generated from a theoretical question, not from a more inductivist need to establish a particular text's literariness. The fourth problem—"the means by which subjectivity is socially constituted and constrained"—has similarly conceptual origins in theoretical discussion.

The fifth problem—"the process by which ideologies are produced and sustained"—is most central to New Historicist discussions of Shakespeare. It most closely approximates the problem Stephen Greenblatt considered in his frequently cited (and criticized) article, "Invisible Bullets: Renaissance Authority and Its Subversion, *Henry IV* and *Henry V*," and other articles in my sample; and it helps foreground the difference between, for instance, Barish's and Greenblatt's treatment of the problem of Hal's casting off Falstaff. Critics who identify themselves as New Historicists, as well as those working from closely connected perspectives perhaps critical of New Historicism, often name *power* as the central topic of New Historicism. As Jonathan Dollimore has described it, the New Historicism is "a perspective concerned generally with the interaction in this period between State power and cultural forms and, more specifically, with those genre and practices where State and culture most visibly merge—for example, pastoral, the masque and the institution of patronage" (3).

The New Historicism has been described as Marxist (e.g., Pechter), but that characterization has been disputed, and there has arisen a "subversion-containment debate" (Dollimore 12) in which American New Historicists are seen as finding subversion to be ultimately contained, while critics with a more Marxist perspective—often British "cultural materialists"—see a greater possibility for subversion.[3] There are also American Marxist critiques of the "containment" position attributed to New Historicists. As Frank Lentricchia has described it, Greenblatt's enterprise contains "a strange mix of voices ultimately dominated by Foucauldian tone: the feeling, usually just evoked, almost never argued through, that all social life is organized and controlled down to its oddest and smallest details" (234). Lentricchia criticizes Greenblatt for representing authority as ultimately containing subversion:

> [Greenblatt's] description of power endorses Foucault's theory of power, preserving not only the master's repeated insistence on the concrete institutional character of power, its palpability, as it were, but also his glide into a conception of a power that is elusively and literally undefinable—not finitely anchored but diffused from nowhere to everywhere, and saturating all social relations to the point that all conflicts and "jostlings" among social groups become a mere show of political dissension, a prearranged theater of struggle set upon the substratum of a monolithic agency which produces "opposition" as one of its delusive political effects. (235)

Theodore Leinwand has characterized the subversion-containment debate as follows: "the argument is not with subversion and containment as terms for the debate but with the ratio between them at particular moments. Thus Dollimore reminds us that marginal subjects may and do appropriate dominant discourses, that subversion produced by authority for its own purposes may get out of hand . . . [Dollimore 12–14]" (Leinwand 477–78). In other words, even when critics disagree as to whether there is possibility for subversion or not, they tend to agree on how they define the problem for academic literary work to address: the problem, for New Historicism, is to look at the workings of power and ask whether, how, or to what degree subversion can exist within a hegemonic power structure such as is found in Renaissance England.

For my comparative perspective here, three features of this problem definition are significant: (1) the conceptually driven quality associated with its importation into Shakespearean studies from another realm of discourse, (2) the possibilities for greater knowledge compacting when a disciplinary problem is shared and worked on by many scholars, and (3) the problematics associated with the tension between abstract and particular that the problem demonstrates.

First, the more conceptually driven character of New Historicist work may be seen in the difference between Barish's article and Stephen Greenblatt's "Invisible Bullets," both articles having discussed *Henry IV* and *Henry V*. Barish used the two concepts of "authority" and "rebellion" explicitly and centrally in his problem definition, but Greenblatt's article is, nevertheless, more conceptually driven in using a Foucaultian definition of the subversion-containment problem that moves away from the relatively text-driven and particularistic problems of the New Criticism. In Barish's text-driven approach, the characterization of Falstaff and the dynamics of Shakespearian comedy and history generated the problem of authority and rebellion in *Henry IV*. But for New Historicists influenced by Foucault, the "problem" of authority and subversion has been generated first in other contexts and can then be transferred to literature of any period or place. The fact that Foucault's statements of the problem may have been made in relation to the development of the penitentiary system, for instance (e.g., *Discipline and Punish*), and then imported into an academic discussion about the English Renaissance shows that the problem has not arisen from the particulars of historical context or literary text in the way that I have characterized as text-driven (see chapter 2).

Second, the "subversion-containment debate" opens the possibility of moving toward a more cumulative knowledge making in this subfield of literary studies. Instead of text-driven inquiry potentially spread over every facet of every play of Shakespeare's, a conceptually driven inquiry can develop and then refine ways of looking at texts with an interpretive problem in mind. At the same time, however, the debate in colonial social history between community versus individualism or tradition versus modernization (see chapter 4) suggests that interpretive binaries, as seen in the subversion-containment debate, may afford a less productive form of conceptually driven problem definition than the explanatory problem driving attachment research. Moreover the epideictic tendencies and point-last textual features I will discuss in the second half of this chapter work to counteract the compacting effects of the consensus on exploring subversion versus containment. Whatever cumulative knowledge building is facilitated by consensus in the field's problem definition is undercut or slowed by textual features that fail to promote adjudication among different contributions to the field.

Third, the abstraction in Renaissance New Historicist problem definition is potentially problematic. We have seen the tension felt by social historians between abstracting general patterns and exploring the particulars of differing social and historical contexts. Shifts within the study of literature in the last twenty years reveal the same problematic between abstracting and particularizing.

Barish's 1965 article showed simultaneously a universalizing and a contextualizing strand that can be taken as roughly typical of earlier criticism. In articulating the problem of authority versus rebellion in the *Henry* plays, Barish may have been influenced by social currents in the 1960s, but he presented his generalized reader and the conflict between authority and rebellion as a difference without historical significance. This ahistorical and generalizing tendency in Barish's article, however, was counterbalanced by a historicizing and particularizing tendency in his close attention to the constraints of genre in Shakespearean comedy and history, to the specifics of the *Henry* plays, to constraints derived (however tinged with interpretation) from the historical fact of Henry V having succeeded Henry IV, and to the specifics of Falstaff's comic personality. In all these particulars, Barish discerned a pattern that he did not represent as typical of other writers or other times.

Having seen the tensions that the more generalized academic problems of social science can create within a more particularized tradition of history writing, we may suspect that importing social science concepts into literary problem definition could produce similar tensions. The tension shows up within New Historicist writing on Shakespeare in the issue of choice of cultural texts to bring to bear on Shakespeare's texts and, frequently, in critiques of Greenblatt's use of anecdotes. There is a generalizing process at work if the problem of authority and subversion may be scrutinized in any literary text or any literary period, but at the same time, there is a particularizing or localizing tendency in Renaissance New Historicism that I will discuss further in the second half of this chapter.

First, however, it is worth looking at what some of the critiques of New Historicism imply about the tension between abstracting and particularizing. Lentricchia, for instance, writes as follows about the particularism of Greenblatt's beginnings:

A strong feature of new-historicist rhetoric and substance is on display in the typical beginnings of Greenblatt's essays, where he would violate the traditional literary sensibility with lengthy citations of bizarre, apparently off-center materials: an account, roughly contemporary with Shakespeare—thickly, arcanely detailed—of a social practice (say, exorcism) far removed from the high literary practice of the Renaissance. With that gambit Greenblatt would shock his traditional reader into the awareness that here, at last, is no literary business as usual. Greenblatt's beginnings seem to promise what, in theory, new historicism, so herme-

neutically savvy, isn't supposed to promise—direct access to history's
gritty ground-level texture. (234)

Lentricchia's comments point to the possible falsity in the illusion Greenblatt gives his readers of "access to history's gritty ground-
level" (234). That falseness, I would argue, arises from the unintended
tension between particularism and generality—an attempt to have it
both ways (1) by immersion in the particular, but (2) with a paradigm
sufficiently generalized that it could be used indiscriminately as a
template for analyzing any discourse. The *textual* results of this particular tension will be the subject of the second part of this chapter.

New Historicist—and especially Greenblatt's—yoking of particularistic anecdote and literary text comes in for other kinds of critique
also. Carol Neely and Lynda Boose have critiqued New Historicist
work on Shakespeare from a feminist vantage point relevant to the
issue of abstract versus particular. They have argued, first, that the
cultural texts chosen by New Historicists to illuminate Shakespearean
texts are typically texts written by elite males of the period; though
such texts appear to historicize Shakespeare or to put us in touch, in
Lentricchia's words, with "history's gritty ground-level texture" (234),
they are selectively chosen texts, representing male voices, and therefore serve to reinforce the erasure of women's voices further than
exists in the plays themselves. This charge might be restated, for my
purposes, as a charge that New Historicists generalize from one kind
of text to another without considering the selectivity of the texts
chosen and therefore without considering the tautological process
involved—that the apparently "gritty ground-level texture" is actually
already a generalization from within a particular historical context
that we have no direct access to.

Neely's and Boose's second charge is that through the process
of New Historicist generalizing about the workings of power and
subversion, particulars about women in the plays are being erased.
Neely offered the example of Dollimore's essay on *Measure for Measure* which, she said, "embarks on a potentially interesting Foucaultian exploration of the manipulation of subversion in the play, but
soon elides prostitution with any transgressive sexuality and then
with other forms of social disruption" (Neely 9–10). By this account,
Dollimore has begun at the concrete level with prostitution, generalized that prostitution is an instance of transgressive sexuality, and
then generalized further that transgressive sexuality is an instance of

social disruption. Through the upward movement on the ladder of abstraction, what is at issue in the treatment of women in *Measure for Measure* is no longer an issue *about* women. Neely's charge seems interestingly similar to Richard Levin's charges about "new readings vs. old plays" (see chapter 2).[4]

Lynda Boose made the same charge about Greenblatt's "Fiction and Friction" in which, she wrote, "gender disappears beneath the category of biological sex differentiation, then sex difference becomes elided beneath the relevance of medical treatises to a 1601 account of a hermaphrodite in Rouen, France, and then—through an associational leap much wider than new historicism will usually venture— all of this becomes the contextual stencil through which Greenblatt, in three pages, reads the cross-dressing of comic heroines, the convention of boy actors, the sexual discourse of *Twelfth Night*, the sexual discourse for all Shakespeare's plays, and by implication, for all English Renaissance drama. . . . Suddenly, there is only one gender and there are no more women in Shakespeare's plays" (Boose 730). Again, the charge resembles the one Levin made in the 1970s, that Shakespearean criticism had the habit of erecting the wrong kind of abstractions, so that "the play is not about what it appears to be about" (*New Readings* 200).

Walter Cohen, writing from a Marxist perspective, has made the same charge Boose and Neely have made, but one of his conclusions is particularly interesting:

> First, the assumption of arbitrary connectedness seems to preclude a systematic survey of the available evidence, leading instead to a kind of synecdoche in which a single text or group of texts stands in for all texts and thus exhausts the discursive field. . . . Thus in the extreme case women cease to be historical actors or subjects. They can be victims or objects, but it is not, however, complexly, their experience that matters. (38)

In other words, the generalizing (or synecdochic) impulse tends to move away from the ostensible phenomena of the plays to interpret them as *about* something else.

Having made this charge, Cohen included the following recommendation: "The practice of anticipatory totalization . . . indicates one possible approach: a commitment to coalition politics marked by an ongoing effort to work out a synthetic position satisfactory to the various groups in the coalition" (38). In endorsing "totalization" but not the New Historicist "synecdoche," Cohen appears to have faulted not so much the generalizing tendencies of New Historicism as the particular generalizations it arrives at. The "synthetic position" Cohen could endorse would be one "satisfactory to the various groups in the coalition"; this seems to imply that interpretations of Shakespeare should merit praise to the degree that they please the varying political interests (Marxists, feminists, New Historicists) Cohen has reviewed in his article.

Cohen's recommendation is worth noting for what it says about the kind of disciplinary adjudication or accountability the field might promote. Although Neely and Boose in effect argue that New Historicists have chosen the wrong problem definition, far more of the charges against Renaissance New Historicism seem only to dispute whether New Historicists have chosen the right position in the subversion-containment debate. Cohen appears to argue that interpretations of Shakespeare should be valued according to the good work they may do in allowing groups to feel good about themselves. The progression from the older criticism of Barish and Olson to contemporary New Historicists and some of their critics shows, then, a different pattern from the line-of-descent patterns in either psychology or history. This area of literary studies has moved from a gentlemanly tradition of scholarship toward a more political focus, rather than toward more professionalized and cumulative knowledge making.

Epistemic and Nonepistemic Problem Presentation

Professional self-monitoring, adjudication, or accounting can be directed at a field's problem definition, proposed problem solutions, or methods and criteria for drawing inferences and identifying relevant sources. In the case of Renaissance Historicism, each of these three has been found problematic by one or more critics. Feminist critiques of the field's problem definition, as well as critiques of anecdotes and inferences, all point to the field's lack of well-developed traditions or mechanisms for carrying on a sustained, progressively developing disciplinary conversation for arguing about the field's focus and methods. The kind of disciplinary self-monitoring and adjudicating that professional forums allow is usually performed through epistemic language, but the articles in my sample appear to take differing positions on the value of epistemic language.

I have already suggested that, in typical academic articles in the social sciences and humanities, problem definition and presentation may largely coincide; the problem the article addresses occupies the introduction of the article, is defined there, and then is treated straightforwardly in the remainder of the article. But the problem definition itself (e.g., "subversion vs. containment") may or may not be presented as an epistemic problem. In epistemic problem presentations, academic articles draw attention explicitly and immediately to the epistemology involved in their genesis—to some of the premises, processes, warrants, or methods involved in research and to the community of researchers. I reserve, for chapter 6, discussion of the linguistic markers and syntax involved in epistemic prose, but a typical problem presentation in psychology is likely to employ passages like those italicized below to keep its focus on the disciplinary problem:

> Prior to 1980—when virtually all *research* on infant day-care focused on children reared in high quality, university-based, research-oriented centers—*little if any evidence existed to suggest that* nonmaternal care initiated in the first year of life was associated with any patterns of behavior that could be *regarded as problematical. Two important changes* have taken place *in infant day-care research* since then, and *both of these* may be responsible for *concerns that have been raised* recently about the influence of nonmaternal care as it is routinely experienced in the United States (Belsky, 1986; Belsky, in press; Gamble & Zigler, 1986). First, *investigators have moved* beyond university-sponsored day-care centers *to study* infants cared for in a variety of nonmaternal child-care arrangements. Second, *in response to advances made in studying* security of attachment, *they have focused on assessing* behavior that infants display on reunion with and following separation from their parents since it is the resistance, avoidance, proximity seeking, and contact maintaining of the infant rather than the extent and intensity of his or her distress, that are viewed as being *critical for appraising* attachment security. (Belsky and Rovine, 1988, 157, italicizing mine)

I have italicized some of the words that refer to the epistemic activities of researchers—the explicit focus on how the disciplinary community makes claims, develops its research questions, defines its problems, or appraises its results. The parenthetical references serve as further epistemic markers, tilting the focus toward the research community and away from an unmediated presentation of the phenomenon under scrutiny—in this example, the effect of infant day-care upon security of attachment.

Epistemic—or relatively epistemic—introductions may be found in literary study also. In the older Barish and Olson articles, citing other critics functioned epistemically to draw attention to critical disagreement. In footnotes to his first paragraph, Barish drew attention to a survey of comment on the issue and to four specific critics. Olson, in his first paragraph, cited eight critics or historical scholars. In these two text-driven articles, the references to critics may have been generated by a gentlemanly tradition of politeness in scholarship, rather than by the more specialized and professionalized knowledge-making conventions of the sciences where citations are likely to refer to codified pieces of knowledge in the field (see Small). But to the extent that they referred to other criticism in the field, Barish and Olson wrote epistemic introductions.

In current Renaissance New Historicism, relatively epistemic introductions may again be found. I use the word "relatively" because, as chapter 6 will suggest, we may not find the same degree of epistemic focus in literary argument that exists in a social science. Since the epistemic introduction is something of a norm in academic writing, it is interesting to note epistemic variation *within* the field of literature— variation over time and variation among subgroups of current critics— because epistemic practices in attachment research are relatively homogeneous. If there is more heterogeneity in New Historicism, that tells us something about the field itself. It is possible to debate about exactly who should be considered a Renaissance New Historicist. Just as not all attachment researchers agree in their approaches to the problem of explaining attachment, not all New Historicists agree in their approaches to Shakespeare. There is perhaps more sense of fracturing in the literary discourse, however. Marxists or cultural materialists sometimes take pains to distinguish themselves from New Historicists. Feminists (e.g., Neely and Boose) may argue with New Historicists. Distinctions have been made about the degree to which deconstruction or feminism has affected different New Historicists (Erickson). Among the four articles in the sample whose sentence subjects I examine (chapter 6), those by Howard and Montrose have more epistemic introductions than those by Greenblatt and Mullaney.

Jean Howard can be considered a New Historicist because in her concerns and in the citations she makes to other New Historicists, she is visibly part of the discourse community in which other authors in my sample write. But her critique of some New Historicist practices ("The New Historicism") also suggests some difference in her stance. She describes the New Historicism as not monolithic in its methods and theoretical perspectives but as united by a number of similar assumptions about historical criticism. I have already referred to Howard's relatively epistemic introduction (chapter 2) to "Renaissance Antitheatricality and the Politics of Gender and Rank in *Much Ado About Nothing*" (1987). Her first paragraph might be described as a model of the epistemic introduction, with clearly delineated parts as follows:

1. She begins by generalizing about concrete patterns in the play, its recurring emphasis on theatricality:

> *Much Ado* is filled with playlets, staged shows, actors, and interior dramatists. . . .

2. She characterizes past critical interpretations:

> Consequently, *critics have often thematized* the play as being "about" truth, illusion, and how to live in a world of deceptive appearances. [Rossiter 1961]. *Viewed metadramatically, the play has yielded readings* which have seen in its assorted dramatists and dramatic projects Shakespeare's self-reflexive meditations on his own theatrical craft. [Huston, 1981]. *Much of this criticism* aspires to articulate an unchanging or universal meaning for the play—a task both impossible and impossibly idealist.

3. She introduces her topic:

> *Instead, I am interested* in the historical contingency of meaning and want to explore *Much Ado's* preoccupation with theatrical practices in relationship to a body of Elizabethan texts overtly concerned with the nature, control, and "morality" of theatrical power: namely, the antitheatrical tracts.

4. She specifies the argument she will make about her topic and the method she will use to do so:

> *I will argue that* these tracts—through their discussions of theater—were a site where anxieties about a changing social order were discursively produced and managed. The presentation of theatrical practices

in Shakespeare's *Much Ado,* far from being "above ideology," also participates in the process by which a historically specific understanding of a patriarchal and hierarchical social order is both secured against threats to itself and also laid open to their demystifying power. *In contradistinction to a criticism* committed to the drama's place "above ideology" and to its aesthetic and thematic unity, *a political criticism of Renaissance drama will focus* precisely on the silences and contradictions which reveal the constructed—and interested—nature of dramatic representations and on the ideological functions served by the plays as produced and read at specific historical junctures and through the mediation of specific theatrical and critical practices. (Howard, 163–64, italics mine)

Here, far more than in Barish and Olson, we see an epistemic focus on the disciplinary discourse, rather than a generic reader or a timeless text. The motifs Howard introduces—the historical contingency of meaning, the ideological functions served by the plays—link her to other New Historicist critics. It is especially significant that in introducing her problem she explicitly lays out relationships among old and new criticism and forecasts her own argument. As a result, her introduction is markedly more epistemic (based on the kinds of items I have italicized, see chapter 6) than either the introductions of Barish and Olson, or those of the current New Historicists, Greenblatt and Mullaney, whom I discuss below.

Nonepistemic Problem Presentations

Howard's introduction demonstrates the epistemic introduction as a New Historicist may write it. Here, by way of contrast, are the first sentences of nonepistemic introductions by Greenblatt and Mullaney:

In his notorious police report of 1593 on Christopher Marlowe, the Elizabethan spy Richard Baines informed his superiors that Marlowe had declared, among other monstrous opinions, that "Moses was but a juggler, and that one Heriots, being Sir Walter Ralegh's man, can do more than he." (Stephen Greenblatt, 1985, 18)

In the autumn of 1599, Thomas Platter of Basle visited the London apartments of Walter Cope—gentleman, adventurer, and member of

Elizabeth's Society of Antiquaries—to view Cope's collection of curiosities gathered from around the world. (Steven Mullaney, 1983, 65)

The similarity of Greenblatt's "In . . . 1593" and Mullaney's "In . . . 1599" is more than coincidental. As Howard describes it, "Such has been the influence of Greenblatt's practice . . . that there is now a spate of essays which begin with the painstaking description of a particular historical event, place, or experience and from that supposedly paradigmatic moment sketch a cultural law" ("New Historicism" 39). Greenblatt is perhaps the most influential and most frequently mentioned American New Historicist, his influence appearing in writers like Mullaney and in *Representations*, the University of California Press journal for which Greenblatt is co-chair of the Editorial Board. It is he who is credited with coining the term "New Historicism" in 1982 ("Forms of Power"). His style is influential, yet distinctively personal; Peter Erickson writes that "the format of [Greenblatt's] essays has become his signature, his narrative style conveys a distinctive voice, and his direct self-presentation heightens the role of narrative performance" (332). By looking at samples from Mullaney and Greenblatt together, we get a sense of what is distinctive about this particular strand of American New Historicism and how it departs from an earlier type of literary criticism and other academic writing.

Greenblatt and Mullaney offer a useful pairing for describing the New Historicist interpretive community because both are associated with *Representations* (Greenblatt as both editor and contributor and Mullaney as contributor), their texts are strikingly nonepistemic in similar ways, and they write on similar problems from similar perpectives. The two articles I discuss both focus on a variant of the problem that Barish wrote on earlier—the problem of why Hal rejects Falstaff after acceding to the throne. Greenblatt's article appeared in *Glyph* in 1981, again (with revisions) in Dollimore and Sinfield's *Political Shakespeare* in 1985, and once again in Greenblatt's *Shakespearean Negotiations* in 1988.[5] Mullaney's article, which first appeared in 1983, did not mention Greenblatt in the text of his article, but included the following footnote:

> For an insightful reading of Hal's rehearsal of Francis . . . see Stephen Greenblatt. . . . Greenblatt's emphasis on the "recording" of alien voices complements the focus, in these pages, on the rehearsal of strange cultures. The fact that both essays were produced indepen-

dently and work from quite different primary materials toward a similar perspective on *Henry IV* is a sign, undoubtedly, of the influence of Greenblatt's previous work on my thinking; but the coincidence suggests, as well, that the recording/rehearsal of the strange is a significant process, both in the period and in Shakespeare's second tetralogy. (Mullaney 91)

Mullaney might also have attributed the similarity in their articles to both having been influenced by Foucault's model of power. Perhaps the coincidence in their thinking is less a sign of something *in* the period than of something in the Foucaultian paradigm—a sign that these interpretive binaries may be applied to a wide range of different texts.

I first survey, briefly, how Greenblatt's and Mullaney's problem presentations and definitions differ dramatically from those of Barish and Olson, and less dramatically in definition, but just as dramatically in their epistemics from Jean Howard's problem presentation. I then discuss in greater detail features of this nonepistemic strain of New Historicism evident in Greenblatt's or Mullaney's articles.

First, whereas the earlier critics presented and defined their "problems" immediately and quickly, Greenblatt and Mullaney begin with concrete historical anecdotes that appear to situate us in history. Almost as if they were writing narrative, rather than argument, they immerse us in particulars and defer point making. There appears to be something like a point in Greenblatt's initial talk of "atheism," but atheism is not really the conceptual focus of his article so much as a vehicle for offering striking anecdotes that allow Greenblatt to set up his discussion of Harriot.

Second, they include little or no representation of current professional thinking on their "problems"—only including a few citations to current critics late in their articles. There is nothing like the introductory review of criticism in Barish, Olson, or Howard. Mullaney mentions his indebtedness to Greenblatt in his forty-fifth footnote, but most of the rest of his references are to primary sources or anthropologists and historians outside the disciplinary community of Renaissance New Historicists. Greenblatt—perhaps because he is more established than Mullaney—ignores his own disciplinary circle even more strikingly; of his thirty-one footnotes, most refer to primary historical sources or secondary works by historians and anthropologists. Five refer to literary critics, but none to the Renaissance New Historicists who are part of Greenblatt's own interpretive community.

Third, their focus is not *textual* in the way that Barish's and Olson's were. Consider the alternatives: Barish and Olson implied that their interpretive problem was inherent in or caused by the text—an assumption current critics are likely to consider naïve. By contrast, the attachment researchers see their problem as professional, defined in the literature of their field and built on others' methods and findings. The historians in my sample present their problems as simultaneously professional (what has previously been said about migration) and phenomenal (what needs to be learned about colonial history).

One could argue that both Greenblatt and Mullaney focus on the same textual problem that Barish did—the meaning of Hal's rejection of Falstaff. One could even argue that this is an instance of old wine in new bottles, of enterprising critics looking for new ways of promoting themselves through innovation. But such an explanation would not account for current theoretical turning away from "the text itself," for the form current innovation takes, or for the similarity in the ways New Historicists like Greenblatt and Mullaney differ from their predecessors. On the subject of the "text itself," Greenblatt has written, "there has probably never been a time since the early eighteenth century when there was less confidence in the 'text.' . . . it is impossible to take the 'text itself' as the perfect, unsubstitutable, freestanding container of all of its meanings" (*Negotiations* 3).

As to the form their innovation takes, both Greenblatt and Mullaney take half or more of their articles leading up to discussion of Shakespeare. Greenblatt only mentions Shakespeare in one sentence of his fifth paragraph before ignoring him for another nine pages, and Mullaney does not even mention Shakespeare—in his title, introduction, or text—until the fifth page of his article, not referring to *Henry IV* until he is over ten pages into his article. They both defer discussing the literary text, and yet the literary text serves as the culmination or end point of the analysis. We have to assume that these choices are deliberate and indicative of important currents in the academic culture of literature departments.

Anecdotes and Inferences in Greenblatt's "Invisible Bullets"

Greenblatt began his 1988 book, *Shakespearean Negotiations,* as follows:

I began with the desire to speak with the dead.

This desire is a familiar, if unvoiced, motive in literary studies, a motive organized, professionalized, buried beneath thick layers of bureaucratic decorum: literature professors are salaried, middle-class shamans. (1)

His style is consciously nonepistemic—motivated, apparently, by a desire to move away from professionalization and "bureaucratic decorum." There are no signs, here, of desire for disciplinary compacting or progress—only the intimation that disciplines, like bureaucracies, create constraints we might prefer to free ourselves from. The same antidisciplinary tone occurs in H. Aram Veeser's introduction to his edited collection on the New Historicism:

> Conventional scholars—entrenched, self-absorbed, protective of guild loyalties and turf, specialized in the worst senses—have repaired to their disciplinary enclaves and committed a classic *trahison des clercs*. As the first successful counterattack in decades against this profoundly anti-intellectual ethos, the New Historicism has given scholars new opportunities to cross the boundaries separating history, anthropology, art, politics, literature, and economics. . . . (Veeser ix)

In the remainder of this chapter, I will explore some of the textual manifestations of this preference for the narrativized and undisciplinary academic text; in chapter 6, I will examine the linguistic consequences in greater detail, and in chapter 7, some disciplinary and pedagogical consequences.

To see how the goal of New Historical literary criticism may differ from psychology's disciplinary goal of producing knowledge, for instance, Greenblatt's use of anecdotes is crucial. In "Invisible Bullets," we see Greenblatt's characteristic use of concrete anecdote, deferred point-making, and profusion of historical references. Greenblatt uses over eleven pages of his twenty-seven-page article discussing the issue of subversion in terms of writings by Thomas Harriot, Machiavelli, and others before he turns to Shakespeare. The problem in the *Henry* plays, as he defines it, is that of "the production and containment of subversion and disorder" (29). But Greenblatt's lengthy introduction moves from Marlowe to Harriot to Ralegh to Machiavelli and Moses, back to Harriot again, again to Machiavelli, and back to Harriot's representation of Indians in Colonial America in *A Brief and True Report of the New Found Land of Virginia*.

The lengthy introductory section on Harriot exists to clarify an issue Greenblatt perceives to be relevant both outside Shakespeare's texts and within them. There is no attempt to argue that only by understanding Harriot can we understand this issue in Shakespeare, no epistemic attempt to justify the use of Harriot as an example rather than some other Renaissance writer, no attempt to argue that the issue cannot be understood in Shakespeare without recourse to texts by other writers. In short, there is no epistemic justification of the anecdotes or of the frequent switching from Machiavelli to Moses to Numa Pompilius to Ralegh to Marlowe to Harriot.

Critiques of Greenblatt's use of anecdotes illuminate just what is unusual about some New Historicist academic writing. Howard ("New Historicism") has criticized Greenblatt for not explaining why he chooses his presumably representative anecdotes—his reasons for not, in my terms, including specific epistemic justifications and discussions. Anne Barton has charged that he tells stories that are not true, that he detaches a single passage and makes it speak for the whole, and that he makes unsubstantiated imaginative leaps. Carolyn Porter has argued that his method of analogizing in "Invisible Bullets" has the effect of essentializing power and of not allowing the possibility of oppositional voices. Walter Cohen has argued that Greenblatt's commitment to arbitrary connectedness leads to a particular issue being pushed to a logical extreme without constraint from an organizing principle. Though these critiques may originate from diverse premises, they share a sense that there is something problematic about the inferences Greenblatt draws as he moves from nonliterary text (e.g., Walter Harriot's *Report* on Virginia) to Shakespeare's text.[6]

If disciplinary knowledge-building in the usual epistemic mode is not the goal of New Historicism, as Greenblatt sees it, then his desire to "speak with the dead" may be analogous to the impulse within social history to "render" the past, as Megill has called it, to narrate and describe the past in order to bring us in touch with how it felt to live in a past society. As we saw in chapter 4, that impulse has been felt by many modern historians, but it has only found an uneasy and somewhat marginal role within the professional texts historians typically write. We should not be surprised to discover, then, that literary studies may contain a similar tension between, on the one hand, synthesizing, generalizing, explanatory, conceptually driven problems from the social sciences and, on the other, the more narrative, representational, text-driven impulses traditional within the humanities. The critiques directed at Greenblatt's use of anecdotes seem to be one sign of such tension; Barton's charge, for instance, that Greenblatt tells stories that are not true and makes unsubstantiated imaginative leaps hints at a tension between narrative impulses and the explanatory syntheses he draws from actual narratives.

We can see the tension more clearly by looking at sample passages from "Invisible Bullets"—such as the set of claims and representations beginning in paragraph nine of his text. The first eight paragraphs have already performed two tasks. First, a profusion of concrete instances like the following have been cited: "at the other end of the social scale, in the same Dorsetshire parish, a drunken servant named Oliver complained that in the Sunday sermon the preacher had praised Moses excessively but had neglected to mention his fifty-two concubines, and Oliver too found himself under official scrutiny" (18). This small illustration would not, typically, occur in the kind of articles we have seen in psychology; it is not *necessary* as part of Greenblatt's point making, not necessary to any understanding of Harriot, for instance, or Shakespeare; but it gives us a sense of "access to history's gritty-ground level" (Lentricchia 234) and introduces an instance of atheism.

Second, Greenblatt has begun to introduce the superordinate idea—though not in the usual epistemic style—that "religious authority . . . confirms its power in this period by disclosing the threat of atheism" (19). He has referred to Marlowe, Moses, Harriot, Sir Walter Ralegh, Machiavelli, Numa Pompilius, and others, with an emphasis on Machiavelli's thesis that religion's "primary function [is] . . . the achievement of civic discipline" (20).

If we look at how a series of consecutive paragraphs set up an increasingly sweeping general claim, we see Greenblatt's characteristic inferencing patterns. Here is a series of inferences that become increasingly stronger:

> —Now Harriot does not give voice to any of these speculations, but if we look attentively at his account of the first Virginia colony, we find a mind that seems interested in the same set of problems, a mind indeed that seems to be virtually testing the Machiavellian hypotheses. (paragraph 9, p. 21)

> —We have then as in Machiavelli, a sense of religion as a set of beliefs manipulated by the subtlety of the priests to help ensure social order and cohesion. (paragraph 10, p. 21)

—What we have here, I suggest, is the very core of the Machiavellian anthropology that posited the origin of religion in a cunning imposition of socially coercive doctrines by an educated and sophisticated lawgiver upon a simple people. (paragraph 11, p. 22)

—In Harriot then we have one of the earliest instances of a highly significant phenomenon: the testing upon the bodies and minds of non-Europeans or, more generally, the non-civilised, of a hypothesis about the origin and nature of European culture and belief. (paragraph 12, p. 22)

—Harriot tests and seems to confirm the most radically subversive hypothesis in his culture about the origin and function of religion by imposing his religion—with all of its most intense claims to transcendence, unique truth, inescapable coercive force—upon others. (paragraph 13, p. 23)

Greenblatt's claims here move from qualified to sweeping, from the admission that Harriot does not "voice . . . these speculations" to the more assertive "Harriot tests and seems to confirm the most radically subversive hypothesis" (20, 23). The subjects of Greenblatt's claims ascend, in degree of generality, from the relatively local "first Virginia colony" to "a simple people" to "non-European" and "European culture." This series of increasingly stronger claims may be justifiable, but Greenblatt's text does not *do* the work of explicit justifying or warranting that his strong claims might suggest. My point, here, is not to quarrel (or agree) with his results, but to draw attention to the way that he gets there, with the assumption that his professional success shows something about textual practices in his field.

One way that Greenblatt attempts to do some warranting appears in a series of statements like "we have then," the typical verbal pattern by which he signals his inferences. Signaling an inference with "we have then" is by no means the norm in the academy (see chapter 6). The use of this generalized "we" might be called evasive in that it represents as consensual what is arguably an individual writer's point of view.[7] "We" is rarely used, in this way, in my psychology sample, somewhat more frequently in the history sample, and significantly more frequently than that in Greenblatt (more so than in the other New Historicists). A more epistemic way to signal an inference would be to write, "This evidence suggests that . . ." or "Harriot's saying X is justification for arguing that . . ."

Those critiquing Greenblatt's use of anecdotes may be responding uneasily to statements like "we have then," but there are other possible causes of uneasiness in the relation between evidence from Harriot and the generalizations Greenblatt derives. In the course of establishing "testing" as a key concept in his point making, Greenblatt offers this evidence from Harriot, "What subtlety soever be in the *Wiroances* and Priests, this opinion worketh so much in many of the common and simple sort of people that it maketh them have great respect to their Governors, and also great care what they do, to avoid torment after death and to enjoy bliss" (21). This sentence, clearly, says nothing about "testing" or about the Machiavellian hypothesis, so whether or not the reader accepts Greenblatt's inference that Harriot is Machiavellian depends upon the reader's interpretation of the sentence—upon whether either (1) Harriot's observation of Indians' respect for governors or (2) Indians' caring what they do confirms Greenblatt's claim that religion is "a set of beliefs manipulated by the subtlety of the priests to help ensure social order and cohesion" (21).

Here is another set of statements used to help justify the inference that Harriot is confirming the Machiavellian hypothesis: a four-sentence paragraph beginning with apparent statements of fact and moving to a generalization about "the coercive power of religious belief" (24).

[1] By October 1586, there were rumours in England that there was little prospect of profit in Virginia, that the colony had been close to starvation, and that the Indians had turned hostile.

[2] Harriot accordingly begins with a descriptive catalogue in which the natural goods of the land are turned into social goods, into "merchantable commodities": "Cedar, a very sweet wood and fine timber; whereof if nests of chests be there made, or timber thereof fitted for sweet and fine bedsteads, tables, desks, lutes, virginals, and many things else, . . . [it] will yield profit" (329–30).

[3] The inventory of these commodities is followed by an inventory of edible plants and animals to prove to readers that the colony need not starve, and then by the account of the Indians, to prove that the colony could impose its will upon them.

[4] The key to this imposition, as I have argued, is the coercive power of religious belief, and the source of this power is the impression

made by advanced technology upon a "backward" people. (Green-blatt 24, my numbering)

The evidential centerpiece of this inference is the quote from Harriot about cedar (sentence [2]), but it is not *self-evident* that there is anything very extraordinary about cataloging the uses of cedar. Nor is it *self-evident* that the juxtaposition of (1) inventoried commodities, (2) inventoried food sources, and (3) the account of the Indians leads to the immediately following conclusion about "the coercive power of religious belief" (24). One may perhaps be permitted to think Greenblatt has not conclusively proved his case when he next writes, "Hence Harriot's text is committed to record what we have called his confirmation of the Machiavellian hypothesis" (24).

Greenblatt's inferencing is vulnerable to criticism for three reasons. First, a concrete statement like "Cedar, a very sweet wood . . ." can be used as evidence for generalizations within the same domain (such as statements about how cedar may be used for furniture and musical instruments), but it cannot be used unequivocally as evidence for abstract statements about religion. The reader is being asked to take Greenblatt's assertion on faith. As in the text-driven literary criticism I have examined, concrete textual items (like the letters in *Cranford* or the cedar in Harriot) lead to divergent interpretations the higher they rise on the ladder of abstraction, and Levin's account of earlier "readings" of Shakespeare makes evident how easily interpretations of Shakespeare's plays may diverge as they move toward higher level abstractions.

Secondly, the sequencing in the four-sentence paragraph moves from statement of fact to assertion; this point-last structure, as I will explain, carries the danger of readers' not following along agreeably because they do not know what point the concrete items are leading toward. Third, Greenblatt's assertion is made without any disciplinary tools for writing explicitly about how and whether inferences are warranted.

What is missing, in the language of Greenblatt's text, is explicit in the epistemic language of the Egeland and Sroufe article, for instance, in my psychology sample. The following paragraph comes from the "Discussion" section of their article and is, therefore, likely to make explicit connections between conclusions and the process of getting to those conclusions. Virtually every clause draws the attention of its professional readers explicitly to the tentativeness of inference making or the possible gaps between phenomenon and explanation:

> These generalizations must be quite tentative, in the form of hypotheses, given the small samples and the anecdotal nature of the data. Other factors cannot be ruled out. In some instances, based on observations and testing of the newborn, the infants were described as especially robust and able to elicit support (from others as well as from mother). In some cases, perhaps, the mother's emotional responsibility was coming through to the infant even when the external appearance was of neglect. And, of course, however reliable the attachment assessments, in some cases these will be in error. We did examine, but did not find, differences between securely and insecurely attached infants in the inadequate care group on (1) results from a battery of personality texts given the mother . . . and (2) degree of maltreatment. We did find a relation between age of onset of observed maltreatment and insecure attachment. It appeared that the earlier the maltreatment, the greater the likelihood of an insecure attachment. It should also be noted that secure attachments in the inadequate care groups or change from insecure to secure appeared to be unrelated to the duration or type of intervention. (Egeland and Sroufe 51)

The authors draw attention to generalizations, drawbacks in their sample, other factors, and the limits of observation or assessment. By contrast, Greenblatt in preferring to "speak with the dead" turns away from epistemic prose—from the professional self-monitoring and epistemic accounting that, it can be argued, provide the disciplinary self-scrutiny and compacting necessary for a field's knowledge making to move forward.

Anecdotes and the Pattern of Deferral: Mullaney's Article

The prototypical academic article introduction, as I have described it, is epistemic in defining its problem and fronting its point in the introduction, along with explicit indication of the methodology or premises that warrant its approach. The point-first nature of the introduction may be said to be an exaggerated version of much paragraph-level organization in the body of the article. Colomb and Williams have discussed two kinds of text structures: point-first and point-last. They suggest that point-first structures appeal to readers pressed for time or interested in efficient reading; point-last structures appeal to readers interested in "the kinds of pleasures we associate with fine, belletristic writing" because point-last structures allow "a richer and more complex unfolding of the Point" (111). Even this brief description suggests how point-last structure departs from the model of cumulative knowledge building in a compact disciplinary field; such knowledge building would presumably be concerned with efficient point-making. Bazerman's study of physicists' purposeful reading supports the view that point-first structures appeal to readers interested in efficiency (*Shaping* 235 f.). The structure Colomb and Williams call "point-last," on the other hand, describes the pattern of Mullaney's deferred point making.

The pattern of deferral is striking in Mullaney's article: he defers problem definition, defers discussion of the Shakespearian text, and defers announcing or developing the abstract terms of his thesis. His article is not only nonepistemic but it is structured inductively in ways that depart markedly from the usual models of academic articles.

First, Mullaney does not represent his twenty-three page article, "Strange Things, Gross Terms, Curious Customs: The Rehearsal of Cultures in the Late Renaissance," as "about" Shakespeare; except for two brief references to Shakespeare, we encounter nothing about Shakespeare or the *Henry IV* plays in the first thirteen pages of the article. The concrete historical material in the introduction is not initially presented as *necessary* or even helpful for our understanding because we do not know what kind of understanding we are moving toward.

Although Mullaney's article works with tropes familiar to anyone reading Renaissance New Historicism, he writes as though there is no disciplinary "problem" of "strangeness" and "rehearsal" defined within the field of New Historicism—as if his interest in this way of looking at the Renaissance and at the *Henry IV* plays is *sui generis*. In one sense, it is *sui generis* because there is no body of disciplinary knowledge concerned with sorting out the connections between the problem of "strangeness" and the *Henry* plays; but in another sense it is not *sui generis* in that it is heavily influenced by discussions of power, knowledge, and subversion in Foucault, Greenblatt, and others. It seems as if, in Mullaney's writing about literature, nonepistemic—or perhaps narrative—priorities have usurped the role of problem definition, making the literary academic simultaneously less inclined to review the work of predecessors and more inclined to interest us in unusual particulars of Renaissance history.

To interest us in these unusual particulars, Mullaney uses a point-last, inductive structure whereby he produces concrete anecdotes first and only later builds toward the kind of point making traditional to academic writing. He begins each section with a concept—initially a low-level abstraction in the form of a verb—that he has arrived at only in concluding the previous section. Then he moves into another anecdote and arrives at a slightly higher-level concept, develops it, and then finally names another concept again at the end of the section.

There is no initial forecasting of where the anecdote is going. And even more than in Greenblatt, Mullaney's initial anecdote is strikingly concrete, with a detailing of items that suggests the novelist, anthropologist, or historian influenced by the Annales school (one of whom, Natalie Zemon Davis, is cited twice in Mullaney's footnotes). The "strange things" in the introduction are not presented merely in the abstract as "strange," but are particularized almost without abstract commentary:

> In the autumn of 1599, Thomas Platter of Basle visited the London apartments of Walter Cope—gentleman, adventurer, and member of Elizabeth's Society of Antiquaries—to view Cope's collection of curiosities gathered from around the world. No catalogue of the objects displayed in the room could presume to be complete. Platter himself records only a selection, but he does take an evident peasure in compiling his list—a *plaisir de conter* akin to that which Jean Céard has found at work in contemporaneous accounts of nature's oddities and marvels, such as the anonymous *Histoire prodigieuses* published in 1598. It is a pleasure in the recollection, literally, of such wonders as an African charm made of teeth, a felt cloak from Arabia, and shoes from many strange lands. An Indian stone axe, "like a thunder bolt." A stringed instrument with but one string. The twisted horn of a bull seal. An embalmed child, or *Mumia*. The bauble and bells of Henry VIII's fool. A unicorn's tail. Inscribed paper made of bark, and an artful Chinese box. A flying rhinoceros (unremarked), a remora (explicated at some length), and flies of a kind that "glow at night in Virginia instead of lights, since there is often no day there for over a month." There are the Queen of England's seal, a number of crowns made of claws, a Madonna made of Indian feathers, an Indian charm made of monkey teeth. A mirror, which "both reflects and multiplies objects." A sea-halcyon's nest. . . . (Mullaney 65)

In this passage, there is one footnote to Céard's 1977 study and one to a 1981 study of sixteenth- and seventeenth-century monsters, the latter appearing in the history journal *Past and Present.* Though these can be considered scholarly references, they are not references to work within Mullaney's own discourse community. There are no references to literary criticism until almost halfway through the article; this is partly because there is no discussion of literature until then, but in a typically epistemic article, Mullaney might have begun by identifying a knowledge problem in his field and identifying how material from outside the field could be helpful in his field. With such a strategy, his introduction would have contained citations to work in literary studies, even if only to explain why such work needed supplementation from work in history or anthropology.

In the passage above, no abstract point is explicitly made. No sense of necessity or logic dictates that the "crowns made of claws"— or any of these other illustrative "strange" items—be included or not. This introductory move goes beyond the introductory anecdote attempting to hook the reader, a familiar convention of essayist writing, and moves toward a hybrid academic genre that draws on both traditional argument and traditional narrative or description, but presents the argument in an unusual way.

Each section of Mullaney's article moves upward from concete to abstract, and each successive section takes up whichever abstraction was the inductive culmination of the preceding section. In the first section, Mullaney introduces Cope's wonder-cabinet as a form of collection; "collection" is thus the superordinate concept of the first (three-page) section. By the end of the section he has linked the idea of "collection" to the idea of the "Other" and of "cultural performance" (68).

He then begins the second section with the concept of cultural "strangeness" or "difference," illustrates a "performance" without yet naming it a "rehearsal," and ends the section by introducing the term "rehearsal" for the first time. The third section moves from "rehearsal" to introducing *Henry IV.* Both the organization of the article and the development of key conceptual terms, then, proceed by the inductive route.

For instance, Mullaney places at the center of the second section a "performance of an alien culture" in Rouen in 1550 when a Brazilian forest landscape was created for Henri II's royal entry into the city. The Rouen anecdote begins with the following sentence, announcing the topic and signaling its importance, but not announcing a point:

> The city of Rouen provides us with an example worth considering
> at some length. . . . (70)

The rest of this paragraph is purely descriptive and does not disclose,
through Mullaney's superordinate terms such as "performance" or
"rehearsal," what the Rouen anecdote exemplifies. The entire paragraph describes the recreation of a Brazilian landscape in Rouen
and refers to "the occasion" three-quarters of the way through the
paragraph before announcing the occasion in the following paragraph.

The next paragraph explains, for the first time, what occasioned
the Rouen "performance" but still defers explaining what its function
was:

> The occasion was Henri II's royal entry into Rouen: an event which
> can hardly explain the genesis of one of the most thorough performances
> of an alien culture staged by the Renaissance, but does at least illuminate
> the pragmatic function of Brazil in the ongoing dramaturgy of city and
> state. . . . (70)

There are eight sentences in this paragraph, and the point—the proposition at the highest conceptual level—is slipped into a grammatically
subordinate position in the seventh sentence as follows (with the point
italicized):

> A castle erected on the margins of the city would be stormed and
> taken: rather than lay siege to gain entry, the monarch granted an
> entry was entertained by the comfortably displaced spectacle of a siege,
> *a dramatic enactment that at once represented the potential for conflict*
> *manifested by a royal visit, and sublimated that potential, recasting it*
> *as a cultural performance to be enjoyed by city and crown alike.* (70,
> italics mine)

In the usual style of the academy, the point italicized above might
have been written in one of two ways: the phenomenon could have
been placed in the grammatical subject position and the point in the
verb:

> The dramatic enactment at Rouen represented the potential for conflict
> . . . and sublimated that potential . . .

Or the epistemic work of the interpreter could be explicitly fronted
in one of these ways:

—I will argue that the dramatic enactment at Rouen represented . . .
—The significance of the dramatic enactment at Rouen appears to be that . . .

Any of these versions would have foregrounded the point more than Mullaney has done by placing his point in a final free modifier, at the end of a sentence that begins with such a bland statement of fact, "A castle . . . would be stormed . . . [and] the monarch . . . was entertained. . . ."

As part of this inductive patterning, Mullaney relies on anecdotes to introduce particulars from which he only later names the abstractions he derives. For instance, after spending three pages of the second section on the incident in Rouen as a "representation of other cultures," Mullaney concludes the section using the Rouen "representation" to move onward to his next abstract term "rehearsal":

> The ethnographic attention and knowledge displayed at Rouen was genuine, amazingly thorough, and richly detailed; the object, however, was not to understand Brazilian culture but to perform it, in a paradoxically self-consuming fashion. Knowledge of another culture in such an instance is directed toward ritual rather than ethnological ends, and the rite involved is one ultimately organized around the elimination of its own pretext: the spectacle of the Other that is thus celebrated and observed, in passing. . . . What we glimpse in the field outside Rouen is not a version of the modern discipline of anthropology, but something preliminary to it; not the interpretation, but what I would call the *rehearsal* of cultures. (Mullaney 73)

This point is truly in last position: last in its sentence, last in its paragraph, and last in this section of Mullaney's text.

From the perspective of how texts are constructed in relation to the epistemics of a discipline, what is most interesting here is that the concrete precedes the abstract and the abstract seems somewhat underdetermined. In Mullaney's inductive point making, there is no explicit hint, yet, of the eventual use he will make of this point in exploring Prince Hal's immersion in the low culture of his contemporaries. A term is not introduced first and then defined and illustrated, but is instead introduced only at the end. There is no forecasting for the reader to indicate where Mullaney is going. This particular inductive movement upward from anecdote to the concept of "representation" and then to the concept of "rehearsal" has taken place, in

Mullaney's text, over the space of roughly three pages, the deferral of point making lasting for those three pages.

The concrete anecdotes and inductive deferral of abstract point making combine with a third element—profusion of anecdotes—to keep the reader somewhat uncertain where the text is heading or what end is served by the article's moving from one historical setting to another. The third section, for instance, uses the term "rehearsal" as a point of embarcation whose direction is initially mysterious; the section begins with definition: "A rehearsal is [a] period of free-play during which alternatives can be staged, unfamiliar roles tried out, the range of one's power to convince or persuade explored with some license . . ." (73). In the next paragraph, Mullaney makes his first mention of Shakespeare but without reference to the *Henry IV* plays ("For Shakespeare and his contemporaries, to recite, rehearse, or perform were synonymous terms . . . " 73). He next introduces the idea that "jurisprudential" concerns could be involved with rehearsal and then launches into another historical anecdote about Edward I's colonizing Wales in the thirteenth century and "rehears[ing]" Welsh culture by having Welsh laws and customs recited.

After briefly referring again to Rouen and then to Foucault's work on madness, Mullaney turns to Phillip Stubbes's 1583 account and Sir Thomas Browne's 1649 account "of the country, alien, heathen, or otherwise strange ways they would see repressed, but must first review or rehearse at some length" (76). As he brings the third section to a close, Mullaney returns to Thomas Platter, briefly narrating his visits to other Renaissance amusements and then finally refers for the first time to Hal and *I Henry IV*. The profusion of historical instances—Rouen, Wales, Stubbes, Browne, Platter—has finally led to Shakespeare, but the reader has not received any signals from the text to indicate that Rouen was leading to Wales, Wales to Stubbes, Stubbes to Brown, Brown to Platter, and Platter to Shakespeare.

Some Disciplinary Consequences of the Anecdotal Style

In both Greenblatt and Mullaney, we have seen an anecdotal style—one that is nonepistemic, not explicitly focused on disciplinary knowledge making, and more liable to cite primary sources than sources within the disciplinary community. Mullaney's pattern of deferred point making differs from Greenblatt's, but their articles are similarly nonepistemic. Both tend to write a point-last prose. Colomb and Williams characterize the drawbacks of the point-last structures as follows: "This structure runs the risk of at best alienating and at worst losing those readers who are unable or unwilling to give the writer the care and attention the text demands. Here the danger is less that details will get lost in the shuffle than that Points will" (112). The compact disciplinary enterprise illustrated in attachment research could not afford to adopt point-last structures, but New Historicism apparently can.

From what we now know about text structures and discourse communities, there seem to be three ways to look at how Greenblatt's and Mullaney's prose structure can affect readers. The first possibility is that their prose should be read like a narrative—perhaps like a detective story, with the reader kept in suspense. Greenblatt's disavowal of "bureaucratic decorum" (*Negotiations* 1) would then be consistent with his turning away from the point-first structure that serves professional or disciplinary purposes, in an attempt to emulate the literary qualities of the work he studies.

A second possibility is that point-last prose may alienate some readers but not others and it is those others who are the desired readers. Perhaps New Historicists who write nonepistemic, point-last prose are in effect "preaching to the converted," writing for others in their discourse community who are already familiar with, for instance, Foucaultian tropes and therefore will not be bothered by any lack of pointedness. If accessibility for the larger community of literary scholars is impeded by the point-last structure of New Historicist prose, it leads to the possibility that New Historicist prose has elitist effects—elitist not in the sense of shutting out the man-in-the-street, for all professional academic prose does that. But point-last academic prose may be more likely than point-first prose to shut out the circle of academic readers who lie just outside the circle of insiders to the discourse community. If relatively few Ph.D.s in literature can readily follow the conceptual point making in an article on Renaissance New Historicism by comparison to the percentage of Ph.D.s in psychology who can follow the point making in attachment research, then questions about elitism may arise within the profession.

The third possibility is that nonepistemic, point-last New Historicist prose is not meant to be communicative in the same way that, for instance, attachment research is meant to be—that it is, instead, a form of epideictic rhetoric, a rhetoric of self-display calculated to celebrate the values of the community or show the writer's virtuosity.

Cumulative knowledge building, knowledge compacting, and disciplinary adjudication appear to be less important, to some practitioners of the New Historicism, than other epideictic goals involving celebration or promotion. But even within epideictic rhetoric, there exist variations in what is celebrated or promoted. Fahnestock and Secor have argued that much literary criticism may be described as epideictic rhetoric in that it "create[s] and reinforce[s] communities of scholars sharing the same values" ("Rhetoric of Literary Criticism" 94). This kind of reinforcing and sharing might take the form of a traditional kind of celebration, as in funeral orations or other ceremonial praise. But whereas literary studies may once have celebrated literature, the focus of celebration—or what is reinforced in the community of scholars—shifts when a discourse community focuses on repudiating its New Critical past, reshaping its canon, or uncovering the repression in past societies.

Epideictic rhetoric may, in the modern academy, have shifted away from traditional celebration toward performance. Michael Carter's characterization of scholarship as the "rhetoric of display" offers the possibility that in current literary discourse what is being promoted or celebrated may not be literature itself or a community's interpretations, but a scholar's personal virtuosity. That is, scholars display prowess, privilege originality, and amplify on paradoxical themes. Elbow, too, finds an element of display in academic literary discourse ("Reflections" 147), and Shumway has commented that "it has become less important for a contributor to be right than to be noticed. . . . in literary studies, being wrong ceased to matter very much once the dominant practice shifted from historical scholarship to New Critical interpretation" (833).

These descriptions help explain how Greenblatt's and Mullaney's narrativized and nonepistemic prose departs from more traditional academic prose. If the function of academic prose, among some literary practitioners, is not to create or evaluate new contributions to disciplinary knowledge, then the point-last structure and relative lack of epistemic language are understandable. If the function of academic contributions, instead, is to display the academic writer's virtuosity and, in the process, celebrate the difficulty of interpretation, then the inductive movement, the profusion of anecdotes, and the general point-last tendencies make sense.

Recognizing affinities between literary study and epideictic discourse may lead to three differing evaluations of current literary study. First, one might decide that epideictic tendencies in literary studies will enhance the value of literature or enhance the value of interpretive activity; if so, epideictic tendencies may not be a cause for lament. New interpretations of Shakespeare will provide constantly renewed reasons for returning to and appreciating the Shakespearean text.

Second, at the opposite extreme, one might decide that an activity so little geared toward point making or knowledge creation has little to recommend it; if so, literary studies may resemble an imposter in the academy, garnering resources for the activities of research while offering only a sham version of research. By this logic, research funding, travel allocations, relief from teaching, or rewards for publication all look like unnecessary benefits accruing to a discipline that has not played by the rules of the research university.

Third, one might instead see the politically conscious discussions of New Historicism as serving to strengthen political resolve through an inverted version of traditional literary celebration—instead of celebrating Shakespeare and the act of interpretation, for instance, it offers anticelebratory emphasis on the darker aspects of our history. Dale Sullivan describes the purpose of epideictic rhetoric as "the creation and maintenance of orthodox opinions within a culture or subculture" ("Ethos" 117). By this logic, one could view literary studies as an embattled minority subculture, increasingly irrelevant in a technological society, faced with dwindling resources (e.g., undergraduate majors, research funding) and yet preserving the values of its subculture.[8] There are, in fact, frequent suggestions among New Historicists, cultural materialists, or cultural critics that there is positive social or political value to be obtained by exposing the workings of power in history. There are potential perils in this approach, however, because if literary studies abandons both the goal of knowledge making and the goal of traditional celebration of literature, then the anticelebratory function may be undermined by its own devaluation of literature; critics elsewhere in the university, legislators, or the public might easily conclude that if literature is not to be celebrated, there is little reason to pay any attention to it at all.

It is not my purpose to judge which of these three evaluations is preferable, but I think it important for scholars to discuss the issues clearly.[9] The disarray in the field of literary studies that Graff and Elbow, for instance, have commented on is rooted in fundamental differences of opinion over these three possible functions of literary studies. But there remains another possibility: that literary studies might strengthen its epistemic activities and assert its knowledge-making powers. The comparatively epistemic academic writing Howard employs suggests that there is more than one course open for literary studies to take.

Language

CHAPTER SIX

Sentence-Level
Differences in Disciplinary
Knowledge Making

The text-level patterns I have explored in the subfields of attachment research, colonial social history, and Renaissance New Historicism are created through language, so we should expect to find some trace of those differences at the sentence level. The traces should be reciprocal, with text-level differences among the disciplines visible at the sentence level and sentence-level differences having text-level consequences. Although the connections between academic knowledge making and text making have begun to come under scrutiny, the connections often have not been made at the sentence level because of the lingering assumption that academic language is transparent and because we have lacked methods of analysis adequate for exploring connections between macro- and micro-levels of structure in academic texts.

Until recently, linguists have worked at the sentence level and rhetoricians at the text level. Text linguists have now begun to connect sentence-level features to larger textual features, but renewed rhetorical interest in contextual variables requires new kinds of analysis (see Huckin). Text linguists ordinarily either have not been concerned with the relatively long, complex texts academics write (e.g., Hoey) or have not been concerned with generically distinctive features of academic writing, particularly writing in the social sciences and humanities. We are now starting to see studies that employ analytic tools derived from linguistics to explore rhetorical differences, as in the different kinds of writing within the academy (e.g., Vande Kopple, "Noun Phrases"; Lovejoy; Swales). It is one such analysis I develop here.

In exploring sentence-level features of professional writing, we need ways of examining how different textual features function in concert with larger rhetorical and knowledge-making goals. Identifying discipline-specific patterns in paragraph length, for instance, will neither tell us much about discursive practices nor help us teach novices to generate disciplinary prose. But once we find that paragraphs are shorter in technical or scientific writing than in writing about literature (Broadhead, Berlin, and Broadhead), we may examine whether differences in paragraph length are generated by other differences in the two discourses, involving, for instance, conventions of economy versus elaboration.

In other words, methods of analyzing sentence-level practices in academic writing need to be informed by and sensitive to the kinds of differences involved in disciplinary knowledge making. In what follows, I analyze the type of conceptual work academic sentences do by analyzing types of epistemic and nonepistemic grammatical subjects in my three subdisciplinary fields. I report here on a classification system useful for examining the kinds of differences in disciplinary knowledge making analyzed in chapters 3, 4, and 5.[1]

Rationale

The classification system I have developed has roots both in theoretical issues in the humanities and social sciences and in discourse analysis. At the theoretical, textual, or macro level, my rationale has already been explained in the preceding chapters: the existence of discipline-specific differences in (1) degrees of particularism and (2) explicit epistemic accounting (a discourse community's self-monitoring or explicit justifications of inferences). These text-level differences suggest kinds of analyses that should be especially fruitful at the sentence- or micro-level and be especially likely to show up in the grammatical subject position. I begin, then, by explaining my focus on the grammatical subject position.

First, if fields in the humanities address more particularistic knowledge problems than fields in the sciences or social sciences, this difference should entail the ways knowledge claims are made and the relation of particular phenomena to conceptual abstractions. Such differences at the conceptual level should involve differences in nouns—either in the kinds of nouns populating professional academic writing or in the structure of their presentation. Nouns in the grammatical subject position may, then, be particularly important.

Second, we have a number of indications that representations of agency are important, and variations in agency are created through variations in sentence subjects. A writer's sense of whether or how "evidence" exists outside its construction by the writer is relevant to epistemological questions about the relation of researcher to data or writer to material. These questions have figured powerfully in contemporary debates about the rhetoric of inquiry, philosophy of science, sociology of knowledge, literary theory, anthropology, and history and should affect the writer's sense of agency. That sense, in turn, involves the grammatical subject position.

The issue of agency arises in relation to method and epistemology when academics address issues like whether to use "I" in scholarly articles. Academics not recognizing or wanting to conceal the constructedness of their accounts might be unlikely to put themselves in the subject position and choose to present data as self-evident. On the other hand, if academics are increasingly aware of the constructedness of their accounts, there should be signs of that awareness in the subject position. Categorizing types of nouns in the subject position is one way to analyze writers' sense of agency and possible discrepancies between epistemological assumption and written practice.

Third, traditional approaches to grammar and style have accorded importance to the grammatical subject position for an entirely different set of reasons. Concerned with readability or grace rather than with specialized or professionalized prose, traditional discussions of style have recognized the importance of the grammatical subject position in creating readable prose. Manuals often urge writers to strengthen sentences and make them more direct by putting the actors or agents in the subject position. Joseph Williams, for instance, offers as his "first principle of clear writing" this two-part advice: "(1) In the subjects of your sentences, name your cast of characters, and

(2) In the verbs of your sentences, name the crucial actions in which you involve those characters" (9). Williams contrasts sentences like the following and urges writers (in general) to write sentences like the second:

> Our lack of pertinent data prevented determination of committee action effectiveness in the targeting of funds to those areas in greatest assistance need.

> Because we lacked pertinent data, we could not determine whether the committee had targeted funds to areas that needed assistance the most. (Williams 8)

Surely the second sentence is more readable, and Williams's advice is useful when applied to ordinary prose.

But decisions about how to represent agency become more complex in the rhetorical contexts of the disciplines. In psychology research, for instance, *who* (or *what*) should be the focus of agency is unclear when, in fact, there are many agents: in the case of attachment research, the psychologist is the agent who chooses experimental subjects, sets up experimental procedures, and then observes parents and infants as they react with each other; but the parents and infants are agents also. These epistemological complexities should complicate our recommendations about what belongs in the grammatical subject position. If a discourse community values explicit warranting of inferences and negotiation among competing explanations, then those values should affect the sense of agency and, consequently, what appears in the grammatical subject position.

In some disciplines, what goes into the grammatical subject position may be affected by changing ideology. For instance, the issue of agency arises in literary studies when there are arguments about the relative unimportance of the autonomous individual (or "subject") in relation to the social contexts that help shape writers. In his critique of New Historicism, Richard Levin ("Bardicide") has argued that Renaissance New Historicists no longer credit Shakespeare with agency but have displaced agency onto texts. As Levin characterizes the New Historicism, Renaissance texts now have "bad moves" and "good moves." In their bad moves, texts project, displace, conceal, or remain silent. In their good moves, they get nervous, reveal, disclose, expose. One need not agree with either Levin's analysis or his evaluation, but his critique is useful in demonstrating how assumptions about agency are likely to have syntactic and semantic consequences. If Shakespeare is no longer seen as the autonomous author intentionally creating effects in his plays, we should expect to see less of "Shakespeare," for instance, as the subject of active verbs in literary studies about Shakespeare. It is consistent with my analysis in this chapter and the last that literary academics appear more concerned with interpretation than with academic text making; literary discussions tend to focus on what shapes writers and selves, rather than on how academic literary texts help negotiate community knowledge claims.

Decisions about agency have important consequences for novices entering a field because certain kinds of agency are probably easier for novices to create. It may be easier for a novice to make arguments with "Shakespeare" or "children" as agents—e.g., "Shakespeare depicts" or "Children are attached to parents"—rather than the more complex sense of agency in "The text displaces" or "Comparison of these figures suggests that children are attached to parents." In a study of writing in grades 4, 8, 12, and 15, Witte and Cherry found four kinds of topical focus, none of the epistemic type in "Comparison of these figures suggests that." This finding suggests that epistemic sentence subjects are not part of the ordinary repertoire of writers even well into the undergraduate years. The move into postgraduate work almost certainly will involve learning new textual practices in some fields. Non-native English students in science and technology appear to need help writing that-nominals (West) of the type found in "Comparison of these figures suggest that." Native English speakers probably experience the same difficulties (in, perhaps, a less acute form). If academic fields are hard to enter because they involve new and perhaps difficult textual practices, we should be concerned to know more about such practices and the effects of the difficulty.

Linguistic Issues

In addition to all these reasons for assigning theoretic and rhetorical importance to the grammatical subject position, there are linguistic issues involved. My focus on the grammatical subject position is intended, first of all, to connect syntactic and semantic analysis. Looking at syntax exclusively in searching for sentence-level signs of conceptual disciplinary work might turn up either no differences or differences that are merely incidental byproducts of unexplained generative principles. For instance, information about syntactic differences among disciplines (e.g., Broadhead, Berlin, and Broadhead's findings about variation in sentence length) cannot by itself explain what generates such differences and whether they correlate with semantic or epistemological differences.

To look at key nouns in a piecemeal way, however, might merely confirm what we already know: that attachment researchers write about children and colonial social historians write about estate holders. To compare the disciplinary discourses, we need a way of canceling out differences in content in order to explore whether there are differences in representation.

The connection between syntax and semantics shows up best in the grammatical subject position of sentences. The subject position is the syntactic element that creates a sense of agency; it is the most important spot for determining what a writer is writing *about* and how questions about epistemology, construction, or agency enter into the writer's thinking. If a writer is writing about children, "children" will show up in that slot in the sentence. If a writer feels it necessary when writing about children to justify how that knowledge is obtained or weighed, words like "reason," "claim," or "evidence" will show up in that slot. Scholars in all three of these sample fields mixed sentences headed by epistemic nouns with sentences headed by nouns like "mothers" and "farmers"—although they did so in different ways, as I will explain.

Disciplinary differences in content can be canceled out by classifying types of nouns in the subject position rather than trying to make sense of the great variety of content-specific nouns. For example, two kinds of sentences in psychology illustrate how a shift in meaning occurs by means of a shift in what occupies the head noun slot: "Children do x" means something different from "Social learning theorists claim that children do x." These contrasted sentences suggest, first of all, why it is better to examine nouns in relation to their syntactic position, rather than examine all of the nouns without regard to syntax. To focus on the grammatical subject, as in the findings I report here, allows us to examine how large or small a role epistemic statements like "Theorists claim that X" play in scholars' arguments. Moreover, placing "theorists" in a class of epistemic nouns allows us to see how that subject is analogous to a subject like "social historians" in history or "Renaissance New Historicists" in literature.

Several kinds of established linguistic analysis are related to my focus on the grammatical sentence subject and the epistemics it reveals. Studies of thematic or topical focus and information management or studies of modality and metadiscourse are related to my method. But those analyses ordinarily serve to explore questions other than the questions I am asking about differing attitudes toward knowing and communicating within disciplinary subfields. I am not proposing that these other methods should be displaced, but that the analysis of grammatical subjects I offer is particularly useful for uncovering differences in disciplinary knowledge- and text-making.

My emphasis on the grammatical subject differs from linguistic approaches emphasizing topic and comment or theme and rheme in two ways. First, I am concerned with *what* writers choose to emphasize among the possible physical and conceptual phenomena in their field of study and what those choices illustrate about the ways of knowing in their disciplines. Instead of asking why or how two consecutive sentences beginning with the topics "data" and "scholars" are comprehensible and coherent for a reader, for instance, I am interested in asking why the psychologist chose "data" rather than, for instance, "parents" as a sentence topic.

Second, those writing about theme and rheme or topic and comment have not altogether agreed in their definitions of those terms and have introduced a degree of variability by not necessarily equating the sentence "topic" with its grammatical subject. Vande Kopple ("Themes") has illustrated some problems with the concepts and terminology of previous studies: if the sentence's "topic" is not always equated with the grammatical subject, then we lack any very clear guidelines for determining what it is (see also Eiler; Faigley; Vande Kopple, "Given"). I have felt justified in avoiding that problem by concentrating solely on the grammatical subject position.

Furthermore, there are justifications for considering the grammatical subject position more important than the topic. In an example I used above—"Comparison of these figures suggests that children"— one might argue that "Comparison" is not the topic. But if "children" is the topic, it still seems significant to me that, as I will demonstrate below, psychologists use epistemic sentence subjects like "comparison" or "evidence" with a relatively high frequency—far higher than their colleagues in literature departments are likely to do. In this sample sentence, "comparison" is a key word because it draws attention to the epistemic work of the discipline, because it shows a carefulness about making statements of fact that may later need to be revised, and because it leads to a *that* noun clause to take care of the information component about children. In other words, it matters— theoretically and linguistically—that the sentence begins with "comparison" and not with "children."

Those who write about topical focus have argued that the "topic" and the grammatical subject position coincide in a large number of instances and that the subject position is the natural place for topical focus to occur (e.g., Lautamatti, Witte). When "subject" and "topic" do not coincide, the usual explanation is that some other strategy involving focus or emphasis has caused the nontopical word to occur in the subject position. I am instead arguing that if the subject position is the natural place for topical focus to occur, whatever we find in the subject position should be taken very seriously as an indication of agency or epistemic accounting. So if seemingly noninformative words like "comparison" occur in the subject position, that occurence is important to explain—not to explain away by designating the topical focus as somewhere else. As Huckin has argued, "There are no two ways of saying exactly the same thing; thus even minor details of language usage can be significant in interpreting the meaning of a text" (88). Differing disciplinary patterns of sentence subject choice can be assumed to have evolved for significant communicative purposes that we need not erase by choosing a method of analysis that ignores them. This is not to say that studies of topical focus might not be helpful in examining disciplinary differences (see, for instance, Lovejoy), merely that we might also learn something about disciplinary differences by the kind of analysis I describe.

My classification of sentence subjects is based, primarily, on the distinction between epistemic and phenomenal and, secondarily, on differences within the epistemic and phenomenal categories. There are other linguistic analyses aimed partly at exploring the epistemic dimension in academic writing but that do not assign the same primacy I assign to epistemic differences. Examinations of how modals are used to convey qualification, assessment, or author's attitude (e.g., Adams Smith, Simpson, Butler) will highlight some of the epistemic qualities highlighted by my classification system. Analysis of *that*-nominals (e.g., West) may uncover textual patterns similar to mine because epistemic sentence subjects tend to be followed by *that* noun clauses. And some of the sentence subjects I classify as epistemic may also be examined as instances of metadiscourse (e.g., Vande Kopple, "Metadiscourse;" Crismore and Vande Kopple; Crismore and Farnsworth). Some of my epistemic classes (Classes 4 and 5) are examples of metadiscourse clauses, but to keep the focus here on the disciplinary differences in epistemic accounting and degrees of particularism, it seems easier and more direct to use a classification system directly tailored to examining such differences.

My method of analysis, then, focuses on the choices expert disciplinary writers make in representing the phenomena they study. To remove the difference in content from consideration, I am abstracting categories of sentence subjects from the individual terms used in the sample texts. For example, the psychologist's interest in "parents" and "children" or the historian's interest in "estate holders" and "children" are comparable kinds of representation: parent/child relations of a particular sort are the phenomena on which attachment psychologists do research just as estate holders' ability to provide land for their children becomes a phenomenon that New England colonial social historians examine. These terms—"parents" or "estate holders"—refer to the class of phenomena under study in each discipline and represent similar kinds or levels of abstraction.

My classification system is not concerned with the ontological status of the phenomena under scrutiny. That is, whatever one might say about how academics construct phenomena or whether the phenomena are "really" out there, much can be said about how academic writers choose to represent their objects of study. The classification system examines how writers in these subfields negotiate between the particular and the abstract and how they represent their epistemological maneuvers. As an example of how the classification system can uncover a field's focus on particulars or abstractions, the psychology sample contains no instances of names of individuals, even though toddlers and parents were the phenomena under scrutiny. The history sample contains a few individuals (e.g., "Henry Curtis") but far more cases of classes or groups (e.g., "farmers" or "fathers"). The literature sample has the highest percentage of individual names occuring in the subject position.

The classification system is also intended to help answer questions about convention and its relative importance in different fields. Despite occasional accusations of "formalism" in academic writing or suggestions that students should "resist" academic norms, we know relatively little about the importance or degree of convention in the disciplines. Work in fields like English for Academic Purposes (or English for Specific Purposes) attempting to specify the nature of sentence-level practices in scientific writing (e.g., Swales, Hopkins and Dudley-Evans, Adams Smith, West) has pointed to standardization or conventionality within the scientific format of Introduction, Methods, Results, and Discussion. But we know far less about professional articles in history and literature or about whether there is a high degree of homogeneity from one writer to another within any particular discourse community in the humanities. Moreover, suggestions from literary studies that academic writing is a form of "bureaucratic decorum" to be overcome (Greenblatt, *Negotiations* 1) indicate that some disciplines may view disciplinary conventions more positively than others.

Before turning to the classification system itself, let me explain several things the system is not intended to do. The classifications are not intended to be evaluative. A discipline characterized by high percentages of Class 2 and 3 subjects is no better or worse than a discipline characterized by high levels of Class 4 and 5 subjects; they are merely different.

The classifications are also not intended to be ends in themselves or to be self-explanatory. Instead, they serve as points of departure for identifying and then interpreting patterns that would otherwise be obscured by differences in content or similarities in syntax. The coding system becomes a sort of heuristic. As I will explain, for instance, Class 3 contains some ambiguities, especially in the literature sample; these ambiguities (because they are far more rare in psychology and history) indicate something about the writing in the literature sample. Identifying this difference between literature and the other two fields can help us explore some distinctive practices in writing about literature.

Finally, the classifications are intended to highlight textual or representational choices rather than underlying truths; that is, the categories do not correspond to degrees of certainty or truth or even to degrees of theoretical loftiness. An item in Class 2 is not more or less "true" or "real" than an item in another class. What is interesting, from my point of view, is how writers construct or present their material textually. One could argue that the word *daughters* is a construct of the historian, a choice that excludes other choices (e.g., *women* or *people*) and therefore no more "real" than a more abstract word like *hypothesis*. I am concerned, however, with textual practices. The term *daughters*, in my classification system, is distinguished by two traits: (1) it is represented as referring to the phenomenal world (unlike such words as *hypothesis, category,* or *rater reliability*) and (2) it refers to a category of phenomena rather than a particular, single phenomenon or entity.

The Classification System

The classification system is initially divided into two larger categories—the phenomenal and epistemic, with the phenomenal consisting of the material that the researcher studies and the epistemic consisting of the methods, conceptual tools, and previous research that the researcher brings to bear on that material. These two categories are subdivided into subcategories that become the coding category to which each sentence subject is assigned.

Here are sample sentences in each of the seven categories; I have given a name to each class to use as a shorthand and have underlined the coded subject in the example that follows:

> *Phenomenal Classes*:
> Class 1: "Particulars"—*Shakespeare* did x.
> Class 2: "Groups"—*Estate holders* tried to do x.
> Class 3: "Attributes"—*Emotional responsivity* was conveyed.

> *Epistemic Classes:*
> Class 4: "Reasons"—The *evidence* suggests that mothers do x.
> Class 5: "Research"—*Sroufe* has argued that x.
> Class 6: "Isms"—The *New Historicism* is characterized by x.
> Class 7: "Audience"—*We* need to see x.

The basic dichotomy between phenomenal and epistemic enables us to distinguish between the phenomena that the researcher writes about (does research on, investigates, etc.) and the concepts, categories, abstractions, or methodological tools the researcher uses to reason about the subject. The coding scheme focuses on ways in which writers present phenomena as self-evident or as requiring explicit epistemological warrants, and it helps characterize the kinds and degrees of abstraction that occur in the disciplines.

Class 1 ("Particulars") contains nouns referring to specific people, places, or objects; the particularized nouns of this class usually refer to named individuals, but at least to particular individuals (or places, objects). Class 2 ("Groups") contains generalized or grouped nouns, still referring to people, places, or objects; for instance, "mothers," "farms," or "Shakespeare's plays" would all be included in Class 2. Class 3 ("Attributes") contains nouns referring to the attributes, properties, action, behavior, or motivations and thoughts of the nouns in Classes 1 and 2. Class 3, therefore, contains the most abstract, least material nouns in the phenomenal category; but nouns included in Class 3 nevertheless are represented as belonging to the phenomenal realm. Thus if a sentence subject in literary writing is "Queen Elizabeth's desires," that subject is categorized in Class 3 because the desires are represented as belonging to Queen Elizabeth, even though it is the academic who has characterized them as belonging there.

The four epistemic classes contain nouns in the subject position represented as belonging to the researcher or referring to the reasoning of academics. Class 4 ("Reasons") contains all-purpose abstractions and words used in reasoning such as "reasons," "argument," "evidence," "significance," or "findings." It also contains field-specific terms such as "ANOVAS," "correlations," "longitudinal studies," or "interviews."

Class 5 ("Research") contains references to scholars in the field, whether generalized (e.g., "historians," "researchers") or named ("Barber writes"). Class 6 ("Isms") contains "isms"—nouns referring to schools of thought such as "Marxism" or "New Historicism." (This class remains largely empty in my sample but is likely to be less empty in a sample of textbook writing.) Finally, Class 7 ("Audience") contains subjects like the generalized "we" (but not the actual "we") and "one" or "you"—words potentially useful either for guiding a reader through the text or for implying areas of agreement among readers.[2]

Differences among the Subfields

Table 1 indicates the overall distribution of sentence subjects in the texts of each disciplinary field.

Table 1
Distribution of Sentence Subjects in Disciplinary Samples
(by percentages)

	Class of Sentence Subject		
	Psychology	*History*	*Literature*
Phenomenal Classes			
Class 1: Particulars	0.1	6.0	30.0
Class 2: Groups	27.0	44.0	10.0
Class 3: Attributes	11.0	26.0	44.0
Epistemic Classes			
Class 4: Reasons	49.0	15.0	7.0
Class 5: Research	12.0	6.0	5.0
Class 6: Isms	0.1	0.0	0.2
Class 7: Audience	1.0	3.0	4.0

Some differences are immediately apparent. Given its relatively low percentage of subjects in the three phenomenal categories, psychology appears comparatively unconcerned with the particular individual subject. History is significantly but only minimally more so. Class 1 nouns ("Particulars") occupied a far greater place in literary studies—30% as compared to .1% in psychology and 6% in history.

Generalized categories of agents (Class 2: "Groups") figured most prominently in history, accounting for nearly half the sentence subjects (44%). They are a significant presence in psychology (27%)—particularly in the Methods sections, where they rose to 42% because sentences like "Mother-infant pairs were chosen" or "Insecurely attached infants did x" were most likely to occur there. The grouping and categorizing present in history and psychology, however, were far less evident in literature (10%). Class 3 subjects ("Attributes") figured most prominently in literature (44%) and least prominently in psychology (11%).

Among the four epistemic categories, Class 4 words ("Reasons") were the most frequent in all fields, but the psychology articles had a far higher percentage of Class 4 words than the other two fields, with 49% as opposed to 15% in history and only 7% in literature. Moreover, if Classes 4 ("Reasons") and 5 ("Research") are considered together as companion ways of referring to work in the epistemic field (through foregrounding research methods, inferences, and findings), the psychology articles had 61% of their sentence subjects in these two epistemic categories, compared with only 21% in history and 12% in literature.

The higher percentage of Class 5 subjects ("Research") in psychology—12% as compared to 6% and 5%—suggests that psychologists place greater importance on cooperative disciplinary knowledge making than historians and literary academics. Price's distinction between fields that have a high percentage of references to the current research front (science and, to a lesser degree, social science) and fields that are more archival (the humanities) is consistent with these differences in the degree of importance assigned to current research through the use of Class 5 subjects.

Class 6 nouns ("Isms") were scarcely present in these three fields—an absence that becomes interesting only when professional articles are contrasted to either theoretical articles or textbook accounts. Further research into undergraduates' writing or the informative writing in textbooks might demonstrate that claims like "Deconstruction dominated . . ." or "Marxism involves the theory . . ." are too sweeping for the kind of knowledge making done at the professional level but are used in textbooks to convey, summarize, or translate knowledge in ways that alter the epistemics professionals would employ.

Class 7 nouns ("Audience")—including the generalized "we"—were relatively infrequent in all fields, but least frequent in psychology and most frequent in literature.

Syntactic and Semantic Consequences

A number of syntactic and semantic consequences arise from these epistemic differences. In a work that is typical of the epistemic style in the psychology sample, Belsky and Rovine foreground methods, inferences, and findings in a way that pushes the phenomenal material to subordinate positions in the sentence, as something entailed or approached by the epistemic route. Here is a strongly epistemic passage from the end of the Belsky and Rovine Introduction; the coded subjects, all Class 4 ("Reasons") or Class 5 ("Research") are italicized and their classification noted in brackets:

> Despite the plethora of factors and processes that our longitudinal data enabled us to explore, *it is important to note* [4] that the investigation on which this report is based was a study of infant and family development rather than that of day-care per se. In terms of addressing the issues raised, *this* [4—this fact about the investigation] has both advantages and disadvantages. Perhaps the most important *disadvantage* [4] is that detailed information on the quality of nonmaternal care experienced by the infant was beyond the scope of our primary data collections. Because quality of care is likely to be a major influence on the development of infants in nonmaternal care (Belsky, 1984; McCartney et al., 1982), the potential *significance* [4] of this limitation should not be underestimated. On the positive side, by not recruiting families for a study of day-care or maternal employment per se and by enrolling families prior to their infants' births rather than well into the first year, *we* [5] may have minimized some of the selection biases that could be associated with recruitment after mothers have returned to work and at a time when parents have some idea of how relationships are working out. (Belsky and Rovine 158–59, italics mine)

This passage is concerned with explaining and justifying to other attachment researchers and child psychologists the research enterprise Belsky and Rovine have undertaken; their exclusive use of Class 4 and 5 subjects directly reflects their focus on convincing the research community.

Two kinds of sentences are particularly worth noting in this regard. Belsky and Rovine make frequent use of the extraposed sentence with a clausal subject, a type of metadiscourse clause I have included in Class 4 because of its epistemic function:[3]

> . . . *it is noteworthy that* the differences in rates of security/insecurity as a function of timing of recruitment is highly reliable in this sample of families with full-time working mothers. . . . (Belsky and Rovine 159, italics mine)

The phenomenal focus of the research—the relation between working parents and their infants—appears only toward the end of the sentence, subordinated, in the hierarchy of clause structure, to the methodological preliminaries, justifications, or qualifications typical of Class 4 ("Reasons") sentence subjects.[4]

A second frequently occurring type of sentence contains a noun *that* clause in the object position that serves to allow the process of reasoning and researching to be foregrounded before the findings are stated in the noun clause:

> The *findings* [4] of Chase-Lansdale and Owen (in press), cited earlier, as well as those from other studies (e.g., Cochran & Robinson, 1983) indicate that boys might be particularly susceptible to any negative consequences of nonmaternal care in the first year. (Belsky & Rovine 158, italics mine)

The epistemic material (*findings*) occurs first in the sentence, followed by an epistemic verb (*indicates*). Finally, a *that* clause, as object of the verb *indicates*, comments on the phenomenal possibility: boys may be more susceptible than girls. The phenomenal clause is presented not as fact, but as research finding, warranted by research but qualified by the possibility that other research might find something different. Linguistically, the sentence represents the psychologist's relation to the phenomena under scrutiny as altogether different from the epistemic relation in a sentence like "Boys are particularly susceptible to nonmaternal care," which presents causal hypothesis as fact.

Variations Within Subparts of Articles

These findings can be further analyzed to show whether writers vary their sentence subjects significantly from one part of an article to another. The standardized format of psychology offers the most obvious opportunity for examining whether subparts of articles use different kinds of sentence subjects to serve different functions within subsections. Table 2 illustrates the averages per subsection in the psychology sample.

Because the Introduction serves to introduce the research subject in the context of knowledge-making work in the disciplinary community, it is not surprising that the Introductions in my sample have a high percentage of Class 4: "Reasons" (42%) and the highest percentage of Class 5: "Research" (24%) of all four sections.

The relatively high percentage of Class 2 sentence subjects ("Groups") in the Methods section reflects one of the key functions of that section, that is, identifying the "subjects" of the experiment.

Table 2
Variation Within Psychology Articles
(by percentages)

	Subparts of articles			
	Introduction	*Methods*	*Results*	*Discussion*
Phenomenal Classes				
Class 1: Particulars	0.0	0.0	0.0	0.3
Class 2: Groups	18.0	42.0	30.0	21.0
Class 3: Attributes	15.0	11.0	5.0	10.0
Epistemic Classes				
Class 4: Reasons	42.0	42.0	60.0	52.0
Class 5: Research	24.0	6.0	5.0	17.0
Class 6: Isms	0.5	0.0	0.0	0.0
Class 7: Audience	1.0	0.5	0.0	1.0

Class 2 sentence subjects appear most useful in the Methods section because experimental subjects are described there matter-of-factly and inferences have little role. The function of the Methods section is to focus on and convey factual information like "The families were maritally intact and of working- and middle-class socioeconomic status" (Belsky and Rovine 159). These patterns in my psychology sample resemble those West found in examining divisions in the scientific research article: the Methods section in his study was least likely to contain *that*-nominals because *that*-nominals—like epistemic sentence subjects—occur in sentences commenting on knowledge claims, and the Methods section "rarely makes claims about other statements" (West 487).

Once the task of identifying experimental subjects has been performed through relatively high use of Class 2 sentence subjects ("Groups") in this sample, the articles return to the more epistemic style in the Results and Discussion sections. The Introductions differ from the Results and Discussion sections less in overall epistemic focus than in the kind of epistemic focus: the larger percentage of Class 5 subjects ("Research") in the Introductions functions to place the research within its research community. Once that task is accomplished, there is less need for Class 5 subjects in subsequent sections.

Without clearly demarcated subsections in the history and literature articles, it is more difficult than in psychology to assess the degree of variation within an article. A typical history article in the sample, however, may contain discernible internal variations, despite a lack of internal gaps or section headings. For instance, John Waters's "Family, Inheritance, and Migration in Colonial New England" contains no internal gaps of subheadings, but Waters's first seven pages introduce the topic with an overview of previous assumptions about Colonial New England families and distinctions about different models of the family (e.g., the joint, stem, and nuclear family). After the introductory seven pages, he turns to specific families for the remainder of the twenty-one-page article, dealing with particulars about the Cruttenden, Lee, Blachley, and Meigs families in eighteenth-century Guilford, Connecticut, and discussing what tax lists, deeds, and other early documents can show about family, inheritance, and migration patterns in Colonial New England. This turn from introduction and theory to particulars is reflected in the ways sentence subject patterns differ from the introduction to the body of the article, as Table 3 demonstrates.

The turn to particular families after the introductory portion of Waters's article generates a rise from 27% to 51% in Class 2 subjects ("Groups") and a corresponding drop in the combined Class 4 and 5 ("Reasons" and "Research") percentages from 46% to 11%.

Some Nonepistemic Patterns among New Historicists

By comparison to the samples from psychology and history, articles in my Renaissance New Historicist sample show a less epistemic focus at the sentence level, just as they did at the text level. Class 4, "Reasons," are less prominent in general in the literary sample (7% as opposed to 49% in psychology and 15% in history). Greenblatt's first paragraph in "Invisible Bullets" has exclusively Class 1 ("Particulars") subjects—for example, "Richard Baines," "Heriots," "Harriot," and "one of his contemporaries" (18). This sentence-level pattern mirrors the text-level patterns in Greenblatt's article that I have discussed in chapter 5: immersing his readers in particulars about individual contemporaries of Shakespeare's, setting the stage inductively for

Table 3
Sentence Subjects by Section in Waters's History Article
(by percentages)

	Subparts of Article	
	Introduction	*Body*
Phenomenal Classes		
Class 1: Particulars	5.0	12.0
Class 2: Groups	27.0	51.0
Class 3: Attributes	17.0	21.0
Epistemic Classes		
Class 4: Reasons	23.0	9.0
Class 5: Research	23.0	2.0
Class 6: Isms	0.0	0.5
Class 7: Audience	6.0	4.0

Shakespeare's appearance only much later in the article. Lentricchia's critique that it is not "hermeneutically savvy" for Greenblatt's beginnings to promise "direct access to history's gritty ground-level texture" (234) suggests that literary academics who are aware of the constructedness of knowledge should take pains to draw attention to their own constructions. The way academics typically draw such attention is through use of Class 4 and 5 "Reasons" and "Research," particularly in their introductions.

Greenblatt's ratio of Class 4 "Reasons" to Class 7 "Audience" also shows a pattern quite different from that in the more epistemic articles. The contrast to Belsky and Rovine in psychology is instructive because they are at the epistemic extreme among psychologists, while Greenblatt is at the nonepistemic extreme among New Historicists. In the more epistemic articles, Class 4 subjects play a larger role than Class 7 subjects:

Table 4
Relative Use of Class 4 "Reasons"
and Class 7 "Audience" in Three Articles
(by percentages)

	Class 4	Class 7
Belsky & Rovine (psychology)	57.0	0.6
Waters (history)	13.0	4.0
Greenblatt (literature)	13.0	10.0

Greenblatt uses Class 4 epistemic subjects only slightly more often than he uses Class 7 subjects—the generalized "we" primarily: for example, "We have then, as in Machiavelli, a sense of religion as . . ." (21). The explanation for the ratio between Class 4 and Class 7 in Greenblatt's article is not that he is unconcerned with theory or hypothesis, but that he either presents his hypotheses without the explicit epistemic accounting present in psychology or else presents his hypotheses as something "we" *believe, know,* or *have*—as an assumption the audience can be counted on to share. He presents his claims frequently as already agreed on.

Greenblatt's sentence subject patterns lead to some interesting ambiguities through the relative lack of epistemic foregrounding. He tends to embed his hypotheses within Class 3 phenomena ("Attributes") without explicit, Class 4, epistemic accounting.[5] For instance, the following sentence *asserts* the existence of "charges" instead of explicitly signaling the inference by which the literary researcher hypothesizes that such charges exist:

> The pervasiveness and frequency of these charges [of atheism made by some Elizabethans] then does not signal the probable existence of a secret society of freethinkers, a School of Night, but rather registers the operation of a religious authority that, whether Catholic or Protestant, characteristically confirms its power in this period by disclosing the threat of atheism. (Greenblatt 19)

The "pervasiveness" and "frequency" of these Class 3 "charges" have not been explicitly addressed or warranted; Greenblatt has begun with three particular instances of charges of atheism—without explicitly explaining why they warrant the generalization that authority "characteristically confirms its power in this period by disclosing the threat of atheism."

The critiques of Greenblatt (see chapter 5) may have their source in these linguistic phenomena. Critics reacting to Greenblatt's shift toward narrative may (whether consciously or not) perceive something missing when phenomenal attributes are asserted without accompanying epistemic accounts. Greenblatt in effect hides the constructedness of his account by reliance on Class 3 "Attributes" rather than Class 4 "Reasons."

Second, he inserts "new" information into the sentence subject position that linguists claim typically belongs to "given" information. Variations among New Historicists highlight what is distinctive about Greenblatt's use of "new" information in the subject position. Jean Howard's critique ("New Historicism") of Greenblatt's lack of epistemic accounting becomes more interesting in that her own work is less likely than Greenblatt's to put new information in the subject position. Howard's article in this sample ("Antitheatricality") contains the relatively high percentage of Class 3 subjects typical of other New Historicists: for example, 38% Class 3 subjects, as opposed to Greenblatt's 44% (or the psychologists' 11%). But Howard tends to use Class 4 or 5 subjects for claim making and to reserve Class 3 subjects for given information; that is, the new information typically appears in the complement following Class 3 subjects, as in the following passage; I have given the claim itself in boldface:

> These *theatrics* [Class 3] make Hero appear a whore and lead directly to her denunciation in the church. This *deception* [Class 3] is **clearly coded as evil:** *it* [Class 3] is engineered by a bastard, involves the transgressive act of a servant wearing the clothes of one of higher rank, and leads to the threat of death for several of the play's characters. (Howard 174, my emphasis)

Here, by contrast, is a sentence of Greenblatt's with its claims given in boldface:

> Hence *Harriot's text* [Class 1] is committed to record **what we have called his confirmation of the Machiavellian hypothesis,** and hence too this *confirmation* [Class 3] is not only **inaccessible as subversion to those on whom the religion is supposedly imposed but functionally**

inaccessible to most readers and quite possibly to Harriot himself. (Greenblatt 24, my emphasis)

His claim that Harriot "confirms" the Machiavellian hypothesis initially occurs in the complement of the first independent clause where linguists expect "new" information to occur. But without further epistemic justification, the claim then slips into the subject position and this "confirmation" becomes the given information of the following clause, thereby losing its explicit marking as claim rather than given fact.

Vande Kopple, in studying the noun phrases of scientific writing, comments on the "responsibility" not to insert in the sentence subject information "that would, if it appeared outside the bounds of a subject, be open to challenge or debate. Readers apparently accept the information in sentence subjects as beyond challenging, and if they are inclined to question or challenge information in a sentence, that information will usually be found in the predicate" ("Noun Phrases" 343–44). These are not merely matters of personal responsibility, however, because they also involve the epistemic repertoire developed within a discourse community. The academic literary community is comparatively reluctant to use epistemic structures like "This hypothesis about Harriot suggests that . . ." (metadiscourse consisting of epistemic sentence subject and *that* noun clause); this reluctance lies behind the placing of claim in the position of given information. Greenblatt's willingness to put unwarranted claims in the sentence subject, along with his particularistic, rather than epistemic focus in introducing his material, are signs that literary studies may contain markedly different knowledge-making practices from the rest of the academy.

Taken together, these sentence-level findings parallel the text-level tendencies I have already discussed: the differing emphasis on negotiating knowledge claims within a research community and the differing degrees of particularism. The greater prominence of both Class 4 "Reasons" and Class 5 "Research" in the psychology sample suggests the importance, in that field, of foregrounding one's negotiations and attempting to build on previous knowledge. For the psychologists in this sample, knowledge of attachment is not unmediated knowledge of the phenomenon but knowledge mediated by the research community, and psychologists have developed a sentence-level repertoire for carrying on and assessing that mediation. At the other extreme, within this sample, New Historicists may focus more or less directly on their Renaissance phenomena without the elaborate means the psychologists have for discussing their own mediations. Renaissance New Historicists' relative lack of sentence-level epistemic language prevents their addressing, refining, and compacting knowledge claims, though it at the same time may serve other narrative and epideictic purposes. The historians in this sample tend to occupy a middle ground between New Historicists and attachment psychologists.

The same parallel exists between sentence- and text-level degrees of particularism in these three samples: the New Historicists are most likely to refer to particulars, the New England social historians are interested in both particulars and group patterns, and the psychologists are interested in generalizable phenomena. These findings raise the question of what relation exists between particularism in a field of study and the tendency to write less epistemic texts. There are several possible connections: academic fields focusing on more socially and historically particularistic phenomena may be comparatively constrained by a lack of generalizable patterns. Generalizable patterns of an "urban" research area (Becher) may make it more possible to build elaborate epistemic frameworks for negotiating knowledge claims.

At the same time, the more particularistic fields like literature and history may find it important not to generalize in such a way as to erase particulars. If literary study serves epideictic goals in addition to (or in lieu of) knowledge-making goals, then particular details may help celebrate and preserve the insights of past writers and current interpretive activity. If such are the goals of literary study, language that is too epistemic could lessen the enjoyment of reading and change its purpose.

Further research is needed to explore these suggestions, but I hope to have shown here some of the potential of this method for examining how approaches to knowledge making may vary in ways that are parallel at text- and sentence-level. Examining the kind and importance of epistemic sentence subjects can illuminate disciplinary differences in warranting practices, uses of abstraction, and cumulative knowledge building within disciplinary fields.

CHAPTER SEVEN

Professional Styles
and Their Consequences

The preceding chapters have suggested that variations in academic writing within the social sciences and humanities are not randomly distributed: the frequency of *that*-noun clauses as sentence objects in psychology ("Research suggests that") or the high incidence of particularized sentence subjects in literature both result from goals of their disciplinary communities. But discussions of academic writing frequently ignore or blur the relation between purpose and language. As a result, efforts to describe, to teach, even to reform academic language are plagued by category confusions and lack of detailed, rhetorically informed linguistic description. These confusions can be avoided by more careful consideration of the varied goals involved in academic writing and how those goals reflect or generate stylistic variation.

In this chapter I will first consider some of the larger professional consequences of the sentence-level differences explored in the last chapter and how the differences among these subdisciplinary styles lend themselves to different rhetorical purposes. I will then discuss the consequences of these disciplinary differences for novices. Finally, I discuss some of the consequences for academic professionals: recent confusions about "academic" writing and some alternative styles that have been proposed.

Consequences of Sentence-Level Variations

The differences in epistemic and phenomenal focus created by sentence subjects are situated within larger linguistic patterns that have been described, variously, as nominal versus verbal (Wells) or synoptic versus dynamic (Halliday).[1] Although linguists and grammarians have differed in their definitions of these binaries, they have tended to agree that (1) the nominal style is associated with the academy and science whereas the verbal or dynamic is associated with conversation, and (2) the nominal style is inferior to the verbal/dynamic style in the ease with which it is comprehended. The strength of this widespread perception is apparent from consulting the injunctions common in grammar and style handbooks. Sheridan Baker urges writers to "Break the noun habit" exemplified in "Teacher militancy is not as marked in Pittsburgh" (Baker 58). William Zinsser warns of "creeping nounism" (109) or the "concept nouns" that create "typical dead sentences"—for example, "The common reaction is incredulous laughter" (108). Richard Lanham characterizes the noun style as "The Official Style" and offers the following example of an indisputably rough-going passage from Talcott Parsons, *The Social System*:

> There is in turn a two-fold structure of this "binding-in." In the first place, by virtue of internalization of the standard, conformity with it tends to be of personal, expressive and/or instrumental significance to ego. In the second place, the structuring of the reactions of alter to ego's action as sanctions is a function of his conformity with the standard. Therefore conformity as a direct mode of the fulfillment of his own need-dispositions tends to coincide with the conformity as a condition of eliciting the favorable and avoiding the unfavorable reactions of others. (Parsons 38, quoted in Lanham 124)

It is no accident that Lanham could find a particularly egregious example of nominalization in the writing of a sociologist. But since the association between nominal style and particular kinds of knowledge making is so apparent to academics discussing the two styles, it seems almost odd that critiques of the nominal style are often made without qualification or without investigation of the linguistic, rhetorical, and epistemic ecosystem in which the nominal style functions.

Since the critiques of the nominal style are so frequently and routinely made, it perhaps makes sense to set out four of my own premises: (1) that evaluation of academic language is altogether appropriate and that self-evaluation is necessary for the professional health of any professional community, (2) that thorough rhetorical and linguistic understanding is a sine qua non for such self-evaluation, (3) that, looked at acontextually, the verbal/dynamic style is indeed superior to the nominal style, but (4) that we cannot look at academic style acontextually.

Epistemic sentence subjects, like those most strikingly present in the psychology sample, constitute only one element functioning in concert with at least three other sentence-level characteristics to promote generalization and communal knowledge building. These four interactive elements are (1) the relatively high incidence of epistemic Class 4 ("Reasons") and Class 5 ("Research") nouns as sentence subjects, (2) a corresponding set of frequently used verb patterns such as the verb "to be," passive constructions, and verbs like "suggest" or "argue" that serve epistemic functions, (3) a highly nominalized structure, and (4) a point-first structure antithetical to keeping the reader in suspense.

Each element plays its role in making knowledge, and each entails the other elements in this linguistic ecosystem. The epistemic Class 4 and 5 sentence subjects occurring with such frequency in psychology tend to keep the reader's focus on the claim-making negotiations of the research community rather than on unmediated phenomena. Frequent epistemic sentence subjects, therefore, have the effect of promoting disciplinary consensus because sustained attention to previous research and to claims of new knowledge can allow a thread of continuity to be built. Attachment researchers continually focus their material through epistemic indications: "here is what we have agreed upon," "here are the areas of disagreement," "here are the ways in which we currently think we might resolve our disagreements."

Not surprisingly, these Class 4 and 5 subjects entail what might be called epistemic verbs, as in the following:

Research *suggests* that . . .
The findings *indicate* that . . .

In addition, passive verbs or the linking verb "to be" are far more commonly used than active verbs by attachment researchers. This combination of epistemic sentence subjects and passive or linking verbs is common in the sciences or social sciences. Cluett (85) reports, for instance, that 70% of sociologist Max Weber's verbs (as translated by Talcott Parsons) were either linking verbs or passives. In my attachment research sample, linking verbs and passives (my italics) occur both with phenomenal (Class 2 and 3) and epistemic (Class 4 and 5) subjects:

> The families [Class 2] *were* maritally intact . . .
> Changes [Class 3] *have taken place* in . . .
> Cross cultural aspects [Class 4] of attachment theory and findings *have been discussed* . . .
> The most important disadvantage [Class 4] *is* . . .
> The significance of this limitation [Class 4] *should not be under-estimated* . . .

Both these stylistic traits—the preponderance of epistemic sentence subjects and linking or passive verbs—function together as part of a larger pattern of "nominal" or, in Halliday's terms, "synoptic" style. Halliday sees the synoptic style as evolving from the more dynamic spoken language in order to store knowledge and create the potential for "structuring, categorising, disciplinising" (149):

> [Writing] creates a new kind of knowledge: scientific knowledge; and a new way of learning, called education. . . . it offered a new perspective on experience: the synoptic one with its definitions, taxonomies and constructions. The world of written language is a nominalised world, with a high lexical density and packed grammatical metaphors. It is these features that enable discourse to become technical. ("Language" 149)

Noun phrases are key ingredients of this synoptic style. In a study of scientific prose, Vande Kopple ("Noun Phrases") found 83% of the total number of words in noun phrases. Using Halliday's characterization of the synoptic, Vande Kopple argues that scientists use complex noun phrases "to refer to a great deal of information available from past work" (343).

There are indications, then, in compact fields within science and social science, that epistemic sentence subjects work in tandem with noun phrases to consolidate disciplinary knowledge. The noun phrase in the subject position, as in the example that follows (my italics), allows the author immediately to identify where her work fits into the larger field of attachment research.[2]

> *The ability to develop socially competent relationships with peers* has long been regarded as one of the most important developmental tasks of childhood. . . . (Cohn 152)

The combination of epistemic subjects and nominal style also appears to aid point-first presentation. It is not accidental that the point-last organization seen in the literary articles by Greenblatt and Mullaney is more likely to represent particular people acting through concrete verbs than is the typical article in attachment research. In the latter field, sentence subjects referring to the state of knowledge in the field keep the disciplinary problem as the focal point through which the phenomenon of attachment is explored. By contrast, the narrative presentation in the Greenblatt and Mullaney articles leads the reader more inductively through the phenomena toward interpretive point making.

In my history and literature samples, the comparatively less epistemic style may also be described as comparatively less nominalized or synoptic than the style of attachment research. The explanation is to be found, again, in the ways that knowledge-making goals and syntactic elements entail each other. The tension between generalizing and preserving the particulars of history among both social historians and Renaissance New Historians occurs most obviously, in my sample, in the high incidence of Class 1 "Particulars" as sentence subjects in New Historicist writing. The greater emphasis on Class 2 "Groups" in the history sample demonstrates a continuing tension in history writing between particulars and generalization. If synoptic style functions to consolidate generalizations, then it is not surprising that fields that are more particularistic also tend to be less synoptic.

The relatively high incidence of Class 4 sentence subjects ("Reasons") in attachment research is related to that field's emphasis on generalization and communal consensus. The items constituting the field's generalizations tend to be isolable or clearly identifiable parts of the larger disciplinary problem, parts that can be found repeatedly:

an attachment classification may apply to any number of children, the phenomenon of clinging is repeatedly observed, classifications by gender or by the experience of child abuse may be used in differing experiments, and so on. With isolable or clearly identifiable items contributing to the field's problem definition, then, it may be easier to develop a class of epistemic sentence subjects than it is in more humanistic fields where disciplinary problems are less abstractable from particular phenomena. Defined problem, common research tradition, and discrete (but potentially cumulative) contributions to the subdisciplinary research problem function together in attachment research to make epistemic sentence subjects like "Research indicates" or "the findings suggest" more possible. Each researcher can add a bit of information or insight to the same problem and identify where that contribution fits in the field's knowledge making.

In New Historicist work, however, Greenblatt's exploration of subversion in Harriott and Shakespeare's *Henry* plays may not add on to Howard's exploration of gender and rank in *Much Ado* in quite the same way that one piece of attachment research may add on to another. Contributions to interpreting Shakespeare may be more holistic, less able to be broken down into discrete bits of cumulative insight. A reader might need to accept or reject the entire interpretation. The reader of a psychology article may need to do the same, as seen in the possibly incompatible explanations of Sroufe's relational and Kagan's temperament perspective. But the eight-author article by Vaughn et al. attests to the possibility of reconciling parts of the relational and temperament perspectives and to the importance attachment researchers place on pushing forward the best consensual explanations they can.

In attachment research, attributes such as "gender" or "class" constitute the 11% of sentence subjects falling into Class 3. These "attributes" are given conventionalized names and are as unambiguous as researchers in the field can make them. By contrast, the New Historicist sample has 44% of its sentence subjects in Class 3 "attributes," and there is an ambiguity surrounding many of these "attributes" because they tend to be localized. They involve interpretation of localized particulars that probably could not be treated consistently, consensually, or conventionally. For instance, the following instances of Class 3 sentence subjects in the Mullaney article suggest the degree to which his interpretation is *sui generis*:

> . . . *the attention directed toward strange ways and customs* [3] reveals an ambivalent and even paradoxical rhythm; in such forums, *the maintainance and production of the strange* [3] takes on its most dramatic form, as a process of cultural production synonymous with cultural performance.
>
> Within and without the wonder-cabinet, *the "spectacle of strangeness"* [3] enjoyed a remarkable currency during the early modern period. (Mullaney 68, my emphasis)

New Historicists are unlikely to find recurring use for such sentence subjects as "maintenance and production of the strange" or "spectacle of strangeness" whereas attachment researchers find many recurrent uses for such subjects as "security of attachment." The conventionalized subjects of attachment research are as logical an outcome of its disciplinary practices as are the nonconventionalized subjects of New Historicism of its comparatively localized, interpretive practices.

Moreover the types of sentence subjects characteristic of New Historicist work lead to patterns of predication different from those in attachment research. Class 1 "Particulars"—constituting 30% of the literary sample—readily lead to more active and concrete verbs than do Class 4 "Reasons" as sentence subjects. Here are some Class 1 subject-verb pairings from the literary sample to illustrate how active verbs may accompany Class 1 subjects:

> Harriot professes (Greenblatt 18)
> Sir Walter Ralegh teased (Greenblatt 18)
> a drunken servant complained (Greenblatt 18)
> Kyd testified (Greenblatt 21)
> Harriot tests (Greenblatt 23)
> Thomas Platter visited (Mullaney 65)
> Platter records (Mullaney 65)
> the room acts (Mullaney 67)
> the woman gave birth (Mullaney 69)
> Henri did not witness (Mullaney 71)
> a man and a woman strike a pose (Mullaney 71)
> Edward conquered (Mullaney 74)
> Stubbes charges (Mullaney 76)
> Stubbes recreates (Mullaney 76)
> Duke Theseus formulates (Montrose 61)
> Forman recorded (Montrose 62)

Titania treats (Montrose 65)
[Titania] dotes (Montrose 65)
Shakespeare engages (Montrose 66)
Egeus wishes (Montrose 67)
Theseus intervenes (Montrose 67)
Hermia must submit (Montrose 67)
Theseus expands (Montrose 67)
the Duke affirms (Montrose 67)
Don Pedro and Don John devise (Howard 163)
he [Claudio] plays (Howard 163)
Northbrooke decries (Howard 165)
Stubbes evokes (Howard 166)
[Stubbes] idealizes (Howard 167)
[Stubbes] despises (Howard 167)
Gosson marshals (Howard 169)

The Elizabethan prose writers whom Greenblatt, Mullaney, Montrose, and Howard discuss are often coupled with the same colorless epistemic verbs we find in accounts of research: Stubbes may "say" or "find" (Howard 166), and Harriot may "write" or "record" (Greenblatt 23). But they also are textually presented in more active and less neutral ways when they "decry," "despise," "charge," or "tease"—verbs that are not part of the typical repertoire of epistemic prose in psychology.

Class 3 "Attributes" (44% of the literary sample) have their own patterns of subject-verb pairing. The neutral linking or passive verbs we would expect to see are still present—"the motives are far from clear" or "the attention directed toward strange ways and customs reveals" (Mullaney 68). But, in addition, the literature sample has concrete, active verbs that are largely absent from comparable discussions of Class 3 "Attributes" in psychology where neutral verbs and passives predominate:

suspicion persisted (Greenblatt 18)
The pervasiveness and frequency of these charges does not signal (Greenblatt 19)
the wisecrack finds its way (Greenblatt 20)
"hellish verses" were lifted (Greenblatt 21)
The history of subsequent English-Algonkian relations casts doubts (Greenblatt 23)

survival of the rulers depends (Greenblatt 23)
tradition undermines (Greenblatt 25)
No catalogue could presume (Mullaney 65)
Platter's designation duplicates (Mullaney 67)
No system determines (Mullaney 67)
the pleasures of the strange are invoked (Mullaney 68)
the "spectacle of strangeness" enjoyed (Mullaney 68)
[the period] licensed (Mullaney 69)
martial triumphs would celebrate (Mullaney 70)
fighting broke out (Mullaney 72)
Elizabeth's display signified (Montrose 64)
The virginal, erotic, and maternal aspects are appropriated
(Montrose 64)
Forman's private dream-text and Shakespeare's public play-text
embody (Montrose 65)
cultural fantasy assimilates (Montrose 66)
Shakespeare engages (Montrose 66)
The diachronic structure restores (Montrose 67)
Shakespeare's play naturalizes (Montrose 68)
Heterosexual desire disrupts (Montrose 68)
presentation participates (Howard 164)
fear dominates (Howard 165)
violence hints (Howard 168)
The image constructs (Howard 170)
Other modes employ (Howard 171)

Lying behind these subject-verb pairings may be a variety of
disciplinary influences. A literary tradition of valuing active verbs may
be partially implicated in the choice of "no catalogue could *presume*"
(Mullaney 65, my emphasis) as well as in "heterosexual desire *dis-*
rupts" (Montrose 68, my emphasis). But theoretical influences from
such writers as Foucault may also affect the active verb that is chosen—
for example, "licensed" or "disrupts."

Disciplinary assumptions about the competing values of freshness or repetition may also be involved in verb choice. Howard's
use of "hints" in "the violence hints" (168) may be analogous to the
psychologist's use of the verb "suggests," but "hints" has a freshness
about it that the conventionalized "suggests" does not have. The
literary use of active verbs may be affected also, then, by a romantic
literary tradition of valuing originality over repetition and convention-

ality; social scientists using the verb "suggests" do so partly because its conventionality allows them to show that they are observing disciplinary constraints about inferencing.

In addition, many of the active verbs chosen by New Historicists might be considered by attachment researchers to be epistemologically suspect. Whereas a "wisecrack *finds its way* into a police file" in Greenblatt (20, my emphasis), a psychologist similarly unable to identify the agent involved might use the verb "appears" or "is found," but then the psychologist would not typically be concerned with anything so particularized as one wisecrack and one police file. Whereas Montrose can write "Shakespeare's play *naturalizes* Amazonomachy in the vicissitudes of courtship" (68, my emphasis), a psychologist might have a number of reasons for not using verbs like "naturalizes": it conveys too much interpretive meaning, perhaps, or is not neutral enough. The psychologist might be more likely to place interpretation or explanation in nouns than in verbs.

Each of these sample disciplinary fields, then, involves sentence-level choices that are deeply embedded in a variety of disciplinary practices, remnants of former preferences, favorite usages, attitudes toward convention, and convictions about knowledge making. Therefore, any suggestions about changes in academic writing need to involve understanding these complexities. Blanket condemnations of passive verbs, for instance, or prescriptions for vividly concrete verbs are largely ineffectual because they take no account of either the historical situatedness or the complex of knowledge-making goals and rhetorical situations represented in different kinds of academic writing.

Some Problematics of Intermediary Prose

If the goals of disciplinary inquiry shape professional writing, the goals of student writing have equally powerful effects on the kinds of prose written for or by undergraduates. Sentence-level traits of epistemic prose, as we have seen, are shaped by concern for exactitude, community judgment, and the ability to compact the knowledge in a field. These goals are not in the foreground, however, when professionals write for novices or when professionals ask novices to write for their professors (see Bartholomae). Situated between the knowledge-making prose of the academic professional and the primary texts of history or literature, there is a broad expanse of intermediary prose—including textbooks and other popularizations—shaped by the desire to share or transmit knowledge from professional to novice. I use the term "intermediary" not because such prose is all of a kind— a vast expanse of stylistically or generically undifferentiated prose— but because it is intended to mediate between novice and professional and its prose features tend to occupy an intermediary position between professionalized and more "verbal," narrative, or informative prose.

It is not my purpose here to explore in detail either the intermediary prose that professionals write or the junior versions of professional writing that are asked of undergraduates. Such inquiries require fuller treatment than is possible here. My analysis of disciplinary prose, nevertheless, suggests principles or methods of analysis important to keep in mind when considering intermediary prose within the academy. A brief look at such prose in psychology, history, and literature suggests issues that need to be resolved if academics are responsible for transmitting knowledge, engaging students in inquiry, or initiating students into the disciplines.

To begin with, these three goals—transmission, engagement, and initiation—may easily compete with each other. The goal of transmitting knowledge is problematic because what constitutes "knowledge" about a particular subject may change or be open to dispute and because many academics reject the notion of transmission altogether. But the aim of transmitting knowledge is also problematic because the intended transmission does not necessarily occur; lectures may be heard but not understood, and texts may be read but not comprehended or remembered. To enable critical thinking involves facing the possible gaps between reading and comprehending, reading and remembering, remembering and comprehending, or comprehending and using.

In general, psychology courses attempt to transmit knowledge through textbooks intended both to convey knowledge and to initiate students into some epistemic awareness of the discipline or into the "professional-in-training" role, as Walvoord and McCarthy have called it. Among the roles students may be placed in as writers, Walvoord and McCarthy have distinguished between the "professional-in-training" and the "text processor" role (9). The "text processor" focuses on summarizing, synthesizing, reviewing, or commenting while the "professional-in-training" focuses on issues or problems and uses a methodology being taught in the course. By this definition, textbooks in developmental psychology place students primarily in the text processor role but also contain elements that foster the professional-in-training role. For example, a developmental textbook by Collins and Kuczaj contains a twenty-nine-page chapter on "Attachment and Early Social Relationships" with the following mix of subsections (my numbering):

1. Theories of Attachment
2. Research Focus on Maternal Bonding
3. Behavioral Signs of Attachment
4. Research Focus on Fathers as Attachment Figures
5. Individual Differences and Development Outcomes
6. Research Focus on "Quality" Day Care
7. Effects of Attachment on Later Development
8. Research Focus on the Benefits of Early Social Contact

At least two kinds of textual presentation are involved in these sections: one promotes transmission of knowledge, and the other stimulates epistemic awareness for professionals in training. The authors write, in their Preface, of the "continuous emergence of new knowledge," and "a rapid emergence of new knowledge as a result of 'explosions' of activity in certain areas of research" (viii). Much of the material in sections 3, 5, and 7 is the core of recent knowledge in the field, knowledge to be transmitted to learners but knowledge that is designated as incomplete and in process. In addition, Collins and Kuczaj have included page-long sections entitled "Research Focus" to "[call] attention to current emphases in research and newly emerging knowledge" and give "examples of new directions in the field" (viii). These sections—four of them in this chapter on attachment—attempt to do more than transmit knowledge; they also, in the authors' words, "show how the principles and methods of developmental psychology can be applied to some of the pressing real-life questions about children" (xi). Throughout all sections, there are parenthetical references to research (in APA format).

Not surprisingly, the focus on research rather than merely on children, in this psychology textbook, leads to epistemic sentences of the type seen in professional prose. For instance, here are the first sentences of each of the five paragraphs in the "Research Focus" on maternal bonding; the section begins and ends with statements about children and parents, but each of the middle paragraphs focuses on the state of knowledge in the field:

> [1] Attachment is a two-way street: parents must form a bond with their babies, as well as infants with their parents. . . .
> [2] In recent years, however, *it has been widely suggested that* the parental bond is facilitated in humans, as it is in some lower species, by immediate contact between mother and baby after birth. . . .
> [3] *Researchers have attempted to test* Klaus and Kennell's hypothesis, and many of their findings support the idea that . . .
> [4] *The difficulty of studying* differences between experiences in the first few minutes after birth have made it impossible to tell whether the effects . . .
> [5] For parents under stress at the beginning of their relationship with infants, early contact appears to help . . . (Collins and Kuczaj 105, my numbering and emphasis)

There are epistemic sentence subjects (italicized) in the second through fourth paragraphs here and similarly epistemic sentence subjects throughout the chapter:

> In a classic longitudinal study, Schaffer and Emerson (1964) interviewed . . . (106)
> Three types of attachment behavior were examined . . . (106)
> A number of experts believe that these varied behaviors share a common characteristic . . . (109)
> This series of events allows researchers to observe . . . (111)
> One indication that the Strange Situation gives us information about some fundamental qualities of attachment is . . . (111)

In psychology, then, the textual genre students are most likely to read (textbooks) resembles the genre that professionals write; the prose is simplified and the proportion of knowledge to epistemic is altered, but the resemblances remain strong. Students are offered models of the epistemic prose they would need to write if they attempt to enter into the discipline.

Yet such textbook writing is not unproblematic. The epistemic indicators lack the purpose they have in professional prose and may be read simply as indicators of authority, rather than as ways of negotiating claims. Furthermore, the less easily read synoptic prose—even in this watered down form—may have two undesirable side effects: (1) its "dry" synoptic features may discourage engagement, and

(2) students' imitations may only display their lack of comprehension. Here, for example, are some unsuccessful novice attempts to mimic professional psychologists' prose:

> *This view* [Class 4] believes in teleology.
> *Contextualism* [Class 6] has both qualitative and quantitative change.
> *Continuum of reproductive casualty* [Class 4] attributes the child's behavior as a result of what occured at birth.
> *Social learning theory* [Class 6] is cross-cultural.
> *The underarousal and the overarousal hypothesis* [Class 4] are necessary to keep the elderly functioning.

In each case, the student has used an epistemic sentence subject and epistemic verb with an inappropriate complement, often attributing to the theory what the theory attributes to the phenomenon (e.g., it is not that social learning theory is cross-cultural, but that social learning theory posits certain learning mechanisms as cross-cultural). Such sentences reveal students' transitional intellectual development; these writers are striving to connect the phenomenal attributes to proposed explanatory models, but in doing so they mix ideas and attributes in inappropriate ways. Such transitional gaffes might be avoided if students were exposed to nothing but verbal style and spared the epistemic and synoptic style of the professional. But to translate the disciplinary knowledge of psychology into less epistemic and synoptic prose would be to erase the traces of knowledge making and negotiation and imply a positivism that most academics would consider intellectually dangerous. If students need to understand that there are competing models of explanation and interpretation and that competing models carry different consequences, exposing them to epistemic and synoptic prose in some way seems unavoidable. Academics will need to work out what is the best way.

Intermediary texts in history present a different kind of problematic. History courses, in contrast to psychology, tend to contain more textual genres. Some are primary sources (of varying genres), but among the secondary texts there are frequently more different kinds of texts than in psychology. The differences among history texts are shaped by the mixture of purposes seen in the history sample—the tension between narrative and analysis, as well as the tension in intermediary texts between receiving knowledge and engaging material. Here is historian John Breihan's statement about the professional-in-training role he envisions for students:

The difference between basic historical study, of the sort that ought to go on in high school, and history as what historians actually *do*—is argument. History textbooks, for example, attempt balanced, comprehensive narratives of past events. Historians don't read them. They read (and write) opinionated arguments about what the past was like, and they often say why contemporary history courses should introduce students to the world of what historians actually do. This usually involves introducing them for the first time to the concept of conflicting opinions in print, which is often difficult for them to grasp, and teaching them to recognize and adopt a critical approach to the opinions of others. This is combined with assigning them to develop their own opinions and to argue them against opposing points of view. (Breihan, quoted in Walvoord and Breihan, in Walvoord and McCarthy 99)

If the genre Breihan wants his students to write is argument, the genre they read in textbooks, nevertheless, is not ordinarily argument. As Breihan indicates, historians use the term "narrative" history to refer to textbooks especially concerned with coverage or with comprehensive chronological accounts. But such "narratives" are not truly narratives if "narrative" suggests something more than chronology. These "narrative" histories are frequently viewed as deficient both in representing the activity of the historian and in communicating with the reader; such textbook histories present interpretation as a series of facts and their concern for coverage results in writing that is too dry for students either to remember easily or to find engaging (for critical studies of history textbooks see, for instance, Crismore).

By contrast, there is another kind of narrative that more closely resembles what advocates of narrative like Hexter or Megill had in mind: narrative that is engaging and fully describes the *what* of history without reducing history to dry facts. I have already described how Robert Gross in *The Minutemen and Their World* draws on sources, methods, and problems in social history but relegates epistemic issues to his endnotes. Gross's success in both commanding the respect of historians and engaging a lay audience is suggested in Michael Zuckerman's comments quoted on the back of *The Minutemen*: "This lovely little book is what the new local history is all about. It captures, intimately and authentically, the life of an eighteenth-century New England town, and it conveys, effectively and ingeniously, the entanglement of that life in the surge of stirring events of a wider world beyond its borders. In its narrative vibrancy and synthetic sweep, it is, I think, the most suggestive and satisfying of the case studies of colonial communities."

Despite Gross's greater concern with narrative and his wider audience, his sentence-level style reflects the stylistic patterns in the sample of academic history articles: his sentence subjects tend to be either individuals (Class 1 "Particulars") or groups (Class 2) within Concord. He thus emphasizes the agency of his historical actors:

> *Concord* arrived at its strategic position in 1775 only after a good deal of foot-dragging. While Bostonians fulminated against British policies in the 1760s and early 1770s, the *yeomen of Concord* were squabbling among themselves in a series of increasingly bitter quarrels that threatened ultimately to divide the town into two warring parties. (Gross 10, my emphasis)

Even when a social scientist might foreground types of government, Gross foregrounds historical actors; he presents a description of Concord's town structure with the typical Concordian as sentence subject and with a relatively verbal style:

> When the eighteenth-century Yankee reflected on government, *he* thought first of his town. Through town meetings, *he* elected his officials, voted his taxes, and provided for the well-ordering of community affairs. *The main business of the town* concerned roads and bridges, schools, and the poor—the staples of local government even today. But *the colonial New England town* claimed authority over anything that happened within its borders. *It* hired a minister to preach. . . . (Gross 10, my emphasis)

The epistemic negotiations of historians are altogether absent from these accounts; instead, these generalized actors—the town, the Yankee, the Concordian—are interspersed with accounts of particular individuals at the point when individuals either become significant actors in the town or when they help embody some pattern of social behavior. In these ways, Gross not only enlivens his prose but also shows both the local sources of historical phenomena and their local impact.

Gross's success at enlivening history for a lay audience while simultaneously commanding the respect of other historians in his field may be both significant and rare. His model suggests that the intermediary prose presented in history courses might be rewritten in more lively and engaging ways. But, just as in psychology, such intermediary prose can contain traps for the unwary. If students reading narrative prose like Gross's organize their own essays chronologically or repeatedly put historical actors in the sentence subject position, their writing may look suspiciously nonanalytical to many historians. Historians frequently object to their students' apparent lack of "analysis," but students may be merely imitating what they read. If they are reading highly epistemic prose in a history course, they may verge on the historical equivalent of the gaffes I have quoted from psychology students, while if they are reading more narrative prose, they may leave out all epistemic accounting. Their writing will appear largely lacking in the kind of sustained argument Breihan advocates.

If novices' attempts to imitate the disciplinary prose they are reading is a potential source of trouble in psychology and history, it is potentially troublesome in literature also where students are often given little or no intermediary prose to read. In the heyday of New Criticism, students in literature courses typically read literature but not literary criticism. Many students felt somewhat mystified about writing a kind of prose they had never read. With the expansion of theory in literary studies, students are now more likely to read secondary sources. Bettina Huber reports that up to half of the literature professors responding to a 1990 MLA survey had recently added literary criticism to their required readings, but the percentage of readings drawn from current criticism remained around 10% for those using such criticism, while primary sources accounted for roughly 85% of the course material (Huber 44).

If we assume that writers learn to write a particular kind of prose through immersion and imitation, then we might picture a Shakespeare course in which 85% of what students read is Shakespearean prose and up to 10% might include such critics as Greenblatt or the others in my sample. Yet neither Shakespeare nor a New Historicist offers, I would think, an ideal model for what a student writer might write about Shakespeare.

A psychology textbook—despite being dry, positivistic, and vulnerable to unintended parody—at least offers students some version of what their own prose might look like. But in a literature class, the only indication of how a student's own knowledge making should proceed may come orally. Lucille McCarthy's ethnographic study of a student in three courses indicates that in a poetry class "Dave's primary concern was to get the right interpretation of the poem, 'the true meaning' as he phrased it. And as Dave wrote, he assumed that his professor knew the true meaning" (246). With this focus on meaning, rather than on text making, the results are not surprising: "Dave never got his own essay structure; rather, he worked down the poem, explicating from beginning to end" (248).

The competing goals of informing, engaging, and initiating that shape intermediary prose contribute to these tensions, but academics should be able to make some progress by sorting out more clearly what these goals entail and what kinds of prose are therefore suitable. It would help to abandon some of the formulations that have restricted us to binary choices—for example, academic or nonacademic, convention or self-expression, accommodation or resistance. If we conceive of degrees from novice to expert practice on a continuum, there may be at least four points along the continuum that novices move through in gaining access to academic discourse:

1. Nonacademic writing
2. Generalized academic writing concerned with stating claims, offering evidence, respecting other's opinions, and learning how to write with authority
3. Novice approximations of particular disciplinary ways of making knowledge
4. Expert, insider prose

We need to explore more carefully how the second and third options might be appropriate at different levels, and how they might differ from each other or from the fourth option, expert prose. Freshman composition might, legitimately, provide a place for both nonacademic writing and a generalized academic prose without venturing further in the direction of any particular disciplinary ways of writing or specialized disciplinary language (Bartholomae; Elbow, "Reflections"; and Dillon seem to endorse this option).

The third point on the continuum is harder to describe but important to explore further; David Russell has highlighted the need for integrating writing into the disciplines in ways that draw on increasingly sophisticated levels of disciplinary understanding (281). If literary interpretation, a historian's understanding of change over time, or a social scientist's sense of explanation are at the heart of what Kinneavy has termed their disciplinary "axiomatics" (18), then instruction needs to aim toward those axiomatics, and novice writers in those fields will be disadvantaged, whether they realize it or not, by failure to comprehend the axiomatics of the disciplines. Novices may need help at this third level as soon as they are assigned essays in courses like history or literature; surely they will need such help in their fields of concentration. I hope that my discussions in the preceding chapters will begin to point toward what might be essential in a novice approximation of professionals' crucial knowledge- and text-making practices.

For graduate students and young professionals, access to professional employment and rewards will require familiarity with the axiomatics in a more exacting and elaborated way. For instance, work with advanced foreign students entering the sciences appears to require far more detailed and explicit understanding of writing practices than most English-speaking professionals would be able to give about their own prose (see, for instance, Hopkins and Dudley-Evans, Swales, Adams Smith, West). But if English-speaking students in the humanities or social sciences appear not to need such explicit help, that appearance may be deceptive. As Patricia Sullivan has demonstrated, graduate students may struggle in confusion if they cannot satisfy their mentors' inexplicit standards. Even after the Ph.D., some young professionals may never know why their fledgling articles are rejected at journals. Whenever qualitative judgments are made about writing, the only fair way to provide access to the rewards involved is to make explicit the principles on which such judgments are made. The lack of attention academics have paid to understanding textual practices in the social sciences and humanities is the best possible guarantee of capriciousness in the system of academic rewards.

Opposition to initiating students into the discourse of the academy usually has its source either in the assumption that academic writing is itself harmful (e.g., too adversarial, too stuffy, too rational, too male, too ready to privilege limited modes of thinking) or that initiating students into discipline-specific ways of writing is too overwhelming or too difficult. The former is an argument that I hope this book helps indirectly to address; many of the complaints about academic writing are based on very slim analysis of academic texts themselves. But the second complaint about initiating students shows a concern with means rather than ends. We need to separate the two concerns and decide, first, whether we want to let students in on our secrets or not and, second, how we can do so most effectively.

If we decide some form of initiation is appropriate, we need not do everything at once. But there still remains the question of how to initiate students into the appropriate stage. Berkenkotter and Huckin caution that genre knowledge is situated knowledge, best "picked up" through immersion, rather than taught. Kate Ronald's account of students' anxiety when asked, as outsiders, to analyze unfamiliar disciplinary conventions should serve to reinforce the caution Berkenkotter and Huckin express; it is entering the disciplinary conversation, rather than analyzing its conventions, that leads to understanding.

If immersion in the disciplinary conversation is essential, then we need to think clearly about the sorts of academic prose we immerse students in. If we ask them to read narrative, they are likely to write narrative. If we ask them to read intermediary, textbook prose that conveys information rather than makes new knowledge, students are unlikely to understand what more genuine knowledge making will look like. The issue of initiation is extremely complex, but understanding the functions and effects of varying kinds of academic prose is an essential first step.

Professional Self-Monitoring and Competing Prose Styles

Concern about the consequences of professional prose should not be limited to its consequences for students. The effectiveness of professional prose and its ethical consequences for professionals are also legitimate issues. For instance, academics still frequently launch attacks on highly epistemic or nominalized academic writing despite the strong connections existing between text-level goals and sentence-level patterns. Such attacks might be judged favorably as instances of responsible professional self-monitoring—i.e., professionals scrutinizing their own practices with an eye to improving efficiency, clarifying goals, and assuring meritocratic procedures for rewarding the best work within a profession. Viewed less favorably, these repeated attacks may indicate either failure to move beyond simplistic understandings of rhetoric or built-in incentives toward wrangling. I suspect that each of these causes is involved, but the wrangling and oversimplification can be diverted toward a more useful kind of self-monitoring if discourse communities better understand the functions of differing styles.

Foremost in any debate about styles should be the question of purpose. If a discourse community aims at making knowledge for solving disciplinary problems and then compacting that knowledge efficiently, the epistemic and synoptic or nominalized style will be the preferred style. Using that style, academics can efficiently review the literature in the field, foreground the connections between previous and current work, warrant inferences, and rely on conventionalized conceptual tools (methods, concepts) to be understood quickly and similarly within the discourse community. This is not to say that all social scientists who hold the same communicative ideal, for instance, will be equally skilled at using the epistemic style. Some will fall into more tedious nominalization than others. We ought to consider the verbal style preferable to the nominal style whenever the verbal style can be used to communicate what the writer needs to communicate. We should learn to distinguish between necessary nominalization—or necessary epistemic accounting—and stuffy, pretentious nominalization that impedes communication without advancing knowledge.[3] Close scrutiny of the difference between more and less successful epistemic practice should be a subject for further research by discourse analysts as well as by those concerned to monitor their own professional practices. But discourse analysts and academics from the social sciences and humanities should be ready to dismiss blanket condemnations of the epistemic style itself.

Critiques of academic writing come most often from the humanities, where, as I have suggested, competing goals are already far more evident than in attachment research and where more complicated, discordant expectations are involved. Many of the critiques made by humanists would not advance the goals of a discourse community like that of attachment research. Richard Marius's 1990 critique "On Academic Discourse," for instance, demonstrates the continuing currency of humanists' preference for the dynamic style with its clear agents, strong active verbs, and sentences that "move from short to long constituents" (Vande Kopple, "Rhetoric" 338). Marius criticizes literary critical writing for being "devoid of the sense of language as figure and image" and having "no sensory language, no active metaphorical verbs, nothing that takes advantage of the resources of language to make us respond to it from the memories of our experience" (31). As I hope I have demonstrated, sensory language and active metaphorical verbs are likely to play a very small role in epistemic prose; they will play a larger role in narrative, but narrative aims at something other than knowledge making. So although Marius's critique appears accurate in its analysis, it also seems largely irrelevant to knowledge-making "academic discourse" in general. It is relevant to academic discourse within literary studies, however, if the purpose of literary study is not primarily to make knowledge.

In history, analogous critiques have been focused less on the epistemic style than on whether history can engage a nonspecialist public. Just as in literary studies, however, the critiques often fail to connect rhetorical purpose to style. I have already discussed Bailyn's conviction that historians need to communicate better with a lay audience; Peter Novick describes a number of similar expressions of disciplinary dismay in the 1980s (578–79). Hamerow has discussed the "bureaucratization" of history as sacrificing history's previous role "of establishing a link between what was and what had been, between the individual and the community. It provided insight into human destiny . . . helped create a feeling of shared experience between generations . . . seemed to satisfy a profound instinctive yearning to see human society as the outcome not of some haphazard aggregate of random contingencies but of a long, slow process of organic growth" (658).

But although historians may wish to communicate with the public and the public may yearn for a greater sense of historical understanding, the ramifications of professionalization cannot be understood, evaluated, or even resisted without understanding the kinds of connections I discuss here—connections between purpose and prose style, text level and sentence level, epistemology and readership. Keys to the split between professionals and public are to be found not in whether professionals desire to communicate or whether they are able to find better communicative devices, but in deeply rooted disciplinary practices such as "the rise in evidential standards" that Megill and McCloskey point to in explaining the split (233).

Critiques of academic writing coming from literary studies are particularly interesting because of literature's traditional interest in style and because the range of proposed, but competing, alternatives bears so directly on questions of purpose. Marius's criticism of writing "devoid of the sense of language as figure and image" is directed at sentences like the following: "Feminist theories of pedagogy, too, involve a critique of masterful meaning and an interest in the resistance to reductive appropriation" (31). He finds it paradoxical that this feminist argument endorses the realm of the personal, on the one hand, and, on the other, is written in a style so "dreary" and so "captured by an older, male-dominated academic rhetoric" that it "seem[s] content to address only a tiny inner circle" (30–31). Marius implies, then, that knowledge making is not central to academic literary writing; he does not foreground the knowledge-making functions that are typically practiced in a circle of initiates. Instead, he privileges "kinship" between reader and writer and movement away from the depersonalized abstraction of "male-dominated academic rhetoric" (31).

As an example of more personal and verbal style, Marianna Torgovnick has offered the following passage that "made [her] feel like a writer, not just a critic" after she wrote it:

> Malinowski's body looks like Lord Jim's. It's cased rigidly in white or beige trousers and shirt that sometimes become stained a muddy brown. When this happens, Malinowski summons his servants and has the clothes washed, immediately. For his clothes somehow seem to him an important part of his body, not just a covering for it.
> It's a small body, well fed but not kindly disposed enough toward itself to put on flesh. It has a narrow chest—pale, with just a few hairs and no nipples to speak of. It has thin legs yearning for massive thighs; in fact, if this man does put on weight in later life (and he may) it will show in his thighs first. The buttocks lie flat, unwelcoming, with maybe a stray pimple. The penis is a center of anxiety for him but is in fact no smaller—and no bigger—than anyone else's. It's one of the few points of identification he can settle on between his body and theirs. (25)

This passage has exclusively phenomenal sentence subjects; all but one would be categorized as Class One "Particulars" for their direct reference to a specific person or concrete object. The passage resembles narrative, rather than knowledge making prose; its narrative quality does not, of course, preclude its being highly speculative, but it does mitigate against sustained professional negotiation over the legitimacy of specific academic claims.

Torgovnick acknowledges that the boring "thus-and-therefore style" she displaces might be appropriate "in an era when less criticism was published and the circle of critics was small enough to allow its members to believe they were contributing to the building of a common edifice," yet her reasoning virtually discounts the possibility of such common edifices (26–27):

> . . . It seems pretty clear to me that if all we want to do is to write for professional advancement, to write for a fairly narrow circle of critics

who exist within the same disciplinary boundaries as we do, there is nothing really wrong with the traditional academic style. It fact, it's the right style, the inevitable style, because it says, in every superfluous detail and in every familiar move, You don't need to read me except to write your own project; I am the kind of writing that does not want to be heard.

But when critics want to be read, and especially when they want to be read by a large audience, they have to court their readers. (27)

Key elements of this argument signal either disarray and solipsism in professionalized literary criticism or else confusion about the ways that epistemic and synoptic academic style functions. First, Torgovnick's implication that writing for a narrow discourse community might serve only for self-advancement does not necessarily follow; work in attachment research illustrates that a narrow discourse community can advance knowledge, however much it may also contribute to professional self-advancement. Second, the epistemic and synoptic style is not characterized by "superfluous detail" since, as Halliday indicates, the synoptic style has evolved for the sake of efficiency. Third, the synoptic style is not meant to be savored in the way a narrative would, but it is certainly, among scientists and social scientists, meant to be read. Torgovnick's misconceptions about the synoptic style are symptomatic of peculiarities of current academic literary study: the particularism of subject matter that helps preclude consensual progress, the professional splintering Graff has illustrated, lack of traditions for epistemic textual negotiation, and strong remnants of a traditional interest in dynamic prose styles.

Yet opposing assumptions about purpose may also be found among literary academics. Fredric Jameson has defended the appearance of heaviness in his style by arguing that he is involved in knowledge making like that in the sciences:

[I]t is always surprising how many people in other disciplines still take a relatively belle-lettristic view of the problems of culture and make the assumption, which they would never make in the area of nuclear physics, linguistics, symbolic logic, or urbanism, that such problems can still be laid out with all the leisurely elegance of a coffee-table magazine. . . . [W]hy should there be any reason to feel that these problems [of cultural theory] are less complex than those of bio-chemistry? ("Interview" 87–88)

Jameson's analogy here is arguable: that both the knowledge problems and, consequently, the style of cultural studies resemble the problems and style of the sciences in their complexity. I have already suggested ways in which academic knowledge problems may differ as a result of differences in generalizability and particularism; the difference lies not in complexity *per se*, but in the kind of complexity. Jameson's own stylistic complexity, in fact, arises not from the epistemic features typical of attachment research but from a complex syntax not typical of the sciences.

In the following example, for instance, Jameson's sentence length and complexity does not derive from an epistemic focus on a community of knowledge makers:

> Certainly the first half of *Lord Jim* is one of the most breathtaking exercises in nonstop textual production that our literature has to show, a self-generating sequence of sentences for which narrative and narrator are mere pretexts, the realization of a mechanism of well-nigh random narrative free association, in which the aleatory and seemingly uncontrollable, unverifiable generation of new detail and new anecdotal material out of the old—all the while filling in the exposition, so that it ends up presenting the narrative content as exhaustively as any representational aesthetic—obeys a logic of its own, as yet unidentified in this text taken by itself, but which in the hindsight of the emergent textual aesthetic of our own time we can clearly see to be textuality born fully grown. (*Political* 219)

This sentence shows some kinship with the nominalized style because of the main verb ("is") and the nonconcrete verbs of the embedded clauses. Yet it is syntactically far longer and more complex than most epistemic prose in the psychology sample. At 129 words in length, it is certainly longer than the mean academic sentence length of 24.9 words in the study by Broadhead, Berlin, and Broadhead (231), and Vande Kopple's characterization of the nominal style as involving complex noun phrases but relatively short predicates and complements would not apply here. The sentence shows none of the epistemic foregrounding of disciplinary negotiation seen in the psychology sample but is characterized, instead, by a piling up of final free modifiers at the end of the sentence in a way not characteristic of scientific writing.[4]

Although the Jameson example lacks the epistemic markers seen in attachment research, it still presents a greater challenge to readers than the "verbal" style might. To make linguistically and rhetorically informed evaluations of apparently complex academic style, then, requires at least three kinds of distinctions: (1) different kinds of complexity have different linguistic manifestations; (2) understanding the effects of complexity upon readers involves understanding and evaluating disciplinary goals; and (3) even if a specialist audience is targeted, there may be a point at which complexity becomes nonfunctional for knowledge making within a community of specialists.

Readers are an important consideration in any discussion of style. Jameson's defense of his style links its difficulty to the disciplinary problems of cultural theory, but we have indications that the intended readers of scientific writing do not find nominalized style difficult. The strings of noun phrases used by one attachment researcher probably become familiar to another attachment researcher and are then processed in much the way simpler nouns would be. By comparison, Jameson's densely embedded clauses and final free modifiers might have entirely different effects. Evaluating academic styles in relation to readers, then, involves two separate issues: whether a style is efficient and whether it is exclusionary.

The issue of efficiency raises the question of whether efficiency is valued within a particular field. The scientist's standardized noun phrases and epistemic focus promote agreement or agreed upon procedures for negotiating disagreement about knowledge claims. The epistemic style of attachment research can, similarly, be said to have evolved for the sake of disciplinary efficiency. But it is questionable whether Mullaney's and Greenblatt's point-last organization or Jameson's complex style have evolved for communicative efficiency of the kind attachment researchers might prize. So although Jameson likens his difficult style to that of scientific writing, we have no reason to believe the two resemble each other.

The issue of exclusion has been raised in several forms that are often collapsed into one, but we ought to consider at least three possible sets of readers: the nonacademic public, academics outside the field of specialization, and academics within the field of specialization. Historians' laments about not reaching the public or some feminists' concerns about reaching non academic women focus on whether academic prose is exclusionary for a nonacademic public. The analysis I have offered throughout this book suggests that such concerns may involve serious misunderstanding about the function of professional prose.

If one turns to academics outside the field of specialization, the issue in the social sciences should involve whether prose that is designed to create and compact knowledge needs to be readable to academics in other fields. Presumably attachment researchers might progress on their disciplinary problem by reading material from closely related fields of specialization such as temperament or clinical studies of family interaction. There will be psychologists who specialize in other areas (like peer relations or aggression) who occasionally need to read the literature on attachment. But there will also be psychologists in fields like cognition or physiology who would not have occasion to read work in attachment. Similarly, the attachment researcher might have occasion to read work on cognition in order to develop cognitive models of attachment or might read physiological psychology in order to work on the physiological correlates of attachment. When reading in these specialties outside attachment research, the attachment researcher might not be concerned with the same fine-tuned distinctions that a specialist in the field would care about. The issue of exclusion would probably not arise.

In history or literary studies, questions about exclusion become more complex whenever academics feel the phenomena they study should be widely known and appreciated for reasons of general importance. Because such fields have goals additional to the goal of making knowledge, they tend to privilege greater access to the material they write about. A number of recent literary commentators have suggested that, even among professionals in literature, academic literary style may involve exclusion whenever it goes beyond optimal communication for reasons involving power or self-display.

Such critiques are often combined with a desire to reach a wider audience and a critique of the seeming evils of professionalism. Cathy Popkin, for instance, has objected to the "barrage of assurance and self-importance" in " 'yackademic' assault" (173). Olivia Frey has advocated "a nurturing relationship" among writers (517). Jane Tompkins would prefer a criticism that "would always take off from personal experience" and "be in some way a chronicle of my hours and days" (126). The *Chronicle of Higher Education* has hyperbolically hailed this "new brand of scholarship" involving "getting personal in print" (Heller A8). Camille Paglia has gained attention by flamboyant charges, such as that "Academe needs deprofessionalization and de-yuppification" (B1).

Critiques of the academy and suggestions of the importance of resistance have been too plentiful for me to examine here. But several recurring elements of the critiques deserve to be addressed in the light of descriptive studies of the type I have offered here. Three charges are frequently made about academic writing: (1) that argument is given too much importance, (2) that academics are unkind in critiquing each others' work, and (3) that too much importance is placed on objectivity.

These critiques can be considered misinformed and provincial. Coming from literary studies where, in some instances, narrative has usurped knowledge making, self-display has replaced epistemic accounting, and objectivity is routinely used as a whipping boy, the charges do not ring true. It is at least equally possible that academics ought to prefer better arguments, more extensive negotiations about professional contributions, and more objective scrutiny of the discursive practices in any discourse community. As academics, we ought, indeed, to raise questions about how we affect each other and whether we have become a group who blight and wither each other by adopting an adversarial ethos. But we also ought to consider whether self-display and nonepistemic, exclusionary, point-last prose have their own blighting effects—and, if so, whether such effects arise from commitment to rational negotiation within a discourse community or lack of such commitment.

The charges coming especially from literary studies should be seen as reflecting the tensions I have already discussed. Perhaps in the social sciences the tendency toward professional self-display is kept in check—though not altogether muted—by epistemic conventions working together with well-defined disciplinary problems to sift what contributes to communal problem solving from what does not. By this argument, a similar tendency toward professional self-display may exist in the humanities without the same kinds of checks on it. The lesser importance of epistemic conventions may make individual self-assertion relatively more important than communal negotiation. And the partially epideictic goals of celebrating literature or history may easily mutate into related epideictic goals of self-display. If there is no "truth"—however elusive—to aim for and no well-defined disciplinary problem to contribute to, there are correspondingly fewer checks upon self-assertion and self-display.

We need more descriptive, rhetorically and linguistically informed research into academic writing in the humanities and social sciences if we are going to explore how academic practices vary, how we may expand access to professional rewards, how we are to use the full range of our abilities effectively, and how we are to confront our knowledge problems more clearly.

Appendix
Notes
References
Index

APPENDIX

The Sample

The sample consists of journal-length articles written in the 1980s and published in key disciplinary forums. One article (Howard) in the literature sample appeared first in an edited collection, and another (Greenblatt) first appeared in a journal, but the version used here was altered and reprinted in an edited collection. In choosing articles, I focused on writers who cited each other or were in other ways demonstrably participating in the same subdisiplinary discourse.

Articles from the sample subfields were as follows:

Psychology

Belsky, Jay, and Michael J. Rovine. "Nonmaternal Care in the First Year of Life and the Security of Infant-Parent Attachment." *Child Development* 59 (1988): 157–67.

Carlson, Vicki, Dante Cicchetti, Douglas Barnett, and Karen Braunwald. "Disorganized/Disoriented Attachment Relationships in Maltreated Infants." *Developmental Psychology* 25 (1989): 525–31.

Cohn, Deborah A. "Child-Mother Attachment of Six-Year-Olds and

Social Competence at School." *Child Development* 61 (1990): 152–62.

Egeland, Byron, and L. Alan Sroufe. "Attachment and Early Maltreatment." *Child Development* 52 (1981): 44–52.

History

Archer, Richard. "New England Mosaic: A Demographic Analysis for the Seventeenth Century." *William and Mary Quarterly* 3rd ser. 47 (1990): 477–502.

Ditz, Toby L. "Ownership and Obligation: Inheritance and Patriarchal Households in Connecticut, 1750–1820." *William and Mary Quarterly* 3rd ser. 47 (1990): 235–65.

Tracy, Patricia J. "Re-considering Migration Within Colonial New England." *Journal of Social History* 23 (1989): 93–113.

Waters, John J. "Family, Inheritance, and Migration in Colonial New England: The Evidence from Guilford, Connecticut." *William and Mary Quarterly* 3rd ser. 39 (1982): 64–86.

Literature

Greenblatt, Stephen. "Invisible Bullets: Renaissance Authority and its Subversion, *Henry IV* and *Henry V*." *Political Shakespeare: New Essays in Cultural Materialism*. Ed. Jonathan Dollimore and Alan Sinfield. Ithaca: Cornell UP, 1985. 18–47.

Howard, Jean E. "Renaissance Antitheatricality and the Politics of Gender and Rank in *Much Ado About Nothing*." *Shakespeare Reproduced: The Text in History and Ideology*. Ed. Jean E. Howard and Marion F. O'Connor. New York: Methuen, 1987. 163–87.

Montrose, Louis A. " 'Shaping Fantasies': Figurations of Gender and Power in Elizabethan Culture." *Representations* 2 (1983): 61–94.

Mullaney, Steven. "Strange Things, Gross Terms, Curious Customs: The Rehearsal of Cultures in the Late Renaissance." *Representations* 3 (1983): 40–67. Reprinted in *Representing the English Renaissance*. Ed. Stephen Greenblatt. Berkeley: U of California P, 1988. 65–92.

NOTES

1. Introduction

1. Among the conflicting philosophies contributing to the writing-across-the-curriculum movement are (1) the desire to initiate novices into the conventions of the disciplines; and (2) the desire to increase access to complex disciplinary knowledge by removing some of its difficulties. For discussion of these and other conflicting assumptions, see David Russell, Chris Anson, or the collected articles in *Writing, Teaching, and Learning in the Disciplines* edited by Anne Herrington and Charles Moran.

2. See Susan Miller (*Carnivals*) on the low status of composition studies within the university, Robert J. Connors ("Overwork") on some of the history by which writing courses came to be associated with an underclass of instructors, Sue Ellen Holbrook on the feminization of composition studies, and Ellen Strenski on the pressures operating against writing-across-the-curriculum at research universities. Russell's study of writing in the disciplines discusses how confining formal writing instruction to marginalized general composition courses

has helped universities attempt to satisfy the competing goals of expanding access (equity) and excellence.

3. Throughout I will use the word "text" to refer to the articles and books that are the primary knowledge-making textual activity of the professional academic. I will not use the word "text" to refer to "textbooks" unless I so indicate explicitly. Textbooks have altogether different textual properties from those of the primary knowledge-making academic texts. I will return to some of the problems entailed by the gap between textbooks and texts in chapter 7.

4. Patricia Sullivan's study of faculty attitudes toward writing in graduate literature courses suggests how much literary scholars marginalize the role of writing, take for granted the transparency of academic writing, and assume their graduate students can guess what kinds of topics and argumentative structures might be appropriate to the disciplinary study of literature.

5. In refering to "consensus" here, I do not mean to imply there is thorough agreement on all the details of the controversies about interpretation, relativism, science, professionalism, and so forth. But within these controversies, there appears to be some common ground, and it is this common ground on which I focus.

6. See Russell's history of writing in the disciplines.

7. There are also more positive arguments proposed from studies in the rhetoric of inquiry; for some of the variations of approach to the rhetoric of inquiry, see the essays collected by Nelson, Megill, and Mc-Closkey or those collected by Simons. McGee and Lyne describe four routes leading to different rhetorics of inquiry. See also Greg Myers's discussion in chapter 1 or *Writing Biology*, or see George Dillon's discussion of variants of the "it's all rhetoric" argument. Dillon suggests such arguments can lead in disparate directions (5–6).

8. The sample Fahnestock and Secor examined consisted of articles published between 1978 and 1982, a transitional period in literary criticism influenced by both older New Criticism and newer poststructuralist theory. The sample I examine in chapters 5 and 6 comes from the 1980s and exemplifies "New Historicist" writing whose intellectual influences vary from the articles Fahnestock and Secor examined.

9. In classical rhetoric, the epideictic is distinguished from the deliberative and forensic. I advocate thinking about the "epideictic" as a tendency, rather than a category, partly to avoid superimposing the categories of deliberative and forensic on less epideictic academic writing. Carolyn Miller's discussion of "Genre as Social Action" clari-

fies the importance of distinguishing between closed and open categorization. I assume that open categorization is particularly important with academic writing because variations within academic writing have evolved in relation to the growth of science, increasing professionalization of knowledge, and the growth of the research university. Closed categories might imply that classical modes have existed all along as something like receptacles waiting for academic ideas to be poured into.

10. Philosophers have disagreed in their definitions of rationality, some emphasizing irrationality more than others (e.g., Feyerabend). Toulmin (*Human Understanding*) has argued that philosophy, from early in its history, equated rationality with logicality and therefore stressed formal systems of axioms and principles. For a useful discussion of how these strands in philosophy connect and how, despite apparent disagreements, there is a broad consensus of the sort I describe, see Richard Bernstein. See also Rorty and Giere.

11. According to Susan Cozzens, citation analysts have switched their unit of analysis from the discipline to the subdisciplinary specialty; their reasons are similar to mine.

2. Patterns in Disciplinary Variation

1. The term "human sciences" could be used here to refer to the social sciences and humanities, but since I consider these to be only rough designations and since I examine work in smaller discourse communities, the terms "social sciences" and "humanities" seem useful: they may not infallibly predict what kind of inquiry or text-making comes under their headings, but they continue to be used to organize and refer to clusters of disciplines in the academy.

2. On the importance of research programs or research traditions, see Lakatos and Laudan, respectively. Laudan, for instance, distinguishes between theories and research traditions; research traditions may contain competing theories, but they are held together by the problems scientists in the field consider important.

3. See Katherine Rowan's account of the different types of informative discourse and their subtypes.

4. *American Literature*, for instance, had an index of 4%, *English Literary History* had 8%, and *Studies in English Literature* had 8% (Price 16–21).

5. Kuhn used the term "puzzle-solving" in connection with normal science; I consider it a synonym for problem solving and will use the latter term. See Bernstein on Kuhn and his critics and the debates over rationality and incommensurability; Bernstein argues that Kuhn never meant to claim that scientific inquiry is irrational but to shift the understanding of what constitutes rationality. For work in the rhetoric of inquiry that argues against dichotomizing rhetoric and rationality, see Brown or Nelson.

6. When quoting from sample articles in literature and history, I will abbreviate footnotes and insert them in brackets in my text in order to avoid confusion with my own footnotes. Since part of my concern is how academics in a subfield use others' work in order to make progress on common disciplinary problems, I have not removed them altogether; where relevant, I will comment on how the footnotes serve to adjudicate or compact disciplinary work. Archer's footnote, in this instance, illustrates how much less compact and discrete individual historians' contributions to a disciplinary conversation may be than the contributions of a psychologist who can refer to specific findings by specific contributors. Despite Archer's reference here to "discrete studies," he does not name any or associate any particular studies with particular findings.

7. See Carol Berkenkotter's "Paradigm Debates, Turf Wars, and the Conduct of Sociocognitive Inquiry in Composition" for a discussion of divisive quarrels in the field of composition studies over qualitative versus quantitative methodology—and a plea for tolerance.

8. I am using the term "New Criticism" somewhat loosely. As successive waves of critics have risen to prominence since the 1960s, they have used New Criticism as a whipping boy (see Graff's discussion of this phenomenon, 241): deconstructionists have tended to find older New Critical interpretations naïve, and New Historicists now tend to critique New Criticism as politically conservative. These critiques take for granted, however, benefits of the New Criticism that successive interpretive schools have been able to draw upon. In its heyday, the New Criticism had to assert itself against older historical and textual criticism that tended to take textual explication or analysis for granted. Aside from the particular social or historical milieu in which New Criticism arose and aside from its tendencies to focus on ambivalence or to find organic unity in all texts, the New Criticism validated close reading and textual explication in ways that opened up the fascinations of literature for many students. For discussion of this complex history, see Graff.

9. In my *Anthony Trollope* (1987) I argued that *Mr. Scarborough's Family* is about aging, an aging man's frustrated desire to protect his sons through passing on an inheritance. Because of the nature of his realism, Trollope strikes me as an extreme (and therefore interesting) example of a novelist offering unusually wide possibilities of interpretation. That also was partially responsible for the drop in his reputation at the end of the nineteenth century because, in contrast to writers like George Eliot whose abstract ideas are more explicit, Trollope's apparent recounting of mundane realities appeared to contain no abstract ideas worthy of high "art."

10. A 1982 report for the Modern Language Association noted that the number of items in the annual MLA Bibliography had grown exponentially: 10,054 items in 1956, 47,008 in 1979, and 59,000 in 1980 ("Report" 319).

11. There are further, subtler distinctions that can be made about introductions within the sciences and social sciences, but I am concerned here with the more dramatic variations between epistemic and nonepistemic presentation. For further discussion of epistemic introductions, see Swales and Najjar; see also Bazerman's discussion of disciplinary variation in introductions (*Shaping* chapter 2).

3. Attachment Research: Compact Problem Definition in a Conceptually Driven Field

1. In current New Historicism and its British cousin, cultural materialism, one can find claims that Shakespeare has been used in the service of conservative political ideals and therefore that reinterpreting Shakespeare can have political benefits in current situations. Claims of this sort seem to be made in terms of modern needs and therefore must be more difficult to make persuasive with fields focused upon the past.

2. The dates of publication here obscure the lines of descent. Bowlby had been at work on his theory in the 1950s, even though *Attachment* was not published until 1969. The Ainsworth and Wittig study was published in 1969 in a collection from a 1965 seminar and with a forward by Bowlby.

3. The closest the psychologists in the sample come to writing about an individual child is one sentence more concerned with scrupulous accounting for exceptions than with investigating individual, per-

sonalized, or named cases: "Only one baby remained in group C, the dominant pattern at 12 months" (Egeland and Sroufe 50).

4. See Small's discussion of how cited documents in scientific literature become "concept symbols," similarly characterized in citations. This standardizing is another form of disciplinary compacting.

5. Bowlby and Ainsworth originally wrote largely about the child's relationship to the mother. By the 1970s and eighties, we find more references to "caregivers." The shift to "caregivers" is a sign of the increasing importance of the women's movement. Recent attachment research, because it is more differentiated than the early work, may also ask specific questions about mothers who work or attachment to fathers.

6. The developmentalist's interest in "stability" over time involves the validity, reliability, and stability of the psychologist's classifications and descriptions. A child who is classified as "securely attached" in infancy would be predicted to be secure later on; if such a child turns out to be insecure, the psychologist may look for problems with the initial classification system, with the reliability of the classification decision made for the child, with the understanding of the later behavior, or, potentially, with the whole system of explanation. Another source of "instability" could be environmental—for example, changed behavior of the parent(s).

7. By this definition, ethnographic work in anthropology, for instance, may be closer to the humanities than psychology is; the social sciences need not all be considered to operate in the same direction.

4. Colonial New England Social History: The Problematics of Contemporary History Writing

1. For a discussion of Ranke and the "objectivity question," see Peter Novick.

2. For mid-1970s debates on social history, see the Winter 1976 issue of the *Journal of Social History*; for a 1980 overview of the state of social history, see Stearns.

3. One may distinguish (see White, "History") between chronology and narration: chronology presents sequence over time while narrative represents causal sequence over time. But, in any case, the rhetorical organization seemingly most akin to history writing is narration.

4. While the rhetorican may distinguish between narrative and description, the historian appears to find more salience in the distinction between narrative and description on the one hand and analysis on the other. It is useful to begin by accepting the historian's elision of narrative and description in order to see the tension between those *what* foci and the *whys* of analysis.

5. Greven's *Four Generations* was the outgrowth of his dissertation at Harvard where he studied with Bernard Bailyn. Bailyn's students have done a substantial portion of the major work in Colonial American history. Nevertheless, Colonial American history does not grow from so single a line of descent as did attachment research under the influence of Bowlby and then Ainsworth.

6. I have tried to keep the three sets of samples roughly comparable, but since more articles appear in the same subfield in a short period of time in psychology than in literature, I have had to choose more articles from the early 1980s in literature in order to find a set of comparable articles. In order to keep the history and psychology samples in line with the literature sample, then, I have chosen at least one article from the early 1980s for each set.

7. On the connections and differences between community studies of Colonial New England and local history, see Conzen or Kammen.

5. Renaissance New Historicism: Epistemic and Nonepistemic Textual Patterns

1. I have selected the older articles to compare to my current New Historicist sample according to three principles: (1) they should have some historical orientation so that their differences from current New Historicism arise not simply from the difference between aesthetic and historical treatment; (2) they should treat the same Shakespearean plays treated in the current articles in my sample; and (3) they should be both typical and exemplary of criticism of their day—as measured by their still being cited by influential New Historicists. The Barish article, for instance, is cited by Steven Mullaney ("Strange Things") and the Olson article by Louis Montrose ("Shaping Fantasies"). Barish's more recent work (*The Anti-Theatrical Prejudice*, 1981) is cited by Jean Howard as both a "very fine study" and an instance of

older historicist work that assumes "a transhistorical human essence" (Howard, "New Historicism" 20).

2. The apparent congeniality of the interpretive community that Olson and Barish portray may have resulted from a phenomenon particular to post-World War II American universities; Don Wayne has explained the apparently apolitical dimension of the New Criticism as a "way of opening the halls of academe—especially of English departments—to scholars who didn't happen to come to school equipped with English surnames" by emphasizing "principles of unity, universality, and textual autonomy" (53–54).

3. On the differences between British "cultural materialists" and American "New Historicists" see, for instance, Walter Cohen or Don Wayne. Jonathan Dollimore, often cited for his phrase the "subversion-containment debate," is a British "cultural materialist" and editor of *Political Shakespeare*, the volume in which the version of Greenblatt's "Invisible Bullets" I use here appeared in 1985.

4. Levin has written a series of critiques of the New Historicism; in "The Poetics and Politics of Bardicide," he criticizes Dollimore's claims about displacement in *Meaure for Measure* for reasons similar to Neely's—though certainly without describing his as a feminist critique. In "Feminist Thematics and Shakespearean Tragedy" Levin critiqued feminist criticism, so it is interesting to find that, on this issue of displacement, his critiques of 1970s "readings" are analogous both to his critiques of current political readings and to feminist critiques of the New Historicism.

5. There have been a number of critiques of the version of "Invisible Bullets" that appeared originally in *Glyph* in 1981 (e.g., Howard, "New Historicism"; C. Porter). Greenblatt's successive revisions appear to respond to some of the charges that he emphasized "containment" without leaving enough scope for "subversion." I have chosen to use the version printed in Dollimore and Sinfield on the assumption that it represented work typical of Greenblatt and of New Historicism and that, by appearing in book form, it will have been read more often than the *Glyph* version and had more initial impact than the later version in *Shakespearean Negotiations*. Each of the three is representative of Greenblatt's textual style—my primary concern—but I have preferred not to use the latest version, on the assumption that it has been most written over and therefore is, in a sense, a compromised version.

6. In their study of a sample of literary articles from 1978–

82, Fahnestock and Secor found that "the quantity and typicality of evidence were rarely defended" ("Rhetoric of Literary Criticism" 82). Since their sample did not contain New Historicist articles, we may conclude that the problem of accounting for evidence existed before the New Historicism, but the critiques generated by Greenblatt's article suggest that New Historicists have moved farther away from epistemic accounting or have violated some norm of selecting evidence that was implicit in earlier practices.

7. Commenting on Foucault's use of the same generalized "we", Jane Tompkins describes this use of "we" as "Presumptuous because it presumes that we are really like him, and successful because, especially when an author is famous, and even when he isn't, 'our' instinct . . . is to want to cooperate, to be included in the circle the author is drawing so cosily around 'us'. It is chummy, this 'we'. It feels good, for a little while, until it starts to feel coercive, until 'we' are subscribing to things that 'I' don't believe" (132).

8. David Kaufmann sees the quarrels over theory, professionalization, and politicization as functioning to reinforce the necessity of literary study, but he nevertheless sees literary study as a heroically embattled academic subculture: "To practice theory is to help the very divisions and forms of domination that theory seeks to overcome. By the same token, however, to give up critical, truly critical thought in the academy would be to strangle such thought in the only cradle it has left and to sacrifice what we still have of our best hopes" (528).

9. Interestingly, Carter's 1992 suggestions about the rhetoric of display have been accused of being "blandly cynical . . . [and] likely to provoke more anger and despair than the sort of vacuous cheer he apparently intended to promote" (Baldwin 963). Baldwin focuses his critique of Carter on the despair and anger that academics and taxpayers will feel when they understand what Carter has described. Curiously, however, Baldwin does not suggest that Carter was wrong in his analysis. Carter replies that "We benefit society indirectly just by having the conversation" ("Response" 965).

6. Sentence-Level Differences in Disciplinary Knowledge Making

1. The earlier version of this study (*Written Communication* 9 [1992]: 533–69) focused in more detail on the method I propose

for analyzing academic prose; it contains a fuller description of the classification system, coding procedures, training and interrater reliability. I have not reproduced those details here but have, instead, focused on the interconnections between my textual analysis in chapters 3, 4, and 5, and the sentence-level analysis in this chapter.

2. See the appendix of the earlier version of this study (*Written Communication* 9 [1992]) for a detailed description of the coding system, decisions or procedures involved in coding each class of subjects, and procedures for coding sentences such as cleft sentences or questions.

3. Clauses like "It must be noted that," "It is unclear whether," "It should be added that"—all instances of metadiscourse—imply an explicit concern for epistemic weighing and warranting and have, for that reason, been included in Class 4.

4. A sentence like "It is noteworthy that" is also an example of metadiscourse. Because my goal is to identify academic writers' emphasis—or lack of emphasis—on negotiating claims within their research community, it seems appropriate to include instances of metadiscourse within Class 4.

5. Two phenomena during the scoring process indirectly suggest there is greater epistemic ambiguity in literary studies: the greatest ambiguities (and/or interrater disagreements) arose in deciding whether some items belonged in Class 3 or Class 4, and these ambiguous cases arose more often in scoring the literature sample. Furthermore, it took longer to score the literary articles, another sign of more frequent ambiguity in that sample.

7. Professional Styles and Their Consequences

1. The distinction between "nominal" and "verbal" derives from Rulon Wells. See Cluett, or Halliday ("Order of Nature"), for further refinement and renaming of the nominal versus verbal categorization.

2. Though it seems certain that epistemic sentence subjects work in tandem with noun clauses and linking or passive verbs to create the synoptic style, further research would be needed to clarify what portion of the problem-compacting work of a field like attachment research is carried on by epistemic sentence subjects and what portion by lengthy noun phrases. The results Vande Kopple reports ("Noun Phrases" 331) are enough different from the results Quirk,

Greenbaum, Leech, and Svartvik report (*Comprehensive* 1351) to suggest that disciplinary and other rhetorical differences may be involved in some scientific texts' having higher percentages of complex and multiply modified noun phrases than others. Dubois's study of the piling up of modifiers to the left of a head noun suggests that the scientists she studied were able to move nouns from rheme to theme position in relation to what a reader could presuppose at any point in the text. This suggests that relatively compact, urban research fields may tend to use more prenominal modification than less compact, urban fields. The sentence I quote from attachment research (Cohn 152) has a Class 3 subject that is relatively brief compared to some of the noun strings found in scientific writing; it seems likely that the epistemic work of attachment research is carried on by the complementary functioning of two elements: (1) epistemic (Class 4 and 5) subjects, and (2) noun phrases within phenomenal (Class 2 and 3) subjects that are relatively longer than the phenomenal sentence subjects in literary or historical writing but briefer than those in some of the sciences.

3. Despite his account of the advantages of the synoptic style, Vande Kopple also explains some of its disadvantages ("Noun Phrases"). For cases in which the nominal style has been valued not for its communicative power but for its pretentiousness, see Hake and Williams (on how essays are evaluated by English teachers) or Brown and Herndl (on writing in corporations). Williams's suggestions in *Style* are useful for writers attempting to avoid unnecessary nominalization.

4. Broadhead, Berlin, and Broadhead use Christensen's term "free modifier" in investigating syntactic differences among different academic disciplines. In the sentence I quote from Jameson, the final free modifiers are "a self-generating sequence of sentences . . . pretexts" and "the realization of a mechanism of well-nigh random narrative free association" which latter then has further clauses embedded in it. Broadhead et al. report that there were significant syntactical differences from literature (at one extreme) to science and engineering (at the other extreme); in literary writing they found more multistructure sentences in which "final-position modifiers play a substantially greater role, particularly for supplying details or other modification and development of ideas" (239).

REFERENCES

Ackerman, John M. "Reading, Writing, and Knowing: The Role of Disciplinary Knowledge in Comprehension and Composing." *Research in the Teaching of English* 25 (1991): 133–77.

Adams Smith, Diana E. "Medical Discourse: Aspects of Author's Comment." *ESP Journal* 3 (1984): 25–36.

Ainsworth, Mary D. Salter, Mary C. Blehar, Everett Waters, and Sally Wall. *Patterns of Attachment: A Psychological Study of the Strange Situation.* Hillsdale, NJ: Erlbaum, 1978.

Ainsworth, Mary D. Salter, and Barbara A. Wittig. "Attachment and Exploratory Behavior of One-Year-Olds in a Strange Situation." *Determinants of Infant Behaviour IV.* Ed. B. M. Foss. London: Methuen, 1969. 111–36.

Anson, Chris M. "Toward a Multidimensional Model of Writing in the Academic Disciplines." *Advances in Writing Research, Volume Two: Writing in Academic Disciplines.* Ed. David A. Jolliffe. Norwood, NJ: Ablex, 1988. 1–33.

Appleby, Joyce. "Value and Society." *Colonial British America: Essays in the New History of the Early Modern Era.* Ed. Jack P.

Greene and J. R. Pole. Baltimore: Johns Hopkins UP, 1984. 290–316.

apRoberts, Ruth. *The Moral Trollope*. Athens: Ohio UP, 1971.

Archer, Richard. "New England Mosaic: A Demographic Analysis for the Seventeenth Century." *William and Mary Quarterly* 3rd ser. 47 (1990): 477–502.

Bailyn, Bernard. "The Challenge of Modern Historiography." *American Historical Review* 87 (1982): 1–24.

Baker, Sheridan. *The Practical Stylist*. 3rd ed. New York: Crowell, 1973.

Baldwin, Dean. "A Comment on 'Scholarship as Rhetoric of Display.'" *College English* 54 (1992): 963–65.

Barish, Jonas A. "The Turning Away of Prince Hal." [*Shakespeare Studies* I, 1965, reprinted in *Henry the Fourth, Parts I and II: Critical Essays*. Ed. David Bevington. New York: Garland, 1986. 277–88.

Bartholomae, David. "Inventing the University." *When a Writer Can't Write: Studies in Writer's Block and Other Composing-Process Problems*. Ed. Mike Rose. New York: Guilford, 1985. 134–65.

Barton, Anne. "Perils of Historicism." *New York Review of Books* 28 Mar. 1991: 53–56.

Battersby, James L. "Professionalism, Relativism, and Rationality." *PMLA* 107 (1992): 51–64.

Bazerman, Charles. "How Natural Philosophers Can Cooperate: The Literary Technology of Coordinated Investigation in Joseph Priestley's *History and Present State of Electricity (1767)*." *Textual Dynamics in the Professions: Historical and Contemporary Studies of Writing in Professional Communities*. Ed. Charles Bazerman and James Paradis. Madison: U of Wisconsin P, 1991. 13–44.

———. *Shaping Written Knowledge: The Genre and Activity of the Experimental Article in Science*. Madison: U of Wisconsin P, 1988.

Becher, Tony. *Academic Tribes and Territories: Intellectual Enquiry and the Cultures of Disciplines*. Milton Keynes, England: Society for Research into Higher Education and Open UP, 1989.

Belsky, Jay, and Michael J. Rovine. "Nonmaternal Care in the First Year of Life and the Security of Infant-Parent Attachment." *Child Development* 59 (1988): 157–67.

Bender, Thomas. *Community and Social Change in America.* New Brunswick, NJ: Rutgers UP, 1978.

Berkenkotter, Carol. "Paradigm Debates, Turf Wars, and the Conduct of Sociocognitive Inquiry in Composition." *College Composition and Communication* 42 (1991): 151–69.

Berkenkotter, Carol, and Thomas N. Huckin. "Rethinking Genre from a Sociocognitive Perspective." *Written Communication* 10 (1993): [in press].

Berkenkotter, Carol, Thomas N. Huckin, and John Ackerman. "Conventions, Conversations and the Writer: Case Study of a Student in a Rhetoric Ph.D. Program." *Research in the Teaching of English* 22 (1988): 9–44.

Berlin, James A. *Rhetoric and Reality: Writing Instruction in American Colleges, 1900–1985.* Carbondale: Southern Illinois UP, 1987.

————. *Writing Instruction in Nineteenth-Century American Colleges.* Carbondale: Southern Illinois UP, 1984.

Bernstein, Richard J. *Beyond Objectivism and Relativism: Science, Hermeneutics, and Praxis.* Philadelphia: U of Pennsylvania P, 1983.

Bizzell, Patricia. " 'Cultural Criticism': A Social Approach to Studying Writing." *Rhetoric Review* 7 (1989): 224–30.

Boose, Lynda E. "The Family in Shakespeare Studies; or—Studies in the Family of Shakespeareans; or—The Politics of Politics." *Renaissance Quarterly* 40 (1987): 707–42.

Bowlby, John. *Attachment and Loss: Volume I, Attachment.* New York: Basic, 1969.

Bretherton, Inge, and Everett Waters. Preface. *Growing Points of Attachment Theory and Research.* Ed. Inge Bretherton and Everett Waters. Monographs of the Society for Research in Child Development, vol. 50, nos. 1–2, U of Chicago P, 1985.

Broadhead, Glenn J., James A. Berlin, and Marlis Manley Broadhead. "Sentence Structure in Academic Prose and its Implications for College Writing Teachers." *Research in the Teaching of English* 16 (1982): 225–40.

Brodkey, Linda. *Academic Writing as Social Practice.* Philadelphia: Temple UP, 1987.

Brown, Richard Harvey. "Reason as Rhetorical: On Relations Among Epistemology, Discourse, and Practice." *The Rhetoric of the Human Sciences.* Ed. John S. Nelson, Allan Megill, and Donald N. McCloskey. Madison: U of Wisconsin P, 1987. 184–97.

Brown, Robert L., Jr., and Carl G. Herndl. "An Ethnographic Study of Corporate Writing: Job Status as Reflected in Written Text." *Functional Approaches to Writing: Research Perspectives.* Ed. Barbara Couture. Frances Pinter: London, 1986.

Burke, Peter. *Sociology and History.* London: George Allen & Unwin, 1980.

Butler, Christopher S. "Qualifications in Science: Modal Meanings in Scientific Texts." *The Writing Scholar: Studies in Academic Discourse.* Ed. Walter Nash. Newbury Park, CA: Sage, 1990. 137–70.

Carlson, Vicki, Dante Cicchetti, Douglas Barnett, and Karen Braunwald. "Disorganized/Disoriented Attachment Relationships in Maltreated Infants." *Developmental Psychology* 25 (1989): 525–31.

Carter, Michael. "Scholarship as Rhetoric of Display; Or, Why Is Everybody Saying All Those Terrible Things About Us?" *College English* 54 (1992): 303–13.

———. "Response." *College English* 54 (1992): 965–66.

Chase, Geoffrey. "Accommodation, Resistance and the Politics of Student Writing." *College Composition and Communication* 39 (1988): 13–22.

Cluett, Robert. *Prose Style and Critical Reading.* New York: Teachers College P, 1976.

Cockshut, A. O. J. *Anthony Trollope: A Critical Study.* New York: New York UP, 1955; reprint 1968.

Cohen, Walter. "Political Criticism of Shakespeare." *Shakespeare Reproduced: The Text in History and Ideology.* Ed. Jean E. Howard and Marion F. O'Connor. New York: Methuen, 1987. 18–46.

Cohn, Deborah A. "Child-Mother Attachment of Six-Year-Olds and Social Competence at School." *Child Development* 61 (1990): 152–62.

Collins, W. Andrew, and Stanley A. Kuczaj, II. *Developmental Psychology: Childhood and Adolescence.* New York: Macmillan, 1991.

Colomb, Gregory G., and Joseph M. Williams. "Perceiving Structure in Professional Prose: A Multiply Determined Experience." *Writing in Nonacademic Settings.* Ed. Lee Odell and Dixie Goswami. New York: Guilford, 1985. 87–128.

Connors, Robert J. "Overwork/Underpay: Labor and Status of Composition Teachers since 1880." *Rhetoric Review* 9 (1990): 108–25.

Conzen, Kathleen Neils. "Community Studies, Urban History, and

American Local History." *The Past Before Us: Contemporary Historical Writing in the United States.* Ed. Michael Kammen. Ithaca: Cornell UP, 1980. 270–91.

Cozzens, Susan E. "Comparing the Sciences: Citation Context Analysis of Papers from Neuropharmacology and the Sociology of Science." *Social Studies of Science* 15 (1985): 127–53.

Crismore, Avon. "The Rhetoric of Textbooks: Metadiscourse." *Journal of Curriculum Studies* 16 (1984): 279–96.

Crismore, Avon, and Rodney Farnsworth. "Metadiscourse in Popular and Professional Science Discourse." *The Writing Scholar: Studies in Academic Discourse.* Ed. Walter Nash. Newbury Park, CA: Sage, 1990. 118–36.

Crismore, Avon, and William J. Vande Kopple. "Readers' Learning from Prose: The Effects of Hedges." *Written Communication* 5 (1988): 184–202.

Demos, John. *A Little Commonwealth: Family Life in Plymouth Colony.* New York: Oxford UP, 1970.

Dillon, George L. *Contending Rhetorics: Writing in Academic Disciplines.* Bloomington: Indiana UP, 1991.

Ditz, Toby L. "Ownership and Obligation: Inheritance and Patriarchal Households in Connecticut, 1750–1820." *William and Mary Quarterly* 3rd ser. 41 (1990): 235–65.

Dollimore, Jonathan. "Introduction: Shakespeare, Cultural Materialism and the New Historicism." *Political Shakespeare: New Essays in Cultural Materialism.* Ed. Jonathan Dollimore and Alan Sinfield. Ithaca: Cornell UP, 1985. 2–17.

————. "Transgression and Surveillance in *Measure for Measure.*" *Political Shakespeare: New Essays in Cultural Materialism.* Ed. Jonathan Dollimore and Alan Sinfield. Ithaca: Cornell UP, 1985. 72–87.

Dray, William. " 'Explaining What' in History." Reprinted in *Theories of History.* Ed. Patrick Gardiner. New York: Free, 1959. 403–08.

Dubois, Betty Lou. "The Construction of Noun Phrases in Biomedical Journal Articles." *Proceedings of the 3rd European Symposium on LSP: "Pragmatics and LSP."* Ed. Jørgen Høedt, Lita Lundquist, Heribert Picht, and Jacques Qvistgaard. Copenhagen: Copenhagen School of Economics, 1982. 49–65.

Edwards, Lee R. "Women, Energy, and *Middlemarch.*" *Massachusetts Review* 13 (1972): 223–38.

Egeland, Byron, and L. Alan Sroufe. "Attachment and Early Maltreatment." *Child Development* 52 (1981): 44–52.

Eiler, Mary Ann. "Thematic Distribution as a Heuristic for Written Discourse Function." *Functional Approaches to Writing: Research Perspectives.* Ed. Barbara Couture. London: Frances Pinter, 1986. 49–68.

Elbow, Peter. "Reflections on Academic Discourse: How It Relates to Freshmen and Colleagues." *College English* 53 (1991): 135–55.

———. *What Is English?* New York: MLA, and Urbana, Ill.: NCTE, 1990.

Erickson, Peter. "Rewriting the Renaissance, Rewriting Ourselves." *Shakespeare Quarterly* 38 (1987): 327–37.

Fahnestock, Jeanne, and Marie Secor. *A Rhetoric of Argument.* New York: Random, 1982.

———. "The Rhetoric of Literary Criticism." *Textual Dynamics of the Professions: Historical and Contemporary Studies of Writing in Professional Communities.* Ed. Charles Bazerman and James Paradis. Madison: U of Wisconsin P, 1991. 76–96.

———. "The Stases in Scientific and Literary Argument." *Written Communication* 5 (1988): 427–43.

Faigley, Lester. "The Problem of Topic in Texts." *The Territory of Language: Linguistics, Stylistics, and the Teaching of Composition.* Ed. Donald A. McQuade. Carbondale: Southern Illinois UP, 1986. 123–141.

Faigley, Lester, and Kristine Hansen. "Learning to Write in the Social Sciences." *College Composition and Communication* 36 (1985): 140–49.

Feyerabend, Paul. *Against Method: Outline of an Anarchistic Theory of Knowledge.* London: NLB, 1975.

Foucault, Michel. *Discipline and Punish: The Birth of the Prison.* Trans. Alan Sheridan. New York: Knopf, Vintage, 1979.

———. "What Is an Author?" *Language, Counter-Memory, Practice: Selected Essays and Interviews.* Ed. Donald F. Bouchard. Trans. Donald F. Bouchard and Sherry Simon. Ithaca, NY: Cornell UP, 1977. 113–36.

Frey, Olivia. "Beyond Literary Darwinism: Women's Voices and Critical Discourse." *College English* 52 (1990): 507–26.

Gallie, W. B. *Philosophy and the Historical Understanding* 2nd ed. New York: Schocken, 1968.

Garvey, William D., Nan Lin, and Carnot E. Nelson. "Some Comparisons of Communication Activities in the Physical and Social Sciences." *Communication Among Scientists and Engineers.* Ed.

Carnot E. Nelson and Donald K. Pollock. Lexington: Heath, Lexington, 1970. 61–84.

Geertz, Clifford. *The Interpretation of Cultures.* New York: Basic, 1973.

———. *Local Knowledge: Further Essays in Interpretive Anthropology.* New York: Basic, 1983.

———. *Works and Lives: The Anthropologist as Author.* Stanford: Stanford UP, 1988.

Geisler, Cheryl. "Toward a Sociocognitive Model of Literacy: Constructing Mental Models in a Philosophical Conversation." *Textual Dynamics of the Professions: Historical and Contemporary Studies of Writing in Professional Communities.* Ed. Charles Bazerman and James Paradis. Madison: U of Wisconsin P, 1991. 171–90.

Giere, Ronald N. *Explaining Science: A Cognitive Approach.* Chicago: U of Chicago P, 1988.

Gilbert, G. Nigel, and Michael Mulkay. *Opening Pandora's Box: A Sociological Analysis of Scientists' Discourse.* Cambridge: Cambridge UP, 1984.

Graff, Gerald. *Professing Literature: An Institutional History.* Chicago: U of Chicago P, 1987.

Greenblatt, Stephen. "Fiction and Friction." *Reconstructing Individualism: Autonomy, Individuality, and the Self in Western Thought.* Ed. Thomas C. Heller, Morton Sosna, and David E. Wellbery. Stanford: Stanford UP, 1986. 30–52.

———. "The Forms of Power and the Power of Forms in the Renaissance." *Genre* 15 (1982): 1–4.

———. "Invisible Bullets: Renaissance Authority and Its Subversion, *Henry IV* and *Henry V.*" *Political Shakespeare: New Essays in Cultural Materialism.* Ed. Jonathan Dollimore and Alan Sinfield. Ithaca: Cornell UP, 1985. 18–47.

———. *Shakespearean Negotiations: The Circulation of Social Energy in Renaissance England.* Berkeley: U of California P, 1988.

Greven, Philip J., Jr. *Four Generations: Population, Land, and Family in Colonial Andover, Massachusetts.* Ithaca: Cornell UP, 1970.

Gross, Robert A. *The Minutemen and Their World.* New York: Hill, 1976.

Hake, Rosemary L., and Joseph M. Williams. "Style and Its Consequences: Do as I Do, Not as I Say." *College English* 43 (1981): 433–51.

Halliday, M. A. K. "Language and the Order of Nature." *The Linguistics of Writing: Arguments between Language and Literature.* Ed. Nigel Fabb, Derek Attridge, Alan Durant and Colin MacCabe. Manchester: Manchester UP, 1987. 135–54.

Hamerow, Theodore S. "The Bureaucratization of History." *American History Review* 94 (1989): 654–60.

Hansen, Kristine. "Rhetoric and Epistemology in the Social Sciences: A Contrast of Two Representative Texts." *Advances in Writing Research, Volume Two: Writing in Academic Disciplines.* Ed. David A. Jolliffe. Norwood, NJ: Ablex, 1988. 167–210.

Harris, Joseph. "The Idea of Community in the Study of Writing." *College Composition and Communication* 40 (1989): 11–22.

Haswell, Richard H. "Textual Research and Coherence: Findings, Intuition, Application." *College English* 51 (1989): 305–19.

Heller, Scott. "Experience and Expertise Meet in New Brand of Scholarship." *Chronicle of Higher Education* 6 May 1992: A7-A9.

Hempel, Carl G. "The Function of General Laws in History." *Journal of Philosophy* 39 (1942): 35–48; reprinted in *Aspects of Scientific Explanation.* New York: Free Press, 1965. 231–43.

Henretta, James A. "Families and Farms: *Mentalité* in Pre-Industrial America." *William and Mary Quarterly* 3rd ser. 35 (1978): 3–32.

Herrington, Anne J. "Teaching, Writing, and Learning: A Naturalistic Study of Writing in an Undergraduate Literature Course." *Advances in Writing Research, Volume Two: Writing in Academic Disciplines.* Ed. David A. Jolliffe. Norwood, NJ: Ablex, 1988. 133–66.

———. "Writing in Academic Settings: A Study of the Contexts for Writing in Two College Chemical Engineering Courses." *Research in the Teaching of English* 19 (1985): 331–59.

Herrington, Anne, and Charles Moran, eds. *Writing, Teaching, and Learning in the Disciplines.* New York: MLA, 1992.

Hexter, J. H. *Doing History.* Bloomington: Indiana UP, 1971.

Himmelfarb, Gertrude. "Some Reflections on the New History." *American Historical Review* 94 (1989): 661–70.

Hinde, Robert A. *Biological Bases of Human Social Behavior.* New York: McGraw, 1974.

Hoey, Michael. "Overlapping Patterns of Discourse Organization and Their Implications for Clause Relational Analysis in Problem-Solution Texts." *Study Writing: Linguistic Approaches.* Ed.

Charles R. Cooper and Sidney Greenbaum. Beverly Hills: Sage, 1986. 187–214.

Holbrook, Sue Ellen. "Women's Work: The Feminizing of Composition." *Rhetoric Review* 9 (1991): 201–29.

Hopkins, Andy, and Tony Dudley-Evans. "A Genre-Based Investigation of the Discussion Sections in Articles and Dissertations." *English for Specific Purposes* 7 (1988): 113–21.

Howard, Jean E. "The New Historicism in Renaissance Studies." *English Literary Renaissance* 16 (1986): 13–43.

———. "Renaissance Antitheatricality and the Politics of Gender and Rank in *Much Ado About Nothing*." *Shakespeare Reproduced: The Text in History and Ideology*. Ed. Jean E. Howard and Marion F. O'Connor. New York: Methuen, 1987. 163–87.

Huber, Bettina J. "Today's Literature Classroom: Finding from the MLA's 1990 Survey of Upper-Division Courses." *ADE Bulletin* no. 101 (1992): 36–60.

Huckin, Thomas N. "Context-Sensitive Text Analysis." *Methods and Methodology in Composition Research*. Ed. Gesa Kirsch and Patricia A. Sullivan. Carbondale: Southern Illinois UP, 1992. 84–104.

Huckin, Thomas, and Linda Pesante. "Existential *There*." *Written Communication* 5 (1988): 368–91.

Jameson, Fredric. "Interview." *Diacritics* 12 (1982): 72–91.

———. *The Political Unconscious*. Ithaca: Cornell UP, 1981.

Kammen, Michael. *Selvages & Biases: The Fabric of History in American Culture*. Ithaca: Cornell UP, 1987.

Kaufer, David S., and Cheryl Geisler. "Novelty in Academic Writing." *Written Communication* 6 (1989): 286–311.

Kaufmann, David. "The Profession of Theory." *PMLA* 105 (1990): 519–30.

Kincaid, James. *The Novels of Anthony Trollope*. Oxford: Clarendon, 1977.

Kinneavy, James L. "Writing across the Curriculum." *Profession 83*. New York: MLA, 1983.

Kolb, David. "Learning Styles and Disciplinary Differences." *The Modern American College*. Ed. A. Chickering. San Francisco: Jossey-Bass, 1981. 232–55.

Kuhn, Thomas S. *The Structure of Scientific Revolutions*. 2nd ed. Chicago: U. of Chicago P, 1970.

Lakatos, Imre. *The Methodology of Scientific Research Programmes*. Cambridge: Cambridge UP, 1978.

Lamb, M. E., R. A. Thompson, W. Gardner, and E. L. Charnov. *Infant-Mother Attachment: The Origins and Developmental Significance of Individual Differences in Strange Situation Behavior.* Hillsdale, NJ: Erlbaum, 1985.

Langer, Judith A., and Arthur N. Applebee. *How Writing Shapes Thinking: A Study of Teaching and Learning.* Urbana: NCTE, 1987.

Lanham, Richard A. *Revising Prose.* New York: Scribner's, 1979.

Laslett, Peter. *Family Life and Illicit Love in Earlier Generations: Essays in Historical Sociology.* Cambridge: Cambridge UP, 1977.

Latour, Bruno, and Steve Woolgar. *Laboratory Life: The Construction of Scientific Facts.* Princeton: Princeton UP, 1986.

Laudan, Larry. *Progress and Its Problems: Towards a Theory of Scientific Growth.* Berkeley: U of California P, 1977.

Lautamatti, L. "Observations on the Development of the Topic of Simplified Discourse." *Writing Across Languages: Analysis of L2 text* Ed. U. Connor and R. B. Kaplan. Reading, MA: Addison, 1986. 87–113.

LeFevre, Karen Burke. *Invention as a Social Act.* Carbondale: Southern Illinois UP, 1987.

Leinwand, Theodore B. "Negotiation and New Historicism." *PMLA* 105 (1990): 477–90.

Lentricchia, Frank. "Foucault's Legacy: A New Historicism?" *The New Historicism.* Ed. H. Aram Veeser. New York: Routledge, 1989. 231–42.

Levin, Richard. "Feminist Thematics and Shakespearean Tragedy." *PMLA* 103 (1988): 125–38.

———. *New Readings vs. Old Plays: Recent Trends in the Reinterpretation of English Renaissance Drama.* Chicago: U of Chicago P, 1979.

———. "The Poetics and Politics of Bardicide." *PMLA* 105 (1990): 491–504.

Levine, Lawrence W. "The Unpredictable Past: Reflections on Recent American Historiography." *American Historical Review* 94 (1989): 671–79.

Lloyd, P. C. *Africa in Social Change.* Baltimore: Penguin, 1967.

Lockridge, Kenneth A. *A New England Town: The First Hundred Years: Dedham, Massachusetts, 1636–1736.* New York: Norton, 1970.

Lovejoy, Kim Brian. "Cohesion and Information Strategies in Academic Writing: Anaysis of Passages in Three Disciplines." *Linguistics and Education* 3 (1991): 315–43.

McCarthy, Lucille P. "A Stranger in Strange Lands: A College Student Writing Across the Curriculum." *Research in Teaching English* 21 (1987): 233–65.

MacDonald, Susan Peck. *Anthony Trollope.* Boston: Hall, 1987.

——. "Data Driven and Conceptually Driven Academic Discourse." *Written Communication* 6 (1989): 411–35.

——. "A Method for Analyzing Sentence-Level Differences in Disciplinary Knowledge Making." *Written Communication* 9 (1992): 533–69.

——. "Problem Definition in Academic Writing." *College English* 49 (1987): 315–31.

MacDonald, Susan Peck, and Charles R. Cooper. "Contributions of Academic and Dialogic Journals to Writing about Literature." *Writing, Teaching, and Learning in the Disciplines.* Ed. Anne Herrington and Charles Moran. New York: MLA, 1992. 137–55.

McGee, Michael Calvin, and John R. Lyne. "What Are Nice Folks Like You Doing in a Place Like This? Some Entailments of Treating Knowledge Claims Rhetorically." *The Rhetoric of the Human Sciences.* Ed. John S. Nelson, Allan Megill, and Donald N. McCloskey. Madison: U of Wisconsin P, 1987. 381–406.

Maimon, Elaine. "Preface." *Writing Across the Curriculum: A Guide to Developing Programs.* Ed. Susan H. McLeod and Margot Soven. Newbury Park, CA: Sage, 1992. ix–xiv.

Main, Mary, and J. Solomon. "Discovery of an Insecure-Disorganized/Disoriented Attachment Pattern." *Affective Development in Infancy.* Ed. T. B. Brazelton and M. Yogman. Norwood, NJ: Ablex, 1986. 95–124.

Marius, Richard. "On Academic Discourse." *Profession 90.* New York: MLA, 1990. 28–31.

Marshall, James D. "The Effects of Writing on Students' Understanding of Literary Texts." *Research in the Teaching of English* 21 (1987): 30–63.

Megill, Allan. "Recounting the Past: 'Description,' Explanation, and Narrative in Historiography." *American Historical Review* 94 (1989): 627–53.

Megill, Allan, and Donald N. McCloskey. "The Rhetoric of History." *The Rhetoric of the Human Sciences.* Madison: U of Wisconsin P, 1987. 221–38.

Miller, Carolyn R. "Genre as Social Action." *Quarterly Journal of Speech* 70 (1984): 151–67.

Miller, Susan. *Textual Carnivals: The Politics of Composition.* Carbondale: Southern Illinois UP, 1991.

Montrose, Louis A. "Professing the Renaissance: The Poetics and Politics of Culture." *The New Historicism.* Ed. H. Aram Veeser. New York: Routledge, 1989. 15–36.

———. "Renaissance Literary Studies and the Subject of History." *English Literary Renaissance* 16 (1986): 5–12.

———. " 'Shaping Fantasies': Figurations of Gender and Power in Elizabethan Culture." *Representations* 2 (1983): 61–94.

Mullaney, Steven. "Strange Things, Gross Terms, Curious Customs: The Rehearsal of Cultures in the Late Renaissance." *Representations* 2 (1983), reprinted in *Representing the English Renaissance.* Ed. Stephen Greenblatt. Berkeley: U of California P, 1988. 65–92.

Myers, Greg. *Writing Biology: Texts in the Social Construction of Scientific Knowledge.* Madison: U of Wisconsin P, 1990.

Neely, Carol Thomas. "Constructing the Subject: Feminist Practice and the New Renaissance Discourses." *English Literary Renaissance* 18 (1988): 5–18.

Nelson, John S. "Stories of Science and Politics: Some Rhetorics of Political Research." *The Rhetoric of the Human Sciences.* Ed. John S. Nelson, Allan Megill, and Donald N. McCloskey. Madison: U of Wisconsin P, 1987. 198–220.

Nelson, John S., Allan Megill, and Donald N. McCloskey, eds. *The Rhetoric of the Human Sciences.* Madison, Wisconsin: U of Wisconsin P, 1987.

Newell, George E. "Learning from Writing in Two Content Areas: A Case Study/Protocol Analysis." *Research in the Teaching of English* 18 (1984): 265–87.

North, Stephen M. "Writing in a Philosophy Class: Three Case Studies." *Research in the Teaching of English* 20 (1986): 225–62.

Novick, Peter. *That Noble Dream: The "Objectivity Question" and the American Historical Profession.* Cambridge: Cambridge UP, 1988.

Ohmann, Richard. *Engish in America: A Radical View of the Profession.* New York: Oxford UP, 1976.

Olson, Paul A. "*A Midsummer Night's Dream* and the Meaning of Court Marriage." *ELH* 24 (1957): 95–119.

Paglia, Camille. "Academe Has to Recover Its Spiritual Roots and

Overthrow the Ossified Political Establishment of Invested Self-Interest." *Chronicle of Higher Education* 8 May 1991: B1–B2.

Pearce, W. Barnett, and Victorian Chen. "Ethnography as Sermonic: The Rhetorics of Clifford Geertz and James Clifford." *Rhetoric in the Human Sciences.* Ed. Herbert W. Simons. Newbury Park, CA: Sage, 1989. 119–32.

Pechter, Edward. "The New Historicism and Its Discontents: Politicizing Renaissance Drama." *PMLA* 102 (1987): 292–303.

Perelman, Chaim, and L. Olbrechts-Tyteca. *The New Rhetoric: A Treatise on Argumentation.* Notre Dame: U of Notre Dame P, 1969.

Polhemus, Robert M. *The Changing World of Anthony Trollope.* Berkeley: U of California P, 1968.

Popkin, Cathy. "A Plea to the Wielders of Academic Dis(of)Course." *College English* 54 (1992): 173–81.

Porter, Carolyn. "Are We Being Historical Yet?" *South Atlantic Quarterly* 87 (1988): 745–86.

Porter, James E. "Intertextuality and the Discourse Community." *Rhetoric Review* 5 (1986): 34–47.

Price, Derek J. de Solla. "Citation Measures of Hard Science, Soft Science, Technology, and Nonscience." *Communication Among Scientists and Engineers.* Ed. Carnot E. Nelson and Donald K. Pollock. Lexington: Heath, Lexington, 1970. 3–22.

Quirk, Randolph, Sidney Greenbaum, Geoffrey Leech, and Jan Svartvik. *A Comprehensive Grammar of the English Language.* New York: Longman, 1985.

Rabinow, Paul, and William M. Sullivan. "The Interpetive Turn: Emergence of an Approach." *Interpretive Social Science: A Reader.* Ed. Paul Rabinow and William M. Sullivan. Berkeley: U of California P, 1979. 1–21.

"Report of the Advisory Committee on Documentation Style." *PMLA* 97 (1982): 318–24. (Nine committee members listed.)

Ronald, Kate. "On the Outside Looking In: Students' Analyses of Professional Discourse Communities." *Rhetoric Review* 7 (1988): 130–49.

Rorty, Richard. *Philosophy and the Mirror of Nature.* Princeton: Princeton UP, 1979.

Rosaldo, Renato. "Where Objectivity Lies: The Rhetoric of Anthropology." *The Rhetoric of the Human Sciences.* Ed. John S. Nelson, Allan Megill, and Donald N. McCloskey. Madison: U of Wisconsin P, 1987. 87–110.

Rowan, Katherine E. "A Contemporary Theory of Explanatory Writing." *Written Communication* 5 (1988): 23–56.

Russell, David. *Writing in the Academic Disciplines, 1870–1990: A Curricular History*. Carbondale: Southern Illinois UP, 1991.

Rutman, Darrett B. "Assessing the Little Communities of Early America." *William and Mary Quarterly* 3rd ser. 43 (1986): 163–78.

Sagi, Abraham, and Kathleen S. Lewkowicz. "A Cross-Cultural Evaluation of Attachment Research." *Attachment in Social Networks: Contributions to the Bowlby-Ainsworth Attachment Theory*. Ed. Louis W. C. Tavecchio and Marinus H. van IJzendoorn. Amsterdam: Elsevier Science, 1987. 427–59.

Schorske, Carl E. "History and the Study of Culture." *New Literary History* 21 (1990): 407–20.

Schwegler, Robert A., and Linda K. Shamoon. "Meaning Attribution in Ambiguous Texts in Sociology." *Textual Dynamics of the Professions*. Ed. Charles Bazerman and James Paradis. Madison: U of Wisconsin P, 1991. 216–33.

Scott, Joan Wallach. "History in Crisis? The Others' Side of the Story." *American Historical Review* 94 (1989): 680–92.

———. "Liberal Historians: A Unitary Vision." *Chronicle of Higher Education* 11 Sept., 1991: B1-B2.

Shumway, David R. "Comment on 'Beyond Literary Darwinism.' " *College English* 53 (1991): 831–34.

Simons, Herbert W. "Introduction." *Rhetoric in the Human Sciences*. Ed. Herbert W. Simons. Newbury Park, CA: Sage, 1989. 1–9.

Simpson, Paul. "Modality in Literary-Critical Discourse." *The Writing Scholar: Studies in Academic Discourse*. Ed. Walter Nash. Newbury Park, CA: Sage, 1990. 63–94.

Slakey, Roger. "Trollope's Case for the Moral Imperative." *Nineteenth-Century Fiction* 28 (1973): 383–95.

Small, Henry G. "Cited Documents as Concept Symbols." *Social Studies of Science* 8 (1978): 327–40.

Social Science Research Council, Committee on Historiography. *The Social Sciences in Historical Study*, bulletin 64 (New York, 1954): 86.

Sroufe, L. Alan. "Attachment Classification from the Perspective of Infant-Caregiver Relationships and Infant Temperament." *Child Development* 56 (1985): 1–14.

Sroufe, L. Alan, Nancy E. Fox, and Van R. Pancake. "Attachment and Dependency in Developmental Perspective." *Child Development* 54 (1983): 1615–27.

Sroufe, L. Alan, and Everett Waters. "Attachment as an Organizational Construct." *Child Development* 48 (1977): 1184–99.

Stearns, Peter N. "Toward a Wider Vision: Trends in Social History." *The Past Before Us: Contemporary Historical Writing in the United States.* Ed. Michael Kammen. Ithaca: Cornell UP, 1980. 205–30.

Stone, Lawrence. "Family History in the 1980s: Past Achievements and Future Trends." *The New History: The 1980s and Beyond: Studies in Interdisciplinary History.* Eds. Theodore K. Rabb and Robert I. Rotberg. Pinceton: Princeton UP, 1982. 51–87.

———. "The Revival of Narrative: Reflections on a New Old History." *Past and Present* 85 (1979): 3–24.

Strenski, Ellen. "Writing Across the Curriculum at Research Universities." *Strengthening Programs for Writing Across the Curriculum.* Ed. Susan H. McLeod. San Francisco: Jossey-Bass, 1988. 31–41.

Sullivan, Dale L. "The Ethos of Epideictic Encounter." *Philosophy and Rhetoric* 26 (1993): 113–33.

Sullivan, Patricia A. "Writing in the Graduate Curriculum: Literary Criticism as Composition." *Journal of Advanced Composition* 11 (1991): 283–99.

Swales, John M. *Genre Analysis: English in Academic and Research Settings.* Cambridge: Cambridge UP, 1990.

Swales, John, and Hazem Najjar. "The Writing of Research Article Introductions." *Written Communication* 9 (1987): 175–91.

Tompkins, Jane. "Me and My Shadow." *Gender and Theory: Dialogues on Feminist Criticism.* Ed. Linda Kauffman. Oxford: Blackwell, 1989. 121–39.

Torgovnick, Marianna. "Experimental Critical Writing." *Profession 90.* New York: MLA, 1990. 25–27.

Toulmin, Stephen. *Human Understanding: The Collective Use and Evolution of Concepts.* Princeton: Princeton UP, 1972.

Tracy, Patricia J. "Re-considering Migration Within Colonial New England." *Journal of Social History* 23 (1989): 93–113.

Vande Kopple, William J. "Given and New Information and Some Aspects of the Structures, Semantics, and Pragmatics of Written Texts." *Studying Writing: Linguistic Approaches.* Ed. Charles R. Cooper and Sidney Greenbaum. Beverly Hills: Sage, 1986. 72–111.

———. "Noun Phrases and the Style of Scientific Discourse." *A Rhetoric of Doing: Essays on Written Discourse in Honor of James L. Kinneavy*. Ed. Stephen P. Witte, Neil Nakadate, and Roger D. Cherry. Carbondale: Southern Illinois UP, 1992. 328–48.

———. "Some Exploratory Discourse on Metadiscourse." *College Composition and Communication* 36 (1985): 82–93.

———. "Themes, Thematic Progressions, and Some Implications for Understanding Discourse." *Written Communication* 8 (1991): 311–47.

Van Ghent, Dorothy. *The English Novel: Form and Function*. New York: Harper, 1953.

van IJzendoorn, Marinus H., and Pieter M. Kroonenberg. "Cross-Cultural Patterns of Attachment: A Meta-Analysis of the Strange Situation." *Child Development* 59 (1988): 147–56.

Vaughn, Brian E., Joan Stevenson-Hinde, Everett Waters, Antonis Kotsaftis, Gretchen B. Lefever, Anne Shouldice, Marcel Trudel, and Jay Belsky. "Attachment Security and Temperament in Infancy and Early Childhood: Some Conceptual Clarifications." *Developmental Psychology* 28 (1992): 463–73.

Veeser, H. Aram. "Introduction." *The New Historicism*. Ed. H. Aram Veeser. New York: Routledge, 1989. ix-xvi.

Walvoord, Barbara E., and John R. Breihan. "Arguing and Debating: Breihan's History Course." *Thinking and Writing in College: A Naturalistic Study of Students in Four Disciplines*. Ed. Barbara E. Walvoord and Lucille P. McCarthy. Urbana: NCTE, 1990. 97–143.

Walvoord, Barbara E., and Lucille P. McCarthy. *Thinking and Writing in College: A Naturalistic Study of Students in Four Disciplines*. Urbana: NCTE, 1990.

Waters, Everett. "The Reliability and Stability of Individual Differences in Infant-Mother Attachment." *Child Development* 49 (1978): 483–94.

Waters, John J. "Family, Inheritance, and Migration in Colonial New England: The Evidence from Guilford, Connecticut." *William and Mary Quarterly* 3rd series 39 (1982): 64–86.

———. "Review of *A Little Commonwealth* [Demos], *Four Generations* [Greven], and *A New England Town* [Lockridge]." *William and Mary Quarterly* 3rd Ser. 27 (1970): 657–62.

Wayne, Don E. "Power, Politics, and the Shakespearean Text: Recent Criticism in England and the United States." *Shakespeare Repro-*

duced: The Text in History and Ideology. Ed. Jean E. Howard and Marion F. O'Connor. New York: Methuen, 1987. 47–67.

Wells, Rulon. "Nominal and Verbal Styles." *Style in Language.* Ed. Thomas A. Sebeok. New York: MIT and Wiley, 1960. 213–20.

West, Gregory K. "*That*-Nominal Constructions in Traditional Rhetorical Divisions of Scientific Research Papers." *TESOL Quarterly* 14 (1980): 483–88.

White, Hayden. "The Historical Text as Literary Artifact." *The Writing of History: Literary Form and Historical Understanding.* Ed. Robert H. Canary and Henry Kozicki. Madison: U of Wisconsin P, 1978. 41–62.

Williams, Joseph M. *Style: Ten Lessons in Clarity and Grace* 3rd ed. Glenview, IL: Scott, 1989.

Witte, Stephen P. "Topical Structure and Revision: An Exploratory Study." *College Composition and Communication* 34 (1983): 313–41.

Witte, Stephen P., and Roger D. Cherry. "Writing Processes and Written Products in Composition Research." Ed. Charles R. Cooper and Sidney Greenbaum. *Studying Writing: Linguistic Approaches.* Beverly Hills: Sage, 1986. 112–53.

Zinsser, William. *On Writing Well.* 2nd ed. New York: Harper, 1980.

Zuckerman, Michael. "The Fabrication of Identity in Early America." *William and Mary Quarterly* 3rd ser. 34 (1977): 183–214.

INDEX

Dubois, Betty Lou, 213n.2
Dudley-Evans, Tony, 156, 188

Edwards, Lee, 42
Egeland, Byron, 68, 133, 202, 207–8n.3
Eiler, Mary Ann, 153
Elbow, Peter, 14, 110, 142–43, 187
Eliot, George, 42–43
Epideictic rhetoric, 11–12, 18, 23, 116, 142–44, 169, 197, 204n.9, 211n.9
Epistemic self-consciousness, 12–13, 18–20, 22, 26, 47–50, 61, 197; in problem presentation, 120–24, 160, 207n.11; versus nonepistemic problem presentation, 124–29, 137–42; at the sentence-level, 131, 133–34, 151–54, 160–69, 189. *See also* Knowledge making; Metadiscourse; Sentence subjects
Erickson, Peter, 122, 125
Explanation, 12, 19, 21; in tension with interpretive goals, 32–36, 80, 82, 87, 91, 94, 96–97, 130; in attachment research, 69–73. *See also* Conceptually driven inquiry

Fahnestock, Jeanne, 7, 11, 41–42, 142, 204n.8, 211n.6
Faigley, Lester, 7, 153
Farnsworth, Rodney, 155
Feminism: and academic language, 18, 191–92, 196; and critiques of New Historicism, 118, 122, 210n.4
Feyerabend, Paul, 205n.10
Foucault, Michel, 14, 30, 114, 116, 126, 135, 141, 178, 211n.7
Fox, Nancy E., 48–49, 54–55, 63, 65–66
Frey, Olivia, 18, 196
Function: differences in, 11–12;

90–91; of nominal or epistemic style, 170–75; of intermediary prose, 180, 187; need to understand differences in, 189–91, 195

Gallie, W. B., 81
Garvey, William D., 25–26
Gaskell, Elizabeth, 41–43, 45–46
Geertz, Clifford, 6, 12, 33–36, 76, 82, 95
Geisler, Cheryl, 7, 12
Generalization: versus particularism, 19, 21, 27–28, 32–36; and conceptually driven explanation, 36–42; and particulars versus abstraction in literary studies, 45–47, 115–18, 130–32, 136–37; in attachment research, 72–74; versus particularism in history, 74–76, 80, 86, 92, 101, 103, 105–6; and sentence subjects, 155, 169, 174
Giere, Ronald N., 205n.10
Gilbert, G. Nigel, 8, 22, 37–38
Graff, Gerald, 9, 11, 14, 18, 110, 143, 193, 206n.8
Greenbaum, Sidney, 213n.2
Greenblatt, Stephen, 50, 114–18, 119, 122, 124–36, 140–41, 156, 164–68, 174, 176–79, 186, 195, 201–2, 210nn. 3, 5, 211n.6
Greven, Philip J., Jr., 94, 96–100, 102, 209n.5
Gross, Robert A., 95–96, 102, 107–8, 184–86

Hake, Rosemary L., 213n.3
Halliday, M. A. K., 171, 173, 193, 212n.1
Hamerow, Theodore S., 191
Hansen, Kristine, 7
Harris, Joseph, 14
Hempel, Carl G., 80–81, 95
Henretta, James A., 100–101, 103
Herndl, Carl G., 213n.3
Herrington, Anne J., 7, 203n.1

Positivism, 3, 34–35, 64, 80–82, 87, 95, 183
Price, Derek J. de Solla, 25, 160, 205n.4
Problem definition, 19, 23, 25, 31, 38, 48; and problem presentation, 20, 47–50, 120, 124–27; in attachment research, 53–69; in older Shakespeare criticism, 110–13; in Renaissance New Historicism, 113–21, 135
Professionalization, 16–19, 91, 96, 106, 128, 191, 196; and competing prose styles, 189–97
Progress: notions of, 27–29; in attachment research, 54–71; difficulty of in history and literature, 89–91, 110
Psychology, 5, 94; textbooks in, 180–82. *See also* Attachment research
Purpose. *See* Function

Quirk, Randolph, 212–13n.2

Rabinow, Paul, 33–34, 76
Rationality, 27–31, 47, 71, 205n.10, 206n.5
Readers: lay versus professional, 17, 48, 84, 86, 90–91, 108, 111, 185–86, 195–96; as interpreters, 37–38, 41–42, 73; and effect of point-first and point-last prose, 141
Renaissance New Historicism, 14–15, 20, 24, 45–46, 207n.1, 209n.1, 210nn. 3, 4, 211n.6; epistemic and nonepistemic patterns in, 48–50, 109–44; sentence-level patterns in, 150–51, 159, 164–69, 174–76
Rhetoric and composition studies, 3–4, 6–8, 17, 203nn. 1, 2, 206n.7

Rhetoric of inquiry, 3–4, 9–10, 81, 88, 204n.7, 206n.5
Ronald, Kate, 189
Rorty, Richard, 13, 80, 205n.10
Rosaldo, Renato, 6
Rovine, Michael J., 68, 121, 160–63, 166, 201
Rowan, Katherine E., 205n.3
Russell, David, 4, 9, 187, 203nn. 1, 2, 204n.6
Rutman, Darrett, B., 101

Sample, of articles examined, 15–16, 201–2, 209n.6, 209n.1, 212n.5
Schorske, Carl E., 79
Schwegler, Robert A., 7
Science, 8, 10–11, 13, 33, 37, 81, 87; compact problem definition in, 21–26, 29–31; nominalization and epistemic sentence subjects in, 168, 173, 195
Scott, Joan W., 88–90, 95
Secor, Marie, 7, 11, 41–42, 142, 204n.8, 211n.6
Sentence structure, 16, 20, 107, 160–62, 191–92, 194, 213n.4; extraposed sentences with clausal subject, 161. *See also* Nominalization; Sentence subjects; *That* noun clauses; Verbs
Sentence subjects: epistemic subjects, 138–39, 154–69, 171–75, 181–83, 212–13n.2; nonepistemic patterns in, among New Historicists, 138–39, 164–69; rationale for focusing on, 148–57; as indication of actors or agency, 149–52, 185; classification system for exploring, 151–58; phenomenal subjects, 154–59, 163–69, 175–78, 185, 192; subdisciplinary differences in, 158–69. *See also* Nominalization
Shakespeare criticism, 14, 20, 27,

36, 43–47, 57, 69, 73, 111, 150–51, 209n.1, 210n.2. *See also* Renaissance New Historicism
Shamoon, Linda K., 7
Shouldice, Anne, 63, 66–67, 175
Shumway, David R., 142
Simons, Herbert W., 9–10, 204n.7
Simpson, Paul, 154
Slakey, Roger, 43
Small, Henry G., 122, 208n.4
Social construction of knowledge, 3, 7, 13, 27–28, 165
Social history. *See* New England colonial social history
Social sciences, 4, 8, 10, 13, 21–22, 24–26, 32–33, 35–36, 48, 173, 197, 205n.1; in tension with narrative and interpretive strands in history, 76, 82, 84, 86–87, 90–91, 94–96, 101–5, 117
Sociology, 74–75, 82, 86, 93–94, 97–100, 103–4; of science, 3, 7, 9–10, 22, 29, 38
Sroufe, L. Alan, 48–49, 54–55, 63–68, 71–72, 95, 133, 175, 202, 207–8n.3
Stearns, Peter N., 208n.2
Stevenson-Hinde, Joan, 63, 66–67, 175
Stone, Lawrence, 79, 82–84, 86, 90–96
Strenski, Ellen, 203n.2
Students. *See* Novice writers
Sullivan, Dale L., 11, 143
Sullivan, Patricia A., 188, 204n.4
Sullivan, William M., 33–34, 76
Svartvik, Jan, 213n.2
Swales, John, 7, 148, 156, 188, 207n.11

Textbooks, 4, 180; in psychology, 180–83; in history, 183
Text-driven inquiry, 21, 36–40, 74–77, 91, 96, 100, 116, 129, 133. *See also* Interpretation

Texts: importance of, 3–8, 78, 83–84, 90, 107, 151, 157, 187
That noun clauses, 151, 154, 162–63, 168, 170
Tompkins, Jane, 196, 211n.7
Torgovnick, Marianna, 192–93
Toulmin, Stephen, 13, 22, 24, 29, 31, 80, 110, 205n.10
Tracy, Patricia J., 96–97, 202
Trollope, Anthony, 42–46, 69, 73
Trudel, Marcel, 63, 66–67, 175

Vande Kopple, William, 148, 153, 155, 168, 173, 190, 194, 212n.2, 213n.3
Van Ghent, Dorothy, 41
Vaughn, Brian E., 63, 66–67, 175
Veeser, H. Aram, 128
Verbs, 138, 150, 162, 172–73, 176–79, 190, 194

Wall, Sally, 61–63, 65, 70–71, 73
Walvoord, Barbara E., 7, 180, 184
Waters, Everett, 59, 61–67, 70–73, 175
Waters, John J., 98, 102–6, 164, 166, 202
Wayne, Don E., 210nn. 2, 3
"We" (generalized): as sentence subject, 131, 158, 166, 211n.7
Wells, Rulon, 171, 212n.1
West, Gregory K., 151, 154, 156, 163, 188
White, Hayden, 81, 208n.3
Williams, Joseph M., 134–35, 141, 149–50, 213n.3
Witte, Stephen P., 151, 154
Wittig, Barbara A., 55, 60–61, 72, 207n.2
Woolgar, Steve, 8

Zinsser, William, 171
Zuckerman, Michael, 32, 74, 76, 90, 99–100, 184

Susan Peck MacDonald is currently assistant coordinator of the Dimensions of Culture Program at the University of California, San Diego. She has taught in and administered a variety of freshman composition and writing-in-the-disciplines programs. In addition to her current work on writing in the disciplines, she is author of *Anthony Trollope* and coauthor of a book on the Victorian novel.